Patterns of
Distributed Systems

Pearson Addison-Wesley
Signature Series

Visit informit.com/awss for a complete list of available publications.

The **Pearson Addison-Wesley Signature Series** provides readers with practical and authoritative information on the latest trends in modern technology for computer professionals. The series is based on one simple premise: great books come from great authors.

Books in the Martin Fowler Signature Series are personally chosen by Fowler, and his signature ensures that he has worked closely with authors to define topic coverage, book scope, critical content, and overall uniqueness. The expert signatures also symbolize a promise to our readers: you are reading a future classic.

Connect with InformIT—Visit informit.com/community

Pearson

inform**IT**

O'REILLY

Patterns of Distributed Systems

Unmesh Joshi

✦ Addison-Wesley

Hoboken, New Jersey

Pearson's Commitment to Diversity, Equity, and Inclusion

Pearson is dedicated to creating bias-free content that reflects the diversity of all learners. We embrace the many dimensions of diversity, including but not limited to race, ethnicity, gender, socioeconomic status, ability, age, sexual orientation, and religious or political beliefs.

Education is a powerful force for equity and change in our world. It has the potential to deliver opportunities that improve lives and enable economic mobility. As we work with authors to create content for every product and service, we acknowledge our responsibility to demonstrate inclusivity and incorporate diverse scholarship so that everyone can achieve their potential through learning. As the world's leading learning company, we have a duty to help drive change and live up to our purpose to help more people create a better life for themselves and to create a better world.

Our ambition is to purposefully contribute to a world where:

- Everyone has an equitable and lifelong opportunity to succeed through learning.

- Our educational products and services are inclusive and represent the rich diversity of learners.

- Our educational content accurately reflects the histories and experiences of the learners we serve.

- Our educational content prompts deeper discussions with learners and motivates them to expand their own learning (and worldview).

While we work hard to present unbiased content, we want to hear from you about any concerns or needs with this Pearson product so that we can investigate and address them.

- Please contact us with concerns about any potential bias at https://www.pearson.com/report-bias.html.

*Dedicated to the loving memory of
my father.*

Contents

Foreword

Engineers are often attracted to distributed computing, which promises not only benefits like scalability and fault tolerance but also the prestige of creating clever, talk-worthy computer systems. But the reality is that distributed systems are hard. There are myriads of edge cases, all with subtle interactions and high-dimensional nuance. Every move you make as a systems designer has n-th degree side effects which aren't obvious. You're Sideshow Bob, surrounded by lawn rakes, and every step you take results in a rake in the face—until you've left the field or expended all the rakes. (Oh, and even when you've left the field, there's still a rake or two waiting to be trodden on.)

So how do we avoid, or at least minimize, these pitfalls? The traditional approach has been to accept that distributed systems theory and practice are both hard, and to work your way through textbooks and academic papers with confusing or playful titles, studying numerous proofs so that you can carve out small areas of relative safety and expertise within which to build your system. There's a lot of value in that approach for those that can stay the course. Systems professionals who have grown up that way seem to have a knack for spotting trouble far down the line, and possess a good deal of technical background for reasoning about how to solve problems—or at least minimize their likelihood or impact.

However, in other areas of software engineering, this kind of educational hazing is not so commonplace. Instead of being thrown in at the deep end, we use abstractions to help us gradually learn at greater levels of detail, from higher to lower levels of abstraction, which often maps neatly onto the way software is designed and built. Abstractions allow us to reason about behaviors without getting bogged down in implementation complexity. In a distributed system where complexity is high, some abstractions can be very useful.

In general software engineering, design patterns are a common abstraction. A design pattern is a standardized solution to a recurrent problem in software design. Patterns provide a language that practitioners use to reason about and discuss problems in a well-understood manner. For example, when someone asks, "How does this work?" you may hear something like, "It's just a visitor." Such exchanges, based on a shared understanding of named patterns that solve common problems, are short and information-rich.

The notion of taking something complex and abstracting it into a pattern is both important and fundamental to this book. It applies the pattern approach to the essential building blocks of modern distributed systems, naming the components and describing their behaviors and how they interact. In doing so, it equips you with a pattern language that, within reason, lets you treat a distributed system as a set of composable Lego blocks.

Now, you can talk about "a system that depends on a replicated log with quorum commits" without getting bogged down in the specific details of the data structures and consensus algorithms. Perhaps more importantly, it minimizes the risk of talking past one another because in distributed systems, textbook terms—such as "consistency"—often have several meanings depending on context.

The effect is liberating for practitioners who now have an expressive common vocabulary to expedite and standardize communication. But it's also liberating for learners who can take a structured, breadth-first tour of distributed systems fundamentals, tackling a pattern at a time and observing how those patterns interact or depend on one another. You can also, where needed, go deep into the implementation—this book does not shy away from implementation details either.

My hope is that the patterns in this book will help you teach, learn, and communicate more effectively about distributed systems. It will certainly help you avoid some of the lawn rakes.

—Jim Webber, Chief Scientist, Neo4j

Preface

Why This Book

In 2017, I was involved in developing a software system for a large optical telescope called Thirty Meter Telescope (TMT). We needed to build a core framework and services to be used by various subsystems. The subsystem components had to discover each other and detect component failures. There was also a requirement to store metadata about these components. The service responsible for storing this information had to be fault-tolerant. We couldn't use off-the-shelf products and frameworks due to the unique nature of the telescope ecosystem. We had to build it all from scratch—to create a core framework and services that different subsystems of the software could use. In essence, we had to build a distributed system.

I had designed and architected enterprise systems using products such as Kafka, Cassandra, and MongoDB or cloud services from providers like AWS and GCP. All these products and services are distributed and solve similar problems. For the TMT system, we had to build a solution ourselves. To compare and validate our implementation choices with these proven products, we needed a deeper understanding of the inner workings of some of these products. We had to figure out how all these cloud services and products are built and why they are built that way. Their own documentation often proved too product-specific for that.

Information about how distributed systems are built is scattered across various research papers and doctoral theses. However, these academic sources have their limitations too. They tend to focus on specific aspects, often making only passing references to related topics. For instance, consider a well-written thesis, *Consensus: Bridging Theory and Practice* [Ongaro2014]. It thoroughly explains how to implement the Raft consensus algorithm. But you won't know how Raft is used by products like etcd for tracking group membership and related metadata for other products, such as Kubernetes. Leslie Lamport's famous paper "Time, Clocks, and the Ordering of Events in a Distributed System" [Lamport1978] talks about how to use logical clocks—but you won't know how products like MongoDB use them as a version for the data they store.

I believe that writing code is the best way to test your understanding. Martin Fowler often says, "Code is like the mathematics of our profession. It's where we have to remove the ambiguity." So, to get a deeper understanding of the building blocks of distributed systems, I decided to build miniature versions of these products myself. I started by building a toy version of Kafka. Once I had a reasonable version, I used it to discuss some of the concepts of distributed systems. That worked well. To verify that explaining concepts through code works effectively, I conducted a few workshops within my company, Thoughtworks. Those turned out to be very useful. So I extended this to products like Cassandra, Kubernetes, Akka, Hazelcast, MongoDB, YugabyteDB, CockroachDB, TiKV, and Docker Swarm. I extracted code snippets to understand the building blocks of these products. Not surprisingly, there were a lot of similarities in these building blocks. I happened to discuss this with Martin Fowler a few years back, and he suggested writing about these as patterns. This book is the outcome of my work with Martin to document these common building blocks of distributed system implementations as patterns.

Who This Book Is For

Software architects and developers today face a plethora of choices when it comes to selecting products and cloud services that are distributed by design. These products and services claim to make certain implementation choices. Understanding these choices intuitively can be challenging. Just reading through the documentation is not enough. Consider sentences like "AWS MemoryDB ensures durability with a replicated transactional log" or "Apache Kafka operates independently from ZooKeeper" or "Google Spanner provides external consistency with accurate timing maintained by TrueTime." How do you interpret these?

To get better insights, professionals rely on certifications from product providers. But most certifications are very product-specific. They focus only on the surface features of the product but not the underlying technical principles. Professional developers need to have an intuitive understanding of technical details that are specific enough to be expressed at the source-code level but generic enough to apply to a wide range of situations. Patterns help there. Patterns in this book will enable working professionals to have a good idea of what's happening under the hood of various products and services and thus make informed and effective choices.

I expect most readers of this book to be in this group. In addition to those who work with existing distributed systems, however, there is another group of readers who must build their own distributed systems. I hope the patterns in this book will give that other group a head start. There are numerous references to design alternatives used by various products, which might be useful to these readers.

A Note on Examples

I have provided code examples for most of the patterns. The code examples are based on my own miniature implementations of the various products I studied while working through these patterns. My choice of language is based on what I think most readers are likely to be able to read and understand. Java is a good choice here. The code examples use a minimum of Java language features—mostly methods and classes, which are available in most programming languages. Readers familiar with other programming languages should be able to easily understand these code examples. This book, however, is not intended to be specific for any particular software platform. Once you understand the code examples, you will find similarities in code bases in C++, Rust, Go, Scala, or Zig. My hope is that, once you are familiar with the code examples and the patterns, you will find it easier to navigate the source code of various open-source products.

How to Read This Book

The book has six numbered parts that are divided into two main conceptual sections.

First, a number of narrative chapters cover the essential topics in distributed systems design. These chapters (in Part I) present challenges in distributed system design along with their solutions. However, they don't go into much detail on these solutions.

Detailed solutions, structured as patterns, are provided in the second section of the book (Parts II to VI). The patterns fall into four main categories: replication, partitioning, cluster management, and network communication. Each of these is a key building block of a distributed system.

Consider these patterns as references; there's no need to read them cover to cover. You may read the narrative chapters for an overview of the book's scope, and then explore the patterns based on your interests and requirements.

For additional reference materials, visit https://martinfowler.com/articles/patterns-of-distributed-systems.

I hope these patterns will assist fellow software professionals in making informed decisions in their daily work.

Register your copy of *Patterns of Distributed Systems* on the InformIT site for convenient access to updates and/or corrections as they become available. To start the registration process, go to informit.com/register and log in or create an account. Enter the product ISBN (9780138221980) and click Submit. Look on the Registered Products tab for an Access Bonus Content link next to this product, and follow that link to access any available bonus materials. If you would like to be notified of exclusive offers on new editions and updates, please check the box to receive email from us.

Acknowledgments

First and foremost, the book was only possible because of encouragement from Martin Fowler. He guided me to think in terms of patterns. He also helped me come up with good examples and contributed to the chapters that were very tricky to write.

I want to thank the Thirty Meter Telescope (TMT) team. Working with that team was the trigger for much of this work. I had good conversations about many of these patterns with Mushtaq Ahmed who was leading the TMT project.

Sarthak Makhija validated a lot of these patterns while he worked on building a distributed key-value store.

I have been publishing these patterns periodically on martinfowler.com. While working on these patterns, I sent drafts of new material to the Thoughtworks developer mailing list and asked for feedback. I want to thank the following people for posting their feedback on the mailing list: Rebecca Parsons, Dave Elliman, Samir Seth, Prasanna Pendse, Santosh Mahale, James Lewis, Chris Ford, Kumar Sankara Iyer, Evan Bottcher, Ian Cartwright, and Priyanka Kotwal. Jojo Swords, Gareth Morgan, and Richard Gall from Thoughtworks helped with copyediting the earlier versions published on martinfowler.com.

While working on the patterns, I interacted with many people. Professor Indranil Gupta provided feedback on the Gossip Dissemination pattern. Dahlia Malkhi helped with questions about Google Spanner. Mikhail Bautin, Karthik Ranganathan, and Piyush Jain from the Yugabyte team answered all my questions about some of implementation details in YugabyteDB. The CockroachDB team was very responsive in answering questions about their design choices. Bela Ban, Patrik Nordwall, and Lalith Suresh provided good feedback on the Emergent Leader pattern.

Salim Virji and Jim Webber went through the early manuscript and provided some nice feedback. Richard Sites provided some nice suggestions on the first chapter. I want to extend my heartfelt thanks to Jim Webber for contributing the foreword to this book.

One of the great things about being an employee at Thoughtworks is that they allowed me to spend considerable time on this book. Thanks to the Engineering for Research (E4R) group of Thoughtworks for their support. I want to also thank Sameer Soman, MD, Thoughtworks India, who always encouraged me.

At Pearson, Greg Doench is my acquisition editor, navigating many issues in getting a book to publication. I was glad to work with Julie Nahil as my production editor. It was great to work with Dmitry Kirsanov for copyediting and Alina Kirsanova for composition and indexing.

My family has been a source of constant support. My mother was always very hopeful about the book. My wife, Ashwini, is an excellent software developer herself; she and I had insightful discussions and she provided valuable reviews of early drafts. My daughter, Rujuta, and son, Advait, were sources of my motivation.

About the Author

Unmesh Joshi is a Principal Consultant at Thoughtworks with 24 years of industry experience. As an ardent enthusiast of software architecture, he firmly believes that today's tech landscape requires a profound understanding of distributed systems principles. For the last three years he has been publishing patterns of distributed systems on martinfowler.com. He has also conducted various training sessions around this topic. You can find him on X (formerly Twitter): @unmeshjoshi.

Part I

Narratives

Chapter 1

The Promise and Perils of Distributed Systems

The Limits of a Single Server

In this book, we will discuss distributed systems. But what exactly do we mean when we say "distributed systems"? And why is distribution necessary? Let's start from the basics.

In today's digital world, the majority of our activities rely on networked services. Whether it's ordering food or managing finances, these services run on servers located somewhere. When using cloud services like AWS, GCP, or Azure, these servers are managed by the respective cloud providers. They store data, process user requests, and perform computations using the CPU, memory, network, and disks. These four fundamental physical resources are essential for any computation.

Consider a typical retail application functioning as a networked service, where users can perform actions such as adding items to their shopping cart, making purchases, viewing orders, and querying past orders. The capacity of a single server to handle user requests is ultimately determined by the limitations of four key resources: network bandwidth, disks, CPU, and memory.

The network bandwidth sets the maximum data transfer capacity over the network at any given time. For example, with a network bandwidth of 1Gbps (125MB/s) and 1KB records being written or read, the network can support a maximum of 125,000 requests per second. However, if the record size increases to 5KB, the number of requests that can be passed over the network decreases to only 25,000.

Disk performance depends on several factors, including the type of read or write operations and how well disk caches are used. Mechanical disks are also affected by hardware features such as rotational speed and seek time. Sequential operations usually have better performance than random ones. Moreover, the performance is influenced by concurrent read/write operations and software-based transactional processes. These factors can significantly affect the overall throughput and latency on a single server.

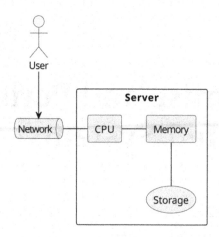

Figure 1.1 *Resources of computation*

Likewise, when the CPU or memory limit is reached, requests must wait for their turn to be processed. When these physical limits are pushed to their capacity, this results in queuing. As more requests pile up, waiting times increase, negatively impacting the server's ability to efficiently handle user requests.

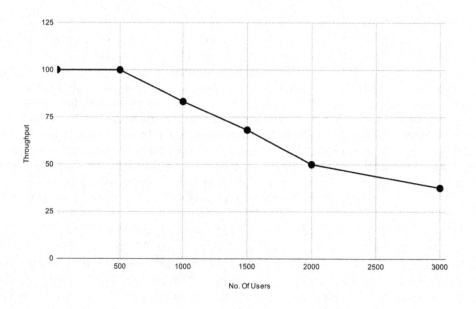

Figure 1.2 *Drop in throughput with increase in requests*

The impact of reaching the limits of these resources becomes evident in the overall throughput of the system, as illustrated in Figure 1.2.

This poses a problem for end users. As the system is expected to accommodate an increasing user base, its performance actually degrades.

To ensure requests are served effectively, you have to divide and process them on multiple servers. This enables the utilization of separate CPUs, networks, memory, and disks to handle user requests. In our example, the workload should be divided so that each server handles approximately five hundred requests.

Separate Business Logic and Data Layer

A common approach is to separate an architecture into two parts. The first part is the stateless component responsible for exposing functionality to end users. This can take the form of a web application or, more commonly, a web API that serves user-facing applications. The second part is the stateful component, which is managed by a database (Figure 1.3).

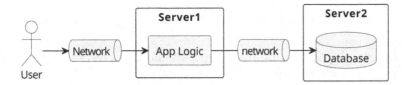

Figure 1.3 *Separating compute and data*

This way, most of the application logic executes on the separate server utilizing a separate network, CPU, memory, and disk. This architecture works particularly well if most users can be served from caches put at different layers in the architecture. It makes sure that only a portion of all requests need to reach the database layer.

As the number of user requests increases, more servers can be added to handle the stateless business logic. This scalability allows the system to accommodate a growing user base and ensures that requests can be processed efficiently. In the event of a server failure, a new server can be introduced to take over the workload and continue serving user requests seamlessly (Figure 1.4).

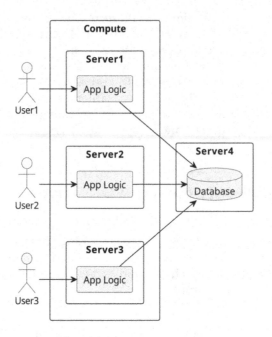

Figure 1.4 *Scaling compute with multiple servers*

This approach is effective for many applications. However, there comes a point when the amount of data stored in stateful databases grows to hundreds of tera-bytes or even petabytes, or the number of requests to the database layer increases significantly. As a result, the simplistic architecture described above runs into limitations stemming from the physical constraints of the four fundamental resources on the server responsible for managing the data.

Partitioning Data

When a software system runs into hardware's physical limits, the best approach to ensure proper request processing is to divide the data and process it on mul-tiple servers (Figure 1.5). This enables the utilization of separate CPUs, networks, memory, and disks to handle requests on smaller data portions.

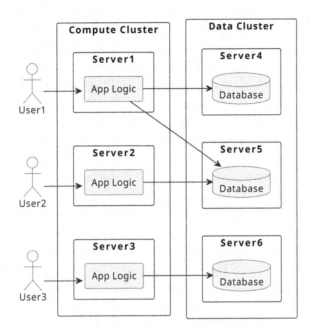

Figure 1.5 *Scaling data by distributing on multiple servers*

A Look at Failures

When we utilize multiple machines with their own disk drives, network intercon-
nects, processors, and memory units, the likelihood of failures becomes a significant concern. Consider the hard disk failure probability. If a disk has a failure
rate of once in 1000 days, the probability of it failing on any given day is 1/1000,
which may not be a major concern on its own. However, if we have 1000 disks,
the probability of at least one disk failing on a given day becomes 1. If the partitioned data is being served from the disk that fails, it will become unavailable
until the disk is recovered.

To gain insights into the types of failures that can occur look at the failure
statistics from Jeff Dean's 2009 talk [Dean2009] on Google's data centers as shown
in Table 1.1. Although these numbers are from 2009, they still provide a valuable
representation of failure patterns.

Table 1.1 *Failure Events per Year for a Cluster in a Data Center from Jeff Dean's 2009 Talk [Dean2009]*

Event	Details
Overheating	Power down most machines in < 5 min (~1–2 days to recover)
PDU Failure	~500–1000 machines suddenly disappear (~6 hours to come back)
Rack Move	Plenty of warning, ~500–1000 machines powered down (~6 hours)
Network Rewiring	Rolling ~5% of machines down over 2-day span
Rack Failures	40–80 machines instantly disappear (1–6 hours to get back)
Racks Go Wonky	40–80 machines see 50% packet loss
Network Maintenances	4 might cause ~30-minute random connectivity losses
Router Reloads	Takes out DNS and external VIPs for a couple minutes
Router Failures	Have to immediately pull traffic for an hour
Minor DNS Blips	Dozens of 30-second blips for DNS
Individual Machine Failures	1000 individual machine failures
Hard Drive Failures	Thousands of hard drive failures

When distributing stateless compute across multiple servers, failures can be managed relatively easily. If a server responsible for handling user requests fails, the requests can be redirected to another server, or a new server can be added to take over the workload. Since stateless compute does not rely on specific data stored on a server, any server can begin serving requests from any user without the need to load specific data beforehand.

Failures become particularly challenging when dealing with data. Creating a separate instance on a random server is not as straightforward. It requires careful consideration to ensure that the servers start in the correct state and coordinate with other nodes to avoid serving incorrect or stale data. This book mainly focuses on systems that face these types of challenges.

To ensure that the system remains functional even if certain components are experiencing failures, simply distributing data across cluster nodes is often insufficient. It is crucial to effectively mask the failures.

Replication: Masking Failures

Replication plays a crucial role in masking failures and ensuring service availability. If data is replicated on multiple machines, even in the event of failures, clients can connect to a server that holds a copy of the data.

However, doing this is not as simple as it sounds. The responsibility for masking failures falls on the software that handles user requests. The software must be able to detect failures and ensure that any inconsistencies are not visible to the users. Understanding the types of errors that a software system experiences is vital for successfully masking these failures.

Let's look at some of the common problems that software systems experience and need to mask from the users of the system.

Process Crash

Software processes can crash unexpectedly due to various reasons. It could be a result of hardware failures or unhandled exceptions in the code. In containerized or cloud environments, monitoring software can automatically restart a process it recognizes as faulty. However, if a user has stored data on the server and received a successful response, it becomes crucial for the software to ensure that the data remains available after the process restarts. Measures need to be in place to handle process crashes and ensure data integrity and availability.

Network Delay

The TCP/IP network protocol operates asynchronously, meaning it does not provide a guaranteed upper bound on message delivery delay. This poses a challenge for software processes that communicate over TCP/IP. They must determine how long to wait for responses from other processes. If a response is not received within the designated time, they need to decide whether to retry or consider the other process as failed. This decision-making becomes crucial for maintaining the reliability and efficiency of communication between processes.

Process Pause

During the execution of a process, it can pause at any given moment. In garbage-collected languages like Java, execution can be interrupted by garbage collection pauses. In extreme cases, these pauses can last tens of seconds. As a result, other processes need to determine whether the paused process has failed. The situation becomes more complex when the paused process resumes and begins sending messages to other processes. The other processes then face a dilemma: Should they ignore the messages or process them, especially if they had previously marked the paused process as failed? Finding the right course of action in these circumstances is a challenging problem.

Unsynchronized Clocks

The clocks in the servers typically utilize quartz crystals. However, the oscillation frequency of a quartz crystal can be influenced by factors like temperature changes or vibrations. This can cause the clocks on different servers to have different times. Servers typically require a service such as NTP[1] that continuously synchronizes their clocks with time sources over the network. However, network faults can disrupt this service, leading to unsynchronized clocks on servers.[2] As a result, when processes need to order messages or determine the sequence of saved data, they cannot rely on the system timestamps because clock timings across servers can be inconsistent.

Defining the Term "Distributed Systems"

We will explore the common solutions to address the challenges posed by these failures. However, before we delve into that, let's establish a definition for distributed systems based on our observations thus far.

A distributed system is a software architecture that consists of multiple interconnected nodes or servers working together to achieve a common goal. These nodes communicate with each other over a network and coordinate their actions to provide a unified and scalable computing environment.

In a distributed system, the workload is distributed across multiple servers, allowing for parallel processing and improved performance. The system is designed to handle large amounts of data and accommodate a high number of concurrent users. Most importantly, it offers fault tolerance and resilience by replicating data and services across multiple nodes, ensuring that the system remains operational even in the presence of failures or network disruptions.

The Patterns Approach

Professionals seeking practical advice need an intuitive understanding of these systems that goes beyond theory. They need detailed and specific explanations

---

1. Network Time Protocol.
2. Even Google's TrueTime clock machinery built using GPS clocks has clock skew. However, that clock skew has a guaranteed upper bound.

that help comprehend real code while remaining applicable to a wide range of systems. The Patterns approach is an excellent tool to fulfill these requirements.

The concept of patterns was initially introduced by architect Christopher Alexander in his book *A Pattern Language* [Alexander1977]. This approach gained popularity in the software industry, thanks to the influential book widely known as the *Gang Of Four* [Gamma1994] book.

Patterns, as a methodology, describe particular problems encountered in software systems, along with concrete solution structures that can be demonstrated by real code. One of the key strengths of patterns lies in their descriptive names and the specific code-level details they provide.

A pattern, by definition, is a "recurring solution" to a problem within a specific context. Therefore, something is only referred to as a pattern if it is observed repeatedly in multiple implementations. Generally, *The Rule of Three*[3] is followed—a pattern should be observed in at least three systems before it can be recognized as a pattern.

The patterns approach, employed in this book, is rooted in the study of actual codebases from various open source projects, such as Apache Kafka,[4] Apache Cassandra,[5] MongoDB,[6] Apache Pulsar,[7] etcd,[8] Apache ZooKeeper,[9] CockroachDB,[10] YugabyteDB,[11] Akka,[12] JGroups,[13] and others. These patterns are grounded in practical examples and can be applied to different software systems. By exploring the insights gained from these codebases, readers can learn to understand and apply these patterns to solve common software challenges.

Another important aspect of patterns is that they are not used in isolation but rather in conjunction with other patterns. Understanding how the patterns interlink makes it much easier to grasp the overall architecture of the system.

The next chapter takes a tour of most of the patterns and shows how they link together.

---

3. https://wiki.c2.com/?RuleOfThree
4. https://kafka.apache.org
5. https://cassandra.apache.org
6. https://www.mongodb.com
7. https://pulsar.apache.org
8. https://etcd.io
9. https://zookeeper.apache.org
10. https://www.cockroachlabs.com
11. https://www.yugabyte.com
12. https://akka.io
13. http://www.jgroups.org

Chapter 2

Overview of the Patterns

by Unmesh Joshi and Martin Fowler

As discussed in the last chapter, distributing data means at least one of two things: partitioning and replication. To start our journey through the patterns in this book, we'll focus on replication first.

Imagine a very minimal data record that captures how many widgets we have in four locations (Figure 2.1).

boston	50
philadelphia	38
london	20
pune	75

Figure 2.1 *An example data record*

We replicate it on three nodes: Jupiter, Saturn, and Neptune (Figure 2.2).

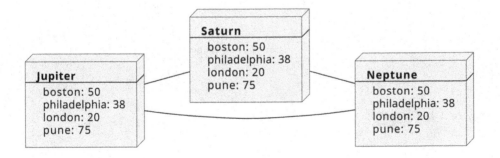

Figure 2.2 *Replicated data record*

Keeping Data Resilient on a Single Server

The first area of potential inconsistency appears with no distribution at all. Consider a case where the data for Boston, London, and Pune are held on different files. In this case, performing a transfer of 40 widgets means changing bos.json to reduce its count to 10 and changing pnq.json to increase its count to 115. But what happens if Neptune crashes after changing Boston's file but before updating Pune's? In that case we would have inconsistent data, destroying 40 widgets (Figure 2.3).

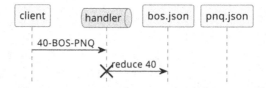

Figure 2.3 *Node crash causes inconsistency*

An effective solution to this is *Write-Ahead Log* (Figure 2.4). With this, the message handler first writes all the information about the required update to a

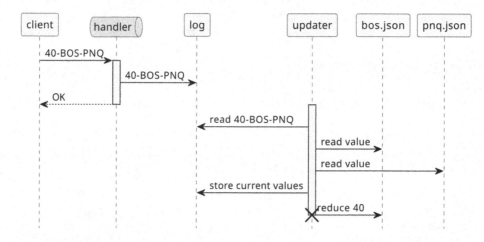

Figure 2.4 *Using WAL*

log file. This is a single write, so is simple to ensure it's done atomically. Once the write is done, the handler can acknowledge to its caller that it has handled the request. Then the handler, or other component, can read the log entry and carry out the updates to the underlying files.

Should Neptune crash after updating Boston, the log should contain enough information for Neptune, when it restarts, to figure out what happened and restore the data to a consistent state, as shown in Figure 2.5. (In this case it would store the previous values in the log before any updates are made to the data file.)

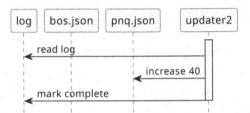

Figure 2.5 *Recovery using WAL*

The log gives us resilience because, for a known prior state, the linear sequence of changes determines the state after the log is executed. This property is important for resilience in a single node scenario but, as we'll see, it's also very valuable for replication. If multiple nodes start at the same state, and they all play the same log entries, we know they will end up at the same state too.

Databases use a Write-Ahead Log, as discussed in the above example, to implement transactions.

Competing Updates

Suppose two different users, Alice and Bob, are connecting to two different cluster nodes to execute their requests. Alice wants to move 30 widgets from Boston to London, while Bob wants to move 40 widgets from Boston to Pune (Figure 2.6).

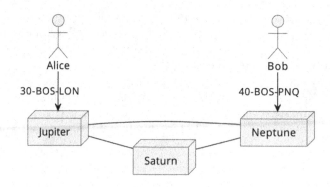

Figure 2.6 *Competing updates*

How should the cluster resolve this? We can't have any node just decide to do an update because we'd quickly run into inconsistency hell as we try to figure out how to get Boston to store antimatter widgets. One of the most straightforward approaches is *Leader and Followers*, where one of the nodes is marked as the leader, and the others are considered followers. In this situation, the leader handles all updates and broadcasts those updates to the followers. Let's say Neptune is the leader in this cluster. Then, Jupiter will forward Alice's A1 request to Neptune (Figure 2.7).

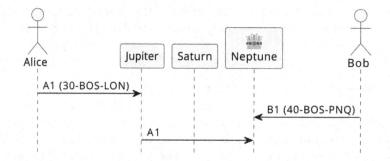

Figure 2.7 *Leader handling all the updates*

Neptune now gets both update requests, so it has the sole discretion as to how to deal with them. It can process the first one it receives (Bob's B1) and reject A1 (Figure 2.8).

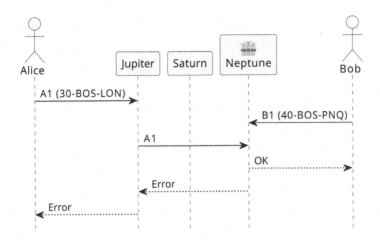

Figure 2.8 *Leader rejecting requests for insufficient widgets*

Dealing with the Leader Failing

That's what happens most of the time—when all goes well. But the point of getting a distributed system to work is what happens when things don't go well. Here's a different case. Neptune receives B1 and sends out its replication messages. But it is unable to contact Saturn. It could replicate only to Jupiter. At this point it loses all connectivity with the other two nodes. This leaves Jupiter and Saturn connected together, but disconnected from their leader (Figure 2.9).

So now what do these nodes do? For a start, how do they even find out what's broken? Neptune can't send Jupiter and Saturn a message saying the connection is broken . . . because the connection is broken. Nodes need a way to find out when connections to their colleagues break. They do this with a *HeartBeat*—or, more strictly, with the absence of a heartbeat.

A heartbeat is a regular message sent between nodes, just to indicate they are alive and communicating. Heartbeat does not necessarily require a distinct message type. When cluster nodes are already engaged in communication, such as when replicating data, the existing messages can serve the purpose of heartbeats. If Saturn doesn't receive a heartbeat from Neptune for a period of time, Saturn marks Neptune as down. Since Neptune is the leader, Saturn now calls for an election for a new leader (Figure 2.10).

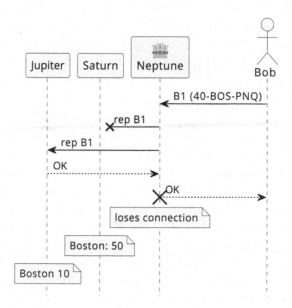

Figure 2.9 *Leader failure*

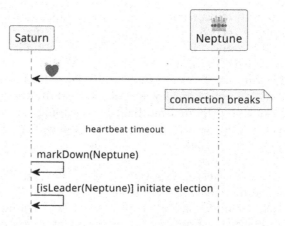

Figure 2.10 *Leader sending heartbeats*

The heartbeat gives us a way to know that Neptune has disconnected, so now we can turn to the problem of how to deal with Bob's request. We need to ensure that once Neptune has confirmed the update to Bob, even if Neptune crashes, the followers can elect a new leader with B1 applied to their data. But we also need to deal with more complication than that, as Neptune may have received multiple messages. Consider the case where there are messages from both Alice (A1) and Bob (B1) handled by Neptune. Neptune successfully replicates them both with Jupiter but is unable to contact Saturn before it crashes, as shown in Figure 2.11.

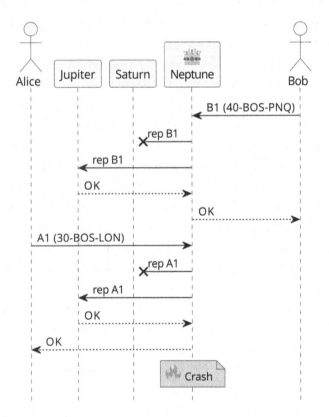

Figure 2.11 *Leader failure—incomplete replication*

In this case, how do Jupiter and Saturn deal with the fact that they have different states?

The answer is essentially the same as discussed earlier for resilience on a single node. If Neptune writes changes into a *Write-Ahead Log* and treats replication as copying those log entries to its followers, then its followers will be able to figure out what the correct state is by examining the log entries (Figure 2.12).

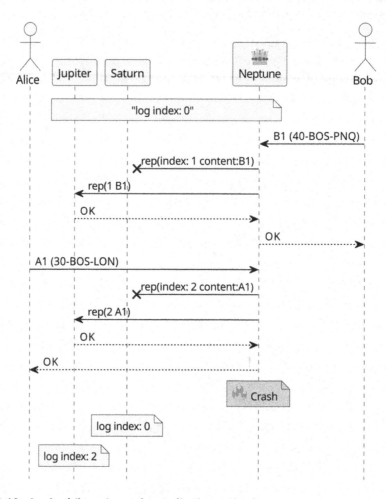

Figure 2.12 *Leader failure—incomplete replication—using log*

When Jupiter and Saturn elect a new leader, they can tell that Jupiter's log has later index entries, and Saturn can apply those log entries to itself to gain a consistent state with Jupiter.

This is also why Neptune can reply to Bob that the update was accepted, even though it hadn't heard back from Saturn. As long as a *Majority Quorum*—that is, a majority—of the nodes in the cluster have successfully replicated the log messages, Neptune can be sure that the cluster will maintain consistency even if the leader disconnects.

Multiple Failures Need a Generation Clock

We assumed here that Jupiter and Saturn can figure out whose log is most up to date. But things can get trickier. Let's say Neptune accepted a request from Bob to move 40 widgets from Boston to Pune but failed before replicating it (Figure 2.13).

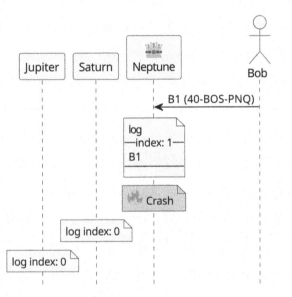

Figure 2.13 *Leader fails before replication.*

Jupiter is elected as a new leader, and accepts a request from Alice to move 30 widgets from Boston to London. But it also crashes before replicating the request to other nodes (Figure 2.14).

In a while, Neptune and Jupiter come back, but before they can talk, Saturn crashes. Neptune is elected as a leader. Neptune checks with itself and Jupiter for the log entries. It will see two separate requests at index 1, the one from Bob which it had accepted and the one from Alice that Jupiter has accepted. Neptune can't tell which one it should pick (Figure 2.15).

To solve this kind of situation, we use a *Generation Clock*. This is a number that increments with each leadership election. It is a key requirement of *Leader and Followers*.

Looking at the previous scenario again, Neptune was leader for generation 1. It adds Bob's entry in its log marking it with its generation (Figure 2.16).

When Jupiter gets elected as a leader, it increments the generation to 2. So when it adds Alice's entry to its log, it's marked for generation 2 (Figure 2.17).

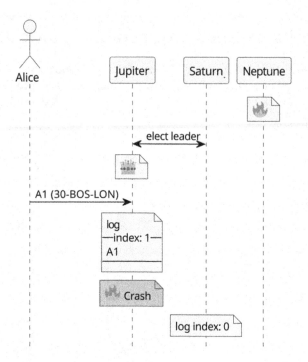

Figure 2.14 *New leader fails before replication.*

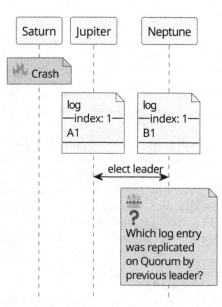

Figure 2.15 *Leader needs to resolve existing log entries.*

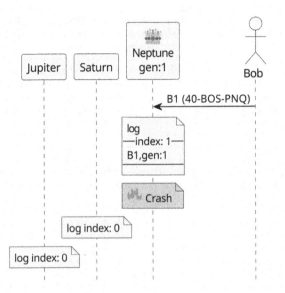

Figure 2.16 *Leader adds generation to log entries.*

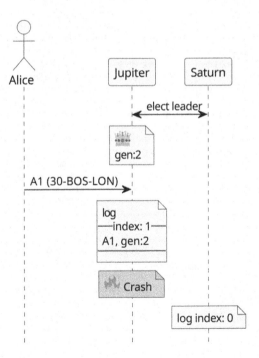

Figure 2.17 *New leader increments generation.*

Now, when Neptune is again elected as a leader, it will be for generation 3. Before it starts serving the client requests, it checks the logs of all the available nodes for entries which are not replicated on the *Majority Quorum*. We call these entries as "uncommitted," as they are not yet applied to data. We will see how each node figures out which entries are incompletely replicated in a while. But once the leader knows about these entries, it completes the replication for those entries. In case of conflict, it safely picks up the entry with higher generation (Figure 2.18).

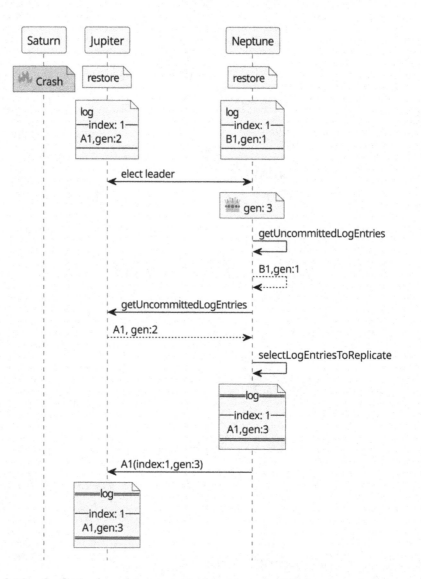

Figure 2.18 *Conflicting log entries are resolved based on generation.*

After selecting the entry with the latest generation, Neptune overwrites the uncommitted entry in its own log with its current generation number and replicates with Jupiter.

Every node tracks the latest generation it knows of the leader. This is helpful in another problem that might occur, as Figure 2.19 demonstrates. When Jupiter became leader, the previous leader, Neptune, might not have crashed, but just temporarily disconnected. It might come back online and send the requests to Jupiter and Saturn. If Jupiter and Saturn have elected a new leader and accepted

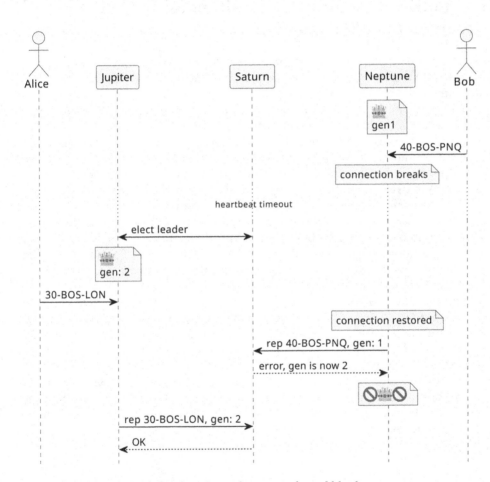

Figure 2.19 *Generation helps detecting stale requests from old leader.*

requests from Alice, what should they do when they suddenly start getting re-quests from Neptune? Generation Clock is useful in this case as well. Every request is sent to cluster nodes, along with the generation clock. So every node can always choose the requests with the higher generation and reject the ones with the lower generation.

Log Entries Cannot Be Committed until They Are Accepted by a Majority Quorum

As seen above, entries like B1 can be overwritten if they haven't been successfully replicated to a *Majority Quorum* of nodes in the cluster. So the leader cannot apply the request to its data store after just appending to its own log—it has to wait until it gets enough acknowledgments from other nodes first. When an update is added to a local log, it is **uncommitted**, until the leader has had replies from a Majority Quorum of other nodes, at which point it becomes **committed**. In the case of the example above, Neptune cannot commit B1 until it hears that at least one other node has accepted it, at which point that other node, plus Neptune itself, makes two out of three nodes—a majority and thus a Majority Quorum.

When Neptune, the leader, receives an update, either from a user (Bob) directly or via a follower, it adds the uncommitted update to its log and then sends replication messages to the other nodes. Once Saturn (for example) replies, that means two nodes have accepted the update, Neptune and Saturn. This is two out of three nodes, which is the majority and thus a Majority Quorum. At that point Neptune can commit the update (Figure 2.20).

The importance of the Majority Quorum is that it applies to decision by the cluster. Should a node fail, any leadership election must involve a Majority Quorum of nodes. Since any committed updates have also been sent to a Major-ity Quorum of nodes, we can be sure that committed updates will be visible during the election.

If Neptune receives Bob's update (B1), replicates, gets an acknowledgment from Saturn, and then crashes, Saturn still has a copy of B1. If the nodes then elect Jupiter as the leader, Jupiter must apply any uncommitted updates—that is, B1—before it can start accepting new ones (Figure 2.21).

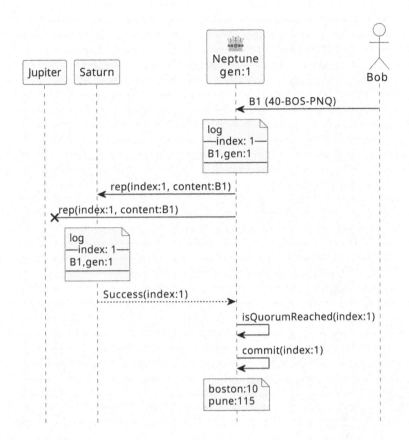

Figure 2.20 *Log entries are committed once they are accepted by a Majority Quorum.*

When the log is large, moving the log across nodes for leader election can be costly. The most commonly used algorithm for *Replicated Log*, Raft [Ongaro2014], optimizes this by electing the leader with the most up-to-date log. In the above example this would elect Saturn as the leader.

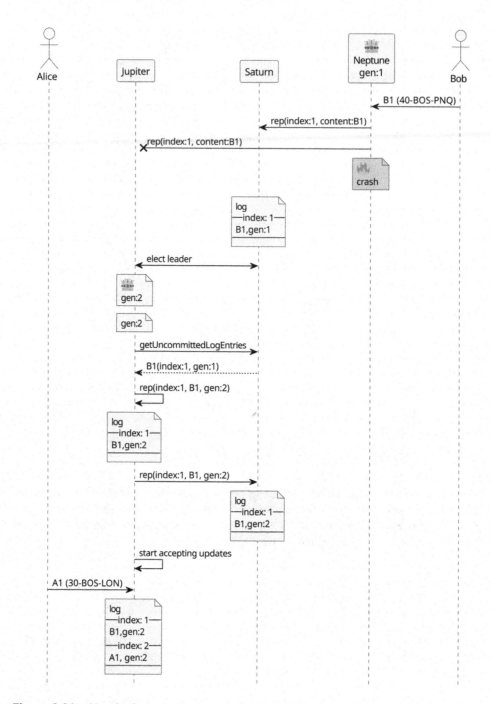

Figure 2.21 *New leader commits uncommitted log entries.*

Followers Commit Based on a High-Water Mark

As we've seen, leaders commit when they get acknowledgments from a *Majority Quorum*—but when do followers commit their log entries? In the three node example we've been using, it's obvious. Since we know the leader must have added the log entry before it replicates, any node knows that it can commit since it and the leader form a Majority Quorum. But that isn't true for larger clusters. In a five-node cluster, a single follower and a leader are only two of five.

A *High-Water Mark* solves this conundrum. Simply put, the High-Water Mark is maintained by the leader and is equal to the index of the latest update to be committed. The leader then adds the High-Water Mark to its *HeartBeat*. Whenever a follower receives a HeartBeat, it knows it can commit all its log entries up to the High-Water Mark.

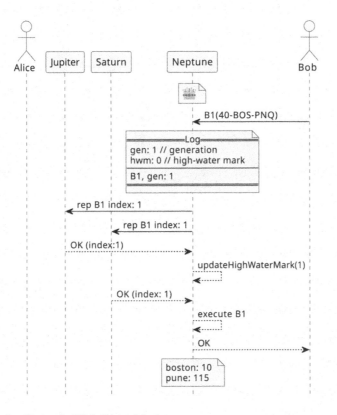

Figure 2.22   *Leader tracks High-Water Mark.*

Let's look at an example of this (Figure 2.22). Bob sends a request (B1) to Neptune. Neptune replicates the request to Jupiter and Saturn. Jupiter acknowledges first, allowing Neptune to increase its High-Water Mark to 1, execute the update against its data store, and return success to Bob. Saturn's acknowledgment is late, and since it's not higher than the High-Water Mark, Neptune takes no action on it.

Neptune now gets three requests from Alice (A1, A2, and A3). Neptune puts all of these into its log and starts sending replication messages. The link between Neptune and Saturn, however, gets tangled and Saturn doesn't get them (Figure 2.23).

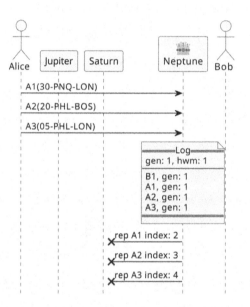

Figure 2.23 *Nodes missing replication of log entries*

After the first two messages, Neptune coincidentally sends out heartbeats, which alert followers to update their High-Water Mark. Jupiter acknowledges A1, allowing Neptune to update its High-Water Mark to 2, execute the update, and notify Alice. But then Neptune crashes before it's able to replicate A3, as shown in Figure 2.24.

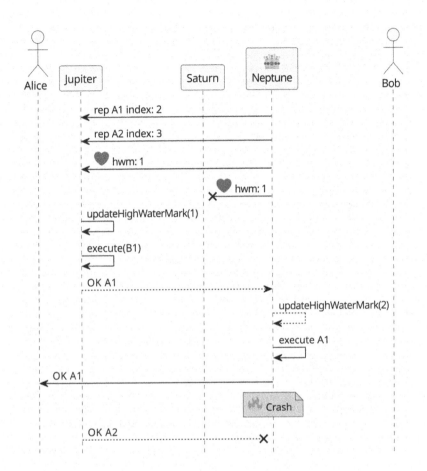

Figure 2.24   *The High-Water Mark is propagated using HeartBeat.*

At this point, here are the states of the nodes:

	Jupiter	Saturn	Neptune
gen	1	1	1
hwm	1	0	2
log	B1 A1 A2	B1	B1 A1 A2 A3

Jupiter and Saturn fail to get HeartBeat from Neptune and thus hold an election for a new leader. Jupiter wins and gathers log entries. In doing this it accepts that A2 reached Majority Quorum and sets its High-Water Mark to 3. Jupiter replicates its log to Saturn, and when Saturn gets a HeartBeat with High-Water Mark of 3 it's able to update its High-Water Mark and execute the updates against its store (Figure 2.25).

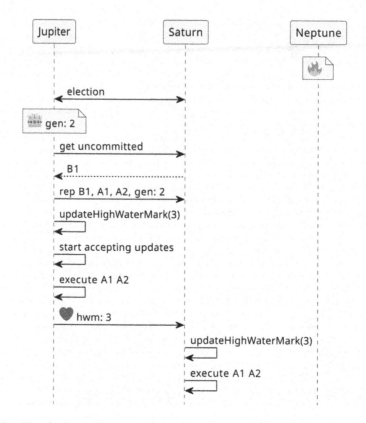

Figure 2.25 *New leader replicates missing log entries and High-Water Mark.*

Now, the state of the nodes is:

	Jupiter	Saturn	Neptune
gen	2	2	1
hwm	3	3	2
log	B1 A1 A2	B1 A1 A2	B1 A1 A2 A3

At this point Alice times out of her A3 request and resends it (A3.2), which routes to Jupiter as the new leader. Just as this happens, Neptune starts back up again. Neptune tries to replicate A3, and is told that there's a new generation of leader, so Neptune accepts that it's now a follower of Jupiter and discards its log down to its High-Water Mark. Jupiter sends replication messages for A2 and A3.2. Once Jupiter gets an acknowledgment for A3.2, it can update its High-Water Mark, execute the update, and respond to Alice (Figure 2.26).

Saturn and Neptune will update their states on the next HeartBeat from Jupiter.

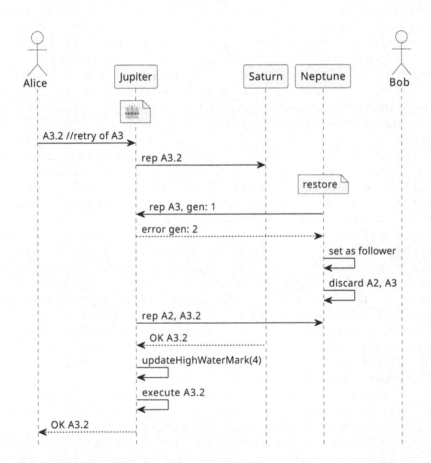

Figure 2.26 *Old leader discards conflicting log entries.*

Leaders Use a Series of Queues to Remain Responsive to Many Clients

A leader has to handle a lot of requests from many clients. Each request takes a fair bit of processing that happens in multiple stages. Requests need to be parsed to understand the request and its payload. Updates need to be persisted to a *Write-Ahead Log*, which means a write to a durable store, and in this context "durable" means "slow." Requests may also be acknowledgments from followers for a replication request—for these, the leader needs to find the request, check to see if it's reached *Majority Quorum* and, if so, update the *High-Water Mark*.

We need to ensure that these operations don't run into problems with multiple threads trying to update the same data at once. Each entry on the Write-Ahead Log needs to be written and processed in full before we start to write another. We don't want clients to wait for other clients to finish their work. At the same time, we do not want other processing stages to be blocked while all of this is going on.

For these reasons, we use a *Singular Update Queue*. Most programming languages these days will have some form of in-memory queue object that handles requests from multiple threads. Singular Update Queue builds on this by allowing client threads to write simple entries onto such an in-memory queue. A separate processing thread takes entries from this work queue, and carries out the processing we discussed above. This way the system remains responsive to clients, but also keeps the processing of requests in a saner, single-threaded world.

Some programming languages, like Go,[14] have first-class support for this mechanism with channels and goroutines.

If Alice and Bob both send messages (A1 and B1) to Neptune, they will be handled by different message handling threads on Neptune. Each of these put the mostly raw message onto the work queue. The thread handling the *Replicated Log* works independently, popping from the head of the queue, unpacking the details, adding to the log, and sending for replication (Figure 2.27).

When Jupiter acknowledges the replication, its response is handled by a message handler, which just puts the raw message on the work queue. The processing thread picks this message, checks Majority Quorum, marks the log entry as committed, and updates the High-Water Mark (Figure 2.28).

In a cluster like this, an update can only be confirmed once a Majority Quorum of nodes accepts the update. But we don't want to leave the message handler blocked while all this goes on. The message handler can possibly deal with more requests while the cluster replicates and reaches Majority Quorum. So, instead of blocking, we use a *Request Waiting List* to track waiting requests and respond

---

14. https://go.dev

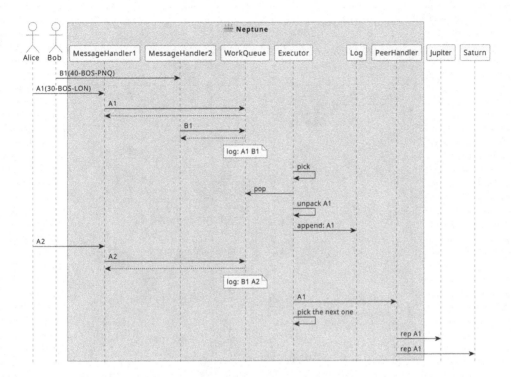

Figure 2.27 *Nodes use queues to decouple processing stages.*

to clients when their requests are actually executed before each request is put on the work queue.

When the leader receives the request, it adds a callback to Request Waiting List that will contain the behavior of notifying Bob when the request succeeds or fails (Figure 2.29).

When Jupiter acknowledges the update, the executor notifies the Request Waiting List, which invokes the callback, notifying Bob of the success of the request (Figure 2.30).

But what if the leader fails before it sends an acknowledgment back to the client? The client then doesn't know if the cluster managed to commit the request or if the leader's failure lost the request. In those circumstances, the client will retry its request, but this leads to a second problem—we don't want to make the same transfer twice.

To avoid executing a retried request again, each cluster node must be an *Idempotent Receiver*. (An idempotent operation is one that can be executed multiple

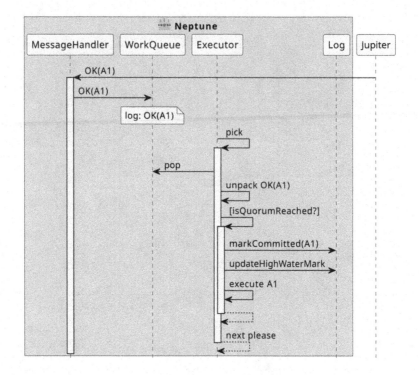

Figure 2.28 *Async processing stage committing log entries*

times with the same effect as if it were executed once. Adding 1 to a variable isn't idempotent, but setting a variable to a value is.)

To implement idempotency, each client registers itself with the leader before sending any requests. The client registration is also replicated across all the replicas similar to any other request. The registered client assigns a unique number to each request. The server can then use client ID and unique request number to store the responses of the executed requests. This mapping is looked up when a client repeats a request. Instead of executing the request again, the server returns the stored response. Now, even a non-idempotent request, such as transferring 40 widgets, can be handled in an idempotent way.

In our example, Bob registers itself before starting to send any requests. The registration request is replicated in the Replicated Log and a unique client ID is returned to Bob. Each cluster node maintains a table with entries for client IDs (Figure 2.31).

Bob now uses client ID, bob, to send the requests. It also assigns a unique number to each request. Here, it sends request 40-BOS-PNQ with request number 1. Whenever the request is executed, the response is stored in the client table (Figure 2.32).

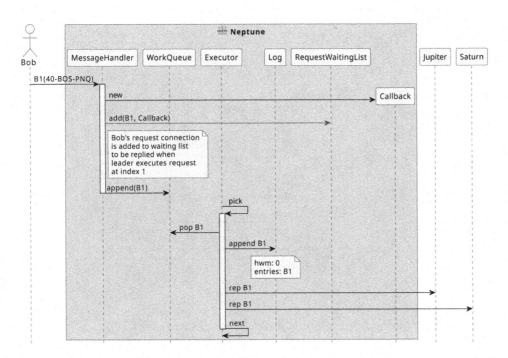

Figure 2.29 *Client requests are tracked in request waiting list.*

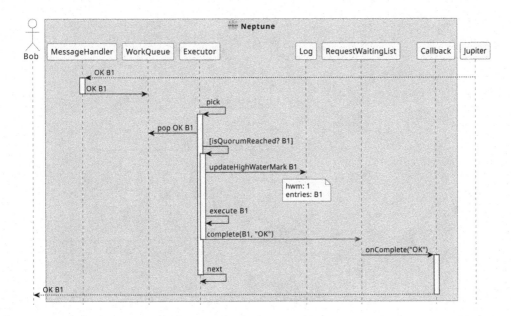

Figure 2.30 *Request waiting list completing client requests*

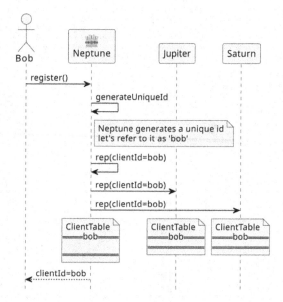

Figure 2.31   *Nodes maintain a client request table for registered clients.*

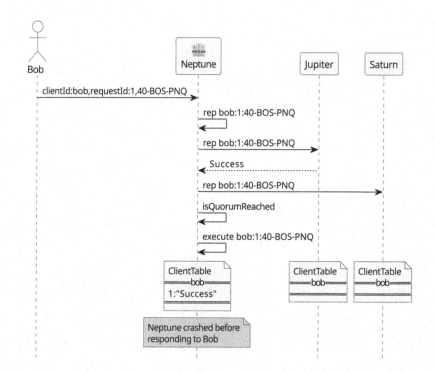

Figure 2.32   *Responses are recorded in the client request table.*

Neptune fails before sending the response to Bob. Jupiter and Saturn now run a leader election as discussed in the previous section. Jupiter will execute the pending log entries. Once it executes the request 40-BOS-PNQ from Bob, it makes an entry in the client table. At this point, Bob has not received the response, so he retries 40-BOS-PNQ again, with Jupiter. But because Jupiter has already executed the request numbered 1 from Bob, it will return the response already stored. This way, the retried request from Bob is not executed again (Figure 2.33).

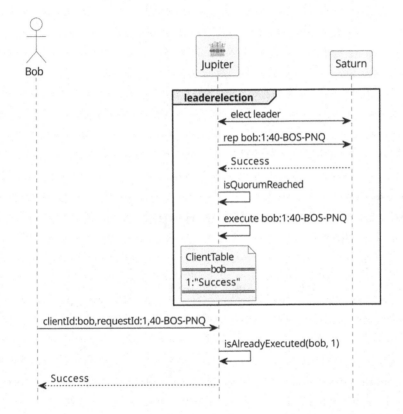

Figure 2.33   *Retried requests are detected by the new leader.*

Given we are replicating an ordered log, nodes have to maintain the order of the entries when there is no guarantee that they will receive messages in the right order.

Given this, any nodes involved in a Replicated Log like Raft are designed to tolerate out-of-order messages, but this adds overhead and degrades performance. So in practice, nodes maintain a *Single-Socket Channel* between leader and followers, as shown in Figure 2.34. ZooKeeper or Apache Kafka are good examples of this implementation.

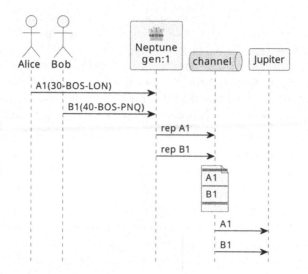

Figure 2.34   *Leader maintains a Single-Socket Channel with follower.*

Followers Can Handle Read Requests to Reduce Load on the Leader

Replicating updates to followers has a couple of benefits. One is that it provides a hot backup of the leader, allowing a follower to step in should a problem occur. But the main reason to do this with a cluster is *Follower Reads*: allowing followers to serve read requests. This reduces load on the leader, enabling it to serve write requests more quickly. This benefit doesn't come for free: The followers will always lag the state of the leader by the amount of time it takes to propagate the log replication. Most of the time, this won't present an issue, but it is an issue in one common case. Once Bob has made his update, he's likely to read the new state. Should his read request go to Saturn, there is a risk that it will beat the replication process and Bob will read stale data (Figure 2.35).

In this situation we want to ensure Bob will read data consistent with what he's written—a property called read-your-writes consistency (Figure 2.36). A way to obtain this is to use *Versioned Value*, storing a version number with each stored record. When Neptune writes Bob's update, it increments the version associated with the data, and returns that version to Bob. When Bob reads data, he supplies that version as part of his request. Saturn can then check the version before responding to a read, if necessary waiting until it's received that version update.

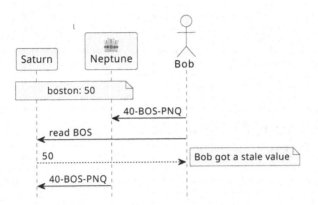

Figure 2.35 *Followers can return stale values.*

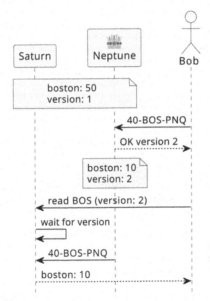

Figure 2.36 *Versions are tracked to ensure read-your-writes consistency.*

Distributed databases such as MongoDB and CockroachDB use *Hybrid Clock* to set a version in the Versioned Value to provide this consistency. Other systems, using *Replicated Log*, can use *High-Water Mark*. In Raft followers all need to ensure their High-Water Mark is the same as the leader before replying to requests. In Apache Kafka, messages are produced in a log, which is very similar to a

Replicated Log. The log index for produced messages is returned to the client on writes, and the client uses it for subsequent reads. If the read request is handled by a follower, it needs to check that it has that log index, similar to the use of Versioned Value discussed above.

A Large Amount of Data Can Be Partitioned over Multiple Nodes

As discussed in the first chapter, there are physical limits for how much data can be handled on a single node. Beyond that, we will need the data to be split up over multiple nodes. The cluster acts as a single database, with its data separated into partitions (also called shards) on different nodes. Since partitioning is done primarily to work around the physical limitations of a single server, it is important that data is as evenly distributed as possible. As the load on the cluster grows, it is common to add more nodes to the cluster. Here are the key requirements for any partitioning scheme:

- Data should be evenly distributed across all the cluster nodes.

- It should be possible to know which cluster node stores a particular data record, without making a request to all the nodes.

- It should be quick and easy to move part of the data to the new nodes.

Almost all data storages can be described as key-value storages. Clients typically store and access data records by some unique identifiers. With a key-value storage, an easy way to achieve the above requirements is to take a hash of each key and map it to a node. Hash values for keys make sure that data is evenly distributed. If the number of partitions is known, a hash can be mapped to its partition simply by

```
partition = hash_of_key % no. of partitions
```

While the modulo operation is easy to use, changing the number of partitions causes the partition for every record to change, so that adding just one extra node to an existing cluster requires moving all the data records across the cluster. This is definitely a no-no when we are dealing with large amount of data. Instead, a common pattern is to define logical partitions, with many more logical partitions than there are physical nodes. To find a node for a record, you first find the record's logical partition, and then look up which node that logical partition is sitting on. The logical partition for a record need never change; if we add a node to the cluster, we reassign some of the logical partitions to it, which only moves the records in those logical partitions.

The most straightforward form of using logical partitions is *Fixed Partitions*.

For example, Akka suggests you should have ten times as many logical partitions (shards) as the number of nodes. Apache Ignite[15] has a default partition count of 1024. That way, mapping of data records to partitions never changes.

Consider a cluster of three nodes: Jupiter, Saturn, and Neptune. We'll use six logical partitions, which is not very realistic but makes it easier to show how they work. Now, if Bob is adding widgets to a Pune, he will interact with the cluster via a client library running on the client machine. This client library will initialize itself by getting the mapping of partitions to cluster nodes (usually from a *Consistent Core* as discussed later). The client library will first find the partition for the key pune by a simple modulo operation.

```
int partition = hash("pune")%6
```

Then it gets the node hosting that partition and forwards the request to that node. In this case, it will send the request to Saturn (Figure 2.37).

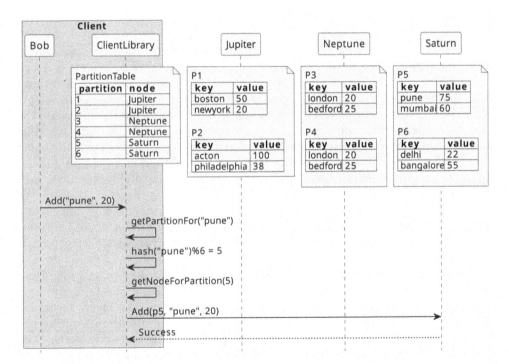

Figure 2.37 *Routing requests to fixed partitions with modulo operation*

---

15. https://ignite.apache.org/docs/latest

If a new node is added, a few partitions can be moved to the new node to balance the load, without needing to change the key-to-partition mapping. Let's say a new node, Uranus, is added to the cluster while Saturn is heavily loaded, possibly because the partitions it is hosting have more data. In that case, some partitions from Saturn can be moved to Uranus (Figure 2.38).

Now, the mapping of keys like `"pune"` to partition is not changing as the value of `hash("pune")%6` will remain the same. The client library will only need to update its partition table. It can do that periodically, or when cluster nodes return an error saying they no longer host the given partition.

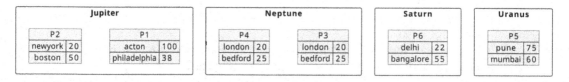

Figure 2.38 *Partitions moved to new nodes to ensure even distribution*

While the hash of Fixed Partitions is simple to produce, it can be limiting because databases often need to support range queries, such as finding a list of cities starting with "p" to "q". If a hash of a key is used for mapping to partitions, a range query may need to access records from all partitions. If such queries are common, *Key-Range Partitions* are a better approach. Key-Range Partitions use the element of the key that appears in common ranges as part of the partition selection algorithm. A simple, indeed naive, example would be to define 26 partitions and map the first letter of the key to each partition. This would allow a p-to-q query to access just two partitions. Generally, the ranges will be slightly broader, such as from "p" to "z".

The client library will have metadata about the partitions, the key ranges, and the nodes where the partitions are hosted. The library uses this data to determine that the p-to-q range is all on partition p3, and only that specific partition is queried by sending a request to Neptune (Figure 2.39).

One of the difficulties with Key-Range Partitions is that key ranges might not be known up front. So most data systems start with a single partition, and only split that partition once it reaches a particular size. So, unlike Fixed Partitions, the mapping from key to partition will change over time. Partition splitting can be performed in a manner that keeps both partitions on the same node. Data movement across nodes happens only if the partitions are eventually relocated to a different node. HBase is a good example of how key-range partitions are implemented; YugabyteDB and CockroachDB also support Key-Range Partitions.

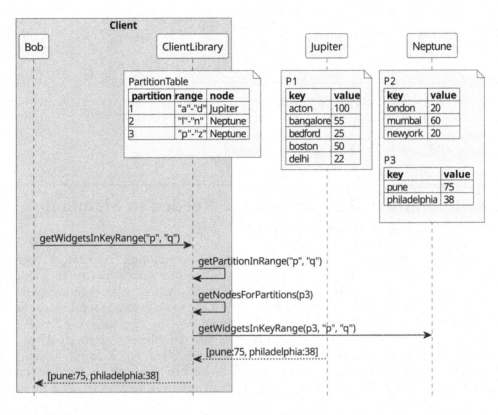

Figure 2.39 *Key-Range Partitions allow range queries.*

Partitions Can Be Replicated for Resilience

While partitioning helps distribute load across the cluster, we still need to resolve issues caused by failures. If a cluster node fails, all the partitions hosted on that node are unavailable. Replicating a partition is just like replicating unpartitioned data, so we use the same patterns for replication that we discussed earlier, centered around *Replicated Log*, as shown in Figure 2.40.

A typical partitioned cluster can be hundreds or thousands of logical partitions. You don't want too much replication, because the more replicas there are, the larger the *Majority Quorum* will be, and thus the slower the response to updates. Three or five replicas strikes a good balance between failure tolerance and performance.

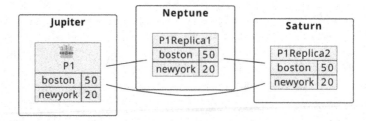

Figure 2.40 *Partitions are replicated for resilience.*

A Minimum of Two Phases Are Needed to Maintain Consistency across Partitions

Introducing partitions adds further complexity to maintaining consistency when operations span across multiple partitions. Consider Alice's desire to move 30 widgets from Boston to London. If Boston and London are on different partitions, we have to maintain consistency not just between multiple replicas of the same data, but also between the different partitions. The *Replicated Log* handles the problem for replicas, but it doesn't help us maintain the consistency between partitions. This is a common distributed system problem. For example, Apache Kafka runs into this when messages need to be produced on multiple topics atomically. MongoDB faces this problem when multiple partitions need to be updated atomically.

Consistency across partitions can be solved by using *Two-Phase Commit*. This nominates one of the nodes as a coordinator (Figure 2.41). Typically the node

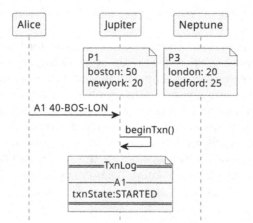

Figure 2.41 *Coordinator tracks transaction state.*

hosting the partition for the first key of the operation is made the coordinator. Let's say Jupiter hosts the partition for Boston, and Neptune hosts the partition for London. Since Jupiter holds the partition for Boston, this message is routed to Jupiter, which is declared the coordinator. As a coordinator, Jupiter needs to do all the bookkeeping for the state of the transaction. All the information needs to be persisted on disk to make sure that in the event of a failure, Jupiter knows about all the pending transactions. So it maintains a separate *Write-Ahead Log* to make this information about the ongoing transaction persistent.

Jupiter tells itself to prepare to reduce Boston's widget count. It also sends a message to Neptune to add widgets to London, as shown in Figure 2.42. However, neither change to the data occurs yet.

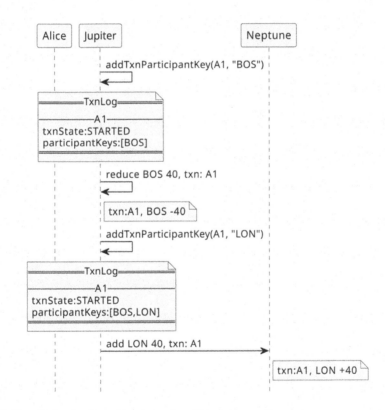

Figure 2.42 *Nodes track pending requests within a transaction.*

Jupiter then coordinates with both nodes, itself and Neptune, to commit the transaction. Both data stores send an accepted message back to the coordinator. Only after both data stores have accepted the transaction, the coordinator commits the transaction and sends an OK back to Alice (Figure 2.43).

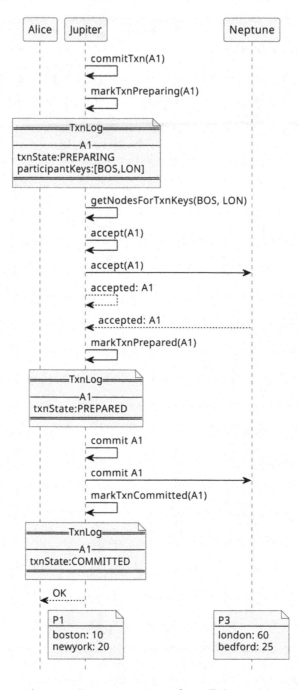

Figure 2.43 *Transaction commits upon acceptance from all the participants.*

This example shows what would happen for nonreplicated partitions, but essentially the same process occurs if they are replicated. The difference is that Jupiter and Neptune would each make the change through a Replicated Log.

Everything we have discussed about various failures is true in this case as well. So, each of the participants in a two-phase commit maintains their own Replicated Log. There is a replicated log maintained for coordinator and for each partition.

In Distributed Systems, Ordering Cannot Depend on System Timestamps

Earlier, we saw that we need to use *Versioned Value* to ensure a client would read values consistent with what they had written. To make it work, it's essential to determine the order in which updates occur.

On a single node, it is easy to implement this just by maintaining a single counter and incrementing it every time a modification is done to any record. Sequence number usage in RocksDB[16] is a good example of that. Let's see how this looks for a single node (Figure 2.44). Alice sends a request to Neptune to reduce 40 widgets from Boston. This creates a new version for Boston with the value of 10. Alice then sends a request to add 40 widgets to London. This creates a new version, with version number 3 for London with the value of 60. Alice then reads the snapshot at version 3. It obviously expects to get Boston's value to be 10, and gets it as expected.

When records are stored across multiple nodes, tracking which records are stored before and after other records becomes tricky. How to increment version numbers to make sure versions across nodes track this before-after relationship?

It is natural to think that system timestamps can be used to version records. Later updates will have higher timestamps, so it will naturally track which records are updated before or after the other. But in practice, this is a big problem because, despite the best efforts of time synchronization tools, different nodes will have slightly different clocks. While these differences are tiny in human terms, they are significant when it comes to computer communications. We have to assume that system timestamps are not monotonic, as discussed in the sidebar "Wall Clocks Are Not Monotonic" of the *Lease* pattern.

To see why this is a problem, let's say records for Boston and London are stored on nodes Jupiter and Neptune respectively. Jupiter's clock shows time as 19:25, but Neptune's clock is lagging behind and shows time as 19:20. Let's say Boston has 50 widgets at timestamp 19:25 and London has 20 widgets at timestamp 19:20 as per Jupiter's and Neptune's clocks respectively. (We're just using

---

16. https://github.com/cockroachdb/pebble/blob/master/docs/rocksdb.md#internal-keys

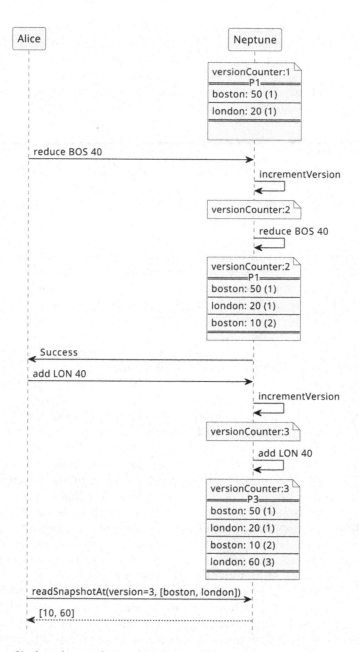

Figure 2.44 *Single node snapshot read—using counter for versions*

time of day in the example, but the actual timestamp would include the date. It would also be UTC to avoid time zone issues.)

Alice sends a message to reduce 40 widgets from Boston. Assuming the clock has progressed 5 seconds, the new version for Boston is created at timestamp 19:30 as per Jupiter's clock.

Alice then sends a message to Neptune, to add 40 widgets to London. This creates a new version for London at timestamp 19:25 as per Neptune's clock. As we can see in Figure 2.45, even though London's record on Neptune was updated "after" Boston's record on Jupiter, it got a lower timestamp.

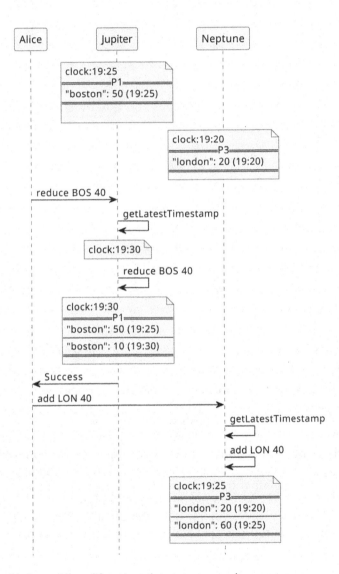

Figure 2.45 *Nodes writing with system timestamp as version*

Now, Alice wants to read the "latest" values for Boston and London. Alice's request is handled by Saturn, which uses its own clock to see what the "latest" timestamp is. If its clock is similar to that of Neptune, it will send read requests to Jupiter and Neptune to read values at timestamp 19:25.

Alice will be puzzled because she will see the latest value for London as 60, but Boston's value from Jupiter will have the old value, 50 (Figure 2.46).

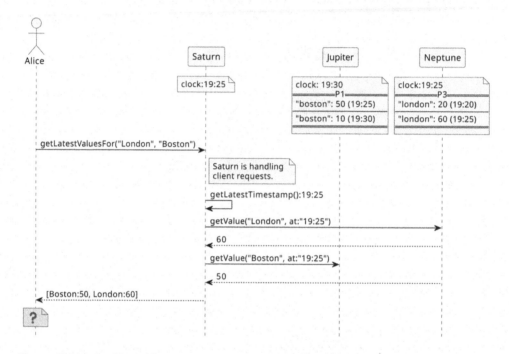

Figure 2.46 *Reading with a system timestamp can return stale values.*

We can use a *Lamport Clock* to track the order of requests across cluster nodes without relying on system timestamps. The trick is to use a simple integer counter per node, but pass it along in requests and responses from and to clients.

Let's take the same example as above. 40 widgets are moved from Boston to London. Both Jupiter and Neptune maintain a simple integer counter. Every time a record is updated, this counter is incremented. But the counter is also passed to the client, which passes it to next operation it does on another node.

Here, when 40 widgets are removed from Boston, the counter at Jupiter is incremented to 2, and a new version for Boston is created at 2. The counter value 2 is passed to Alice. Alice passes it to Neptune when it sends a request to add

40 widgets to London. The important part here is how the counter is incremented on Neptune. Neptune checks its own counter and the one passed to it in the request. It picks the greater value and then increments it to update its own counter. This makes sure that the new version created for London will have a version number of 3 which is greater than the version number for Boston (Figure 2.47).

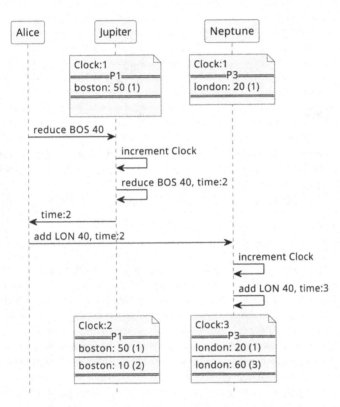

Figure 2.47 *Lamport clock tracks ordering of writes.*

One of the issues with basic Lamport Clock is that versions are tracked by integers with no relation to actual timestamps. For a client to ask for a specific snapshot, it will need to somehow ask for the Lamport timestamp values corresponding to that snapshot. The other, more important issue is that when data on two independent servers is modified by two independent clients, there is no way to order those versions. For example, in the following scenario (Figure 2.48), Bob might have added 20 widgets to London before Alice added 40 widgets to

Boston. There is no way to tell that by looking at the logical versions. That is why Lamport Clock is said to be partially ordered.

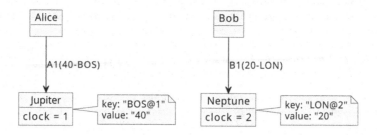

Figure 2.48   *Lamport clock values across servers may not indicate order.*

Therefore, most databases need to use timestamps as versions, so that users can query data based on actual timestamps of the node processing their requests. To work around the problem with computer clocks, *Hybrid Clock*, which combines clock time with a Lamport Clock, is used. When nodes send messages, they include the Hybrid Clock which combines the time of the current server with a Lamport Clock counter. When Neptune receives a message with a timestamp ahead of Neptune's clock, it increments the integer counter part of the Hybrid Clock which ensures its operations sort later than the received message.

With a Hybrid Clock, Alice sends a message to reduce Boston's holding and Jupiter records that operation with its system timestamp and a counter (19:30, 0) which it returns to Alice. Alice then passes this on to Neptune with its request to increase London. Neptune sees that Alice's reported timestamp is (19:30, 0), which is ahead of Neptune's own clock at 19:25. Therefore, Neptune increments the counter, yielding a hybrid timestamp of (19:30, 1), which it uses for its record and acknowledgment to Alice (Figure 2.49).

This solves part of the problem. Even though Neptune's system clock was lagging, the records stored at Neptune after the one stored on Jupiter will have timestamp which is higher. We still have the problem of partial order to solve. If another client, Bob, tries to read and his request is processed by Saturn, whose clock is lagging same as Neptune at 19:25, he would see the old values for both London and Boston. If Alice and Bob now talk to each other, they will find they are seeing different values for the same data.

To prevent this, we use *Clock-Bound Wait*, which waits before storing the value long enough for all of the cluster's nodes' clocks to advance beyond the one assigned to the records.

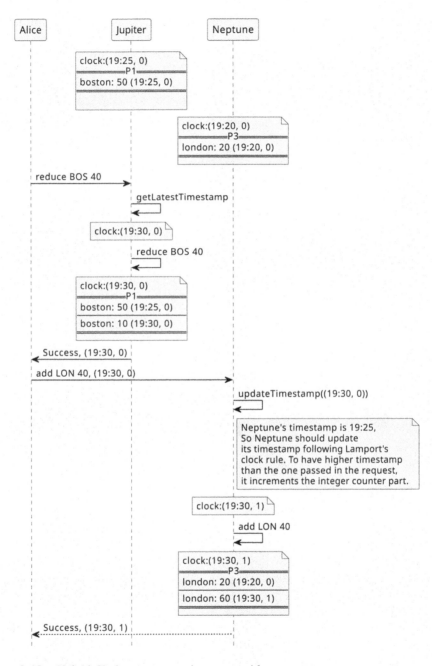

Figure 2.49 *Hybrid Clock uses system timestamp with a counter.*

Consider the example in the previous section. Let's say the maximum clock skew across cluster nodes is 5 seconds. Every write operation can wait for 5 seconds before the values are stored (Figure 2.50).

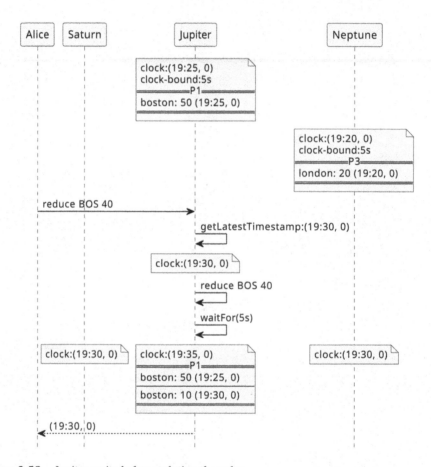

Figure 2.50 *Jupiter waits before updating the value.*

So when the values at 19:30 are stored on Neptune and Jupiter, every node in the cluster is guaranteed to have their clocks showing time higher than 19:30 (Figure 2.51).

Now, if Bob is trying to read the latest value, and his request is initiated on Saturn which has clock lagging same as Neptune, he is guaranteed to get the latest value for Boston—that is, the value written at timestamp 19:30, as Figure 2.52 demonstrates.

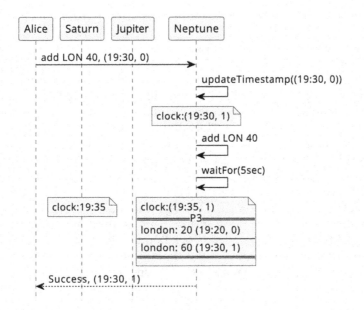

Figure 2.51   *Neptune waits before updating the value.*

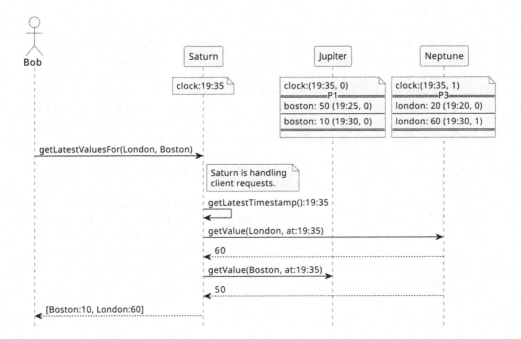

Figure 2.52   *Read requests get latest values with Clock-Bound Wait.*

With this approach, since every node waits for the maximum clock skew, the request initiating on any cluster node is guaranteed to see the latest values irrespective of their own clock values.

The tricky part of this is knowing how much skew there is across all the clocks in the cluster. If we don't wait long enough, we won't get the ordering we need, but if we wait too long, we will reduce the throughput of writes too much. Most open source databases use a technique called as "read restart," as discussed in the section "Read Restart" of the Clock-Bound Wait pattern, to avoid waiting in the write operations.

Databases like MongoDB, YugabyteDB, and CockroachDB use Hybrid Clock. While they can't rely on the clock machinery to give them exact clock skew across cluster nodes, they use Clock-Bound Wait assuming a configurable maximum clock skew. Google developed TrueTime[17] in its data centers to guarantee that the clock skew is no more than 7 ms. This is used by Google's Spanner[18] databases. AWS has a library called Clock Bound which has a similar API to give clock skew across cluster nodes; at the time of writing, the AWS library, unlike TrueTime, does not give a guarantee on the upper bound.

A Consistent Core Can Manage the Membership of a Data Cluster

A cluster can have hundreds or thousands of nodes. Such a cluster is also dynamic, allowing nodes to be added to handle increasing load or removed due to failures or reductions in traffic. We see large clusters regularly with Apache Kafka or Kubernetes clusters and with databases like MongoDB, Cassandra, CockroachDB, or YugabyteDB. To manage such a cluster, we need to keep track of which nodes are part of the cluster. With partitioned data, we have to track the mapping of keys to logical partitions and partitions to nodes. It's important that this management is done in a fault-tolerant way, so that failure of one control node doesn't bring down the whole cluster. Management data also needs strong consistency, otherwise we risk corruption of our data.

As we've seen earlier, *Replicated Log* is an excellent way to achieve this. But a Replicated Log depends on *Majority Quorum*, which cannot scale to thousands of replicas. Therefore the management of a large cluster is given to a *Consistent Core*—a small set of nodes whose responsibility is to manage a larger data cluster. The Consistent Core tracks the data cluster membership with *Lease* and *State Watch* (Figure 2.53).

17. https://cloud.google.com/spanner/docs/true-time-external-consistency
18. https://cloud.google.com/spanner

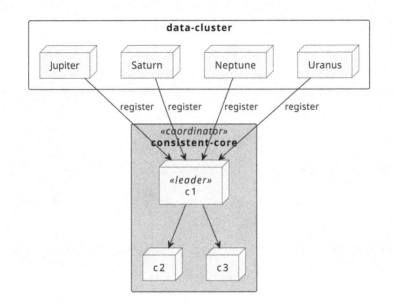

Figure 2.53   *Consistent Core tracks cluster membership.*

This requirement is so common in distributed services that some products include the necessary generic functionalities to utilize a Consistent Core, which includes patterns like Lease and State Watch. Examples of such products are Apache ZooKeeper and etcd, which are often utilized as Consistent Core components.

One use of Lease is for node registration and failure detection of cluster nodes. The ephemeral node implementation in Apache ZooKeeper or the lease functionality in etcd are examples of this. Here, Jupiter, a data cluster node, registers with the Consistent Core with its unique ID or name. The node entries are tracked as leases and renewed with periodic *HeartBeat* (Figure 2.54).

The leader of the Consistent Core periodically checks leases which are not refreshed. If Jupiter crashes and stops sending HeartBeat, its lease will be removed (Figure 2.55).

Leases are replicated, so if a leader fails, the new leader of the Consistent Core will start tracking the leases. Jupiter then needs to connect with the new leader and keep sending the heartbeats.

When a generic Consistent Core like Apache ZooKeeper or etcd is used, a dedicated cluster node, called a **cluster controller**, uses information stored in etcd or ZooKeeper to take decisions on behalf of the cluster. Apache Kafka's controller [Rao2014] is a good example of this. Other nodes need to know when this particular node is down so that someone else can take this responsibility. To do this, the data cluster node registers a State Watch with the Consistent

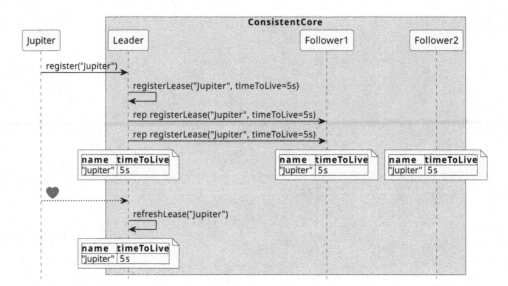

Figure 2.54   *Consistent Core tracks Lease.*

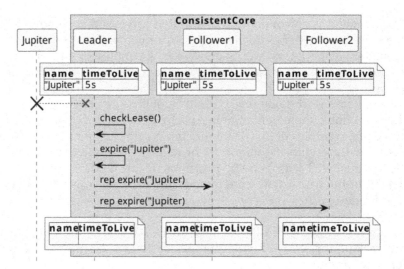

Figure 2.55   *Lease expires if not renewed.*

Core. The Consistent Core notifies all the interested nodes when a particular node fails.

Let's say Jupiter plays the role of cluster controller. Neptune wants to know when Jupiter's lease expires. It registers its interest with the Consistent Core by contacting the core's leader. When the lease for Jupiter expires, indicating that Jupiter is probably no longer up and running, the leader of the consistent core checks to see if any nodes need to be notified. In this case, Neptune is notified with a "lease-deleted" event (Figure 2.56).

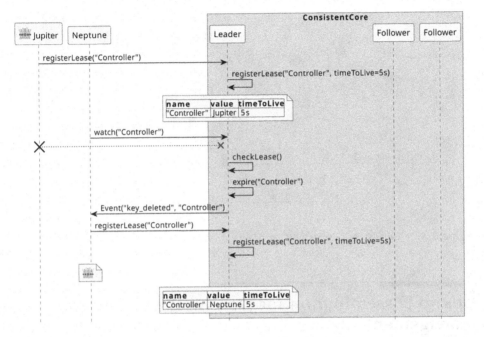

Figure 2.56 *Nodes watch cluster state changes using Consistent Core.*

Replication messages from leader to followers of the Consistent Core are not shown in the diagram.

It's important that Neptune receives all its events in the correct order. While the communication protocol can sort all that out, it is usually more efficient for Neptune to connect to the Consistent Core with a *Single-Socket Channel*.

Apache ZooKeeper and etcd are examples of generic frameworks used by products like Apache Kafka or Kubernetes. Often, it is convenient for clustered software to have their own implementation based on Replicated Log and to do decision making in the Consistent Core itself. Quorum based controller [McCabe2021] for Apache Kafka, the primary cluster of MongoDB, and the master cluster of YugabyteDB are examples of these.

An example of this is when a Consistent Core assigns *Fixed Partitions* to the cluster nodes. Three nodes, Jupiter, Neptune, and Saturn, register with the consistent core. Once the registration is done, the consistent core maps partitions evenly across the cluster nodes (Figure 2.57).

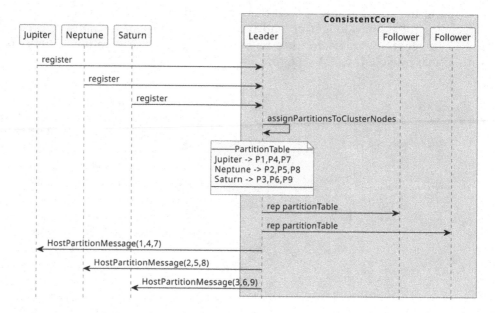

Figure 2.57 *Consistent Core assigns partitions to cluster nodes.*

Gossip Dissemination for Decentralized Cluster Management

Some systems, such as Cassandra, lean more towards eventual consistency, and do not want to rely on a centralized *Consistent Core*. They tolerate some inconsistency in the cluster metadata provided it converges quickly. Metadata, such as the total number of nodes, their network addresses, partitions they host, and so on, still needs to be propagated somehow to everyone. (As we write this, however, there is a proposal to migrate Cassandra to a Consistent Core.)

As discussed in the previous section, there can be thousands of nodes in a cluster. Each node has some information and needs to make sure it reaches every other node. It will incur too much communication overhead if every node talks to every other node. *Gossip Dissemination* is an interesting way out. At regular intervals, each node picks another node at random and sends it the information it has on the state of the cluster. This style of communication has a nice property. In a cluster with n nodes, this information reaches every node in time proportional to log(n). Interestingly, this matches how epidemics spread in large communities. The mathematical branch of epidemiology studies how an epidemic or rumors spread in a society. A disease spreads very quickly even if each person comes into contact with only a few individuals at random. An entire population can become infected from very few interactions. Gossip Dissemination is based on these mathematical models. If nodes send information to a few other nodes regularly, even a large cluster will get that information quickly.

Say, we have eight servers, each having information about a color of the planet they are named after (Figure 2.58). We want all these servers to know every color.

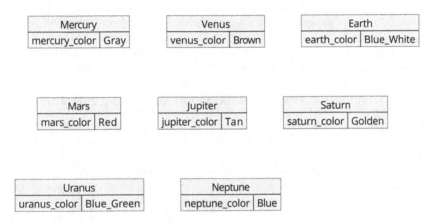

Figure 2.58   *An example cluster. Each node maintains a color.*

To start with, Mercury sends a gossip message to Venus (Figure 2.59).

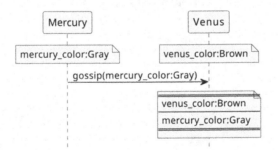

Figure 2.59   *Mercury sending gossip message to Venus*

Then Venus sends gossip message to Neptune. It includes everything it has in the gossip message (Figure 2.60).

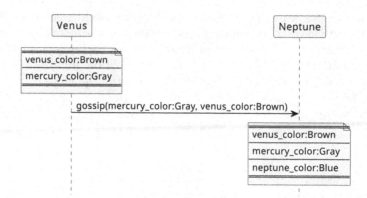

Figure 2.60   *Venus sending gossip message to Neptune*

Meanwhile Jupiter sends gossip message to Mars (Figure 2.61).

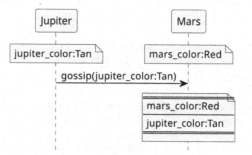

Figure 2.61   *Jupiter sending gossip message to Mars*

Uranus gossips to Earth (Figure 2.62).

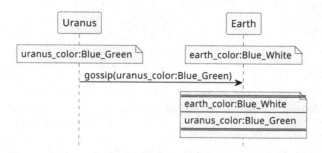

Figure 2.62   *Uranus gossips to Earth.*

Earth gossips to Mars (Figure 2.63).

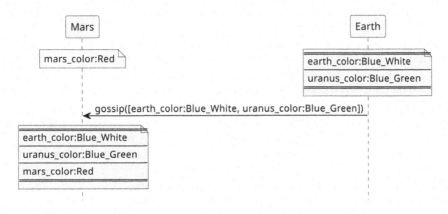

Figure 2.63   *Earth gossips to Mars.*

When Neptune gossips with Mars, Mars will have colors for Mercury, Venus, Neptune, Earth, Jupiter, and Mars (Figure 2.64).

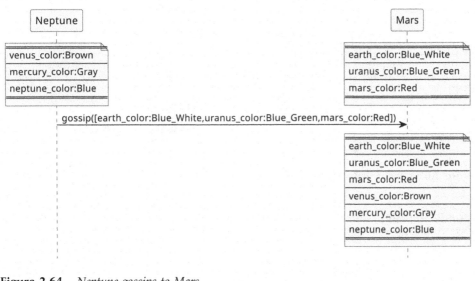

Figure 2.64   *Neptune gossips to Mars.*

This happens at regular intervals at each node. Eventually, and rather quickly, all nodes get the same information. HashiCorp Consul[19] has a very nice convergence simulator[20] which shows how quickly information converges with its gossip implementation.

How is this technique used in real life? One common use is to manage group membership in products like Cassandra. Let's say there is a large cluster of 100 nodes. We need all the nodes to know about each other. The cluster nodes can achieve this by doing a repeated communication, each time with a random node.

To start with, there is at least one special node, which needs to be known to every node. This node is called the seed node. It can either be configured, or there can be a mechanism to know the seed node at startup. The seed node is just one of the nodes in the cluster—it does not implement any special functionality. It only needs to be known to everyone else.

Every node starts by communicating with the seed node and sending its own address to it. The seed node, like any other node, has a scheduled task to repeatedly send what it knows about others to a randomly selected node.

For example, suppose Neptune is the seed node. When Jupiter starts, it sends its own address to Neptune (Figure 2.65).

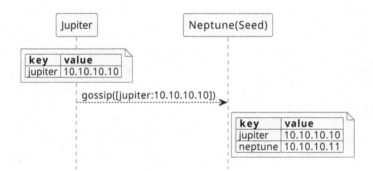

Figure 2.65 *Jupiter gossips to Neptune.*

Then, Saturn starts and sends its own address to Neptune the same way (Figure 2.66).

---

19. https://www.consul.io
20. https://www.serf.io/docs/internals/simulator.html

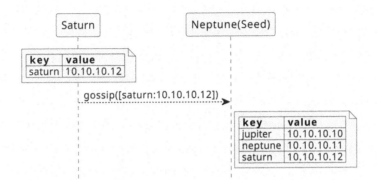

Figure 2.66 *Saturn gossips to Neptune.*

All of Jupiter, Saturn, and Neptune repeatedly pick a random node and send it all the information they have. So in a while, Neptune picks up Jupiter and sends it information that it has. Now both Neptune and Jupiter know about Saturn (Figure 2.67).

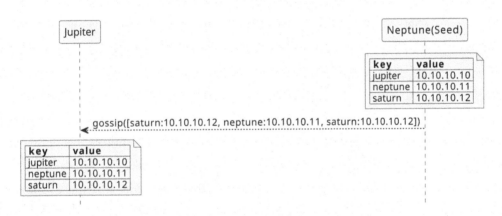

Figure 2.67 *Neptune gossips to Jupiter.*

In the next cycle, either Jupiter or Neptune might pick up Saturn and send it all the information they have. Now, Saturn will know about Jupiter (Figure 2.68). At this point, all three nodes know about each other Figure 2.69).

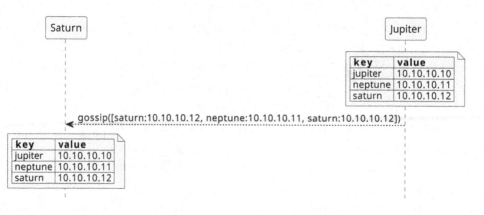

Figure 2.68   *Jupiter gossips to Saturn.*

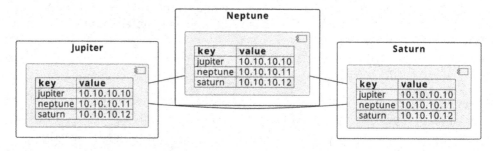

Figure 2.69   *All nodes know about each other.*

Gossip Dissemination is a commonly used technique for information dissemination in large clusters. Products like Cassandra, Akka, or Consul use it for managing group membership information in large clusters.

One major limitation of gossip protocols is that they only provide eventual consistency. When stronger consistency is needed, a Consistent Core implementation is preferred. For example, Cassandra moved from gossip protocol to a smaller consistent core [Tunnicliffe2023] to maintain its metadata.

Some systems, like Akka, designate a single cluster node to act as a cluster coordinator without running an explicit leader election. Similar to Consistent Core, an *Emergent Leader* takes decisions on behalf of the cluster. A common technique is for the nodes to be ordered based on their age in the cluster. The node with the highest age is designated a leader of the cluster to take decisions. Since no explicit election is run, there can be inconsistencies caused by problems like *split brain* as discussed in the section "Split Brain" of the Emergent Leader pattern.

Part II

Patterns of Data Replication

Replicating data is essential for ensuring service continuity to the users. As summarized by the CAP [Brewer1999] theorem, there are design choices that need to be made depending on whether consistency of data in the case of failures is crucial or availability is favored. At one end, there is a technique known as *State Machine Replication* [Schneider1990] to achieve fault tolerance but also guarantee strong consistency. In state machine replication, the storage services, such as a key-value store, are replicated on multiple servers, and the user inputs are executed in the same order on each server. The key implementation technique here is to replicate *Write-Ahead Log* on multiple servers to have a *Replicated Log*. On the other hand, you can have relaxed consistency by using a basic *Majority Quorum* mechanism.

The patterns in this section are primarily focused on the replication mechanism.

Chapter 3

Write-Ahead Log

Provide durability guarantee without the storage data structures to be
flushed to disk, by persisting every state change as a command to the
append only log.
Also known as: Commit Log

Problem

Strong durability guarantee is needed even in the case of the server machines
storing data failing. Once a server agrees to perform an action, it should do so
even if it fails and restarts losing all of its in-memory state.

Solution

Store each state change as a command in a file on a hard disk (Figure 3.1). A
single log is maintained for each server process. It is sequentially appended.
A single log, appended sequentially, simplifies handling of logs at restart and the
subsequent online operations (when the log is appended with new commands).
Each log entry is given a unique identifier. This identifier helps in implementing
certain other operations on the log, such as *Segmented Log*, cleaning the log with
Low-Water Mark, and so on. The log updates can be implemented with *Singular
Update Queue*.

Here's the typical log entry structure:

```
class WALEntry...

  private final Long entryIndex;
  private final byte[] data;
  private final EntryType entryType;
  private final long timeStamp;
```

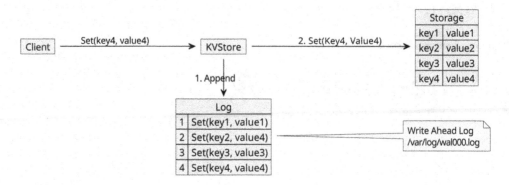

Figure 3.1 *Write-Ahead Log*

The file can be read on every restart and the state can be recovered by replaying all the log entries.

Consider a simple in-memory key-value store:

```
class KVStore...

  private Map<String, String> kv = new HashMap<>();

  public String get(String key) {
      return kv.get(key);
  }

  public void put(String key, String value) {
      appendLog(key, value);
      kv.put(key, value);
  }

  private Long appendLog(String key, String value) {
      return wal.writeEntry(new SetValueCommand(key, value).serialize());
  }
```

The put action is represented as *Command,* which is serialized and stored in the log before updating the in-memory hash map.

```
class SetValueCommand...

  final String key;
  final String value;

  public SetValueCommand(String key, String value) {
      this.key = key;
      this.value = value;
  }

  @Override
  public void serialize(DataOutputStream os) throws IOException {
```

```
        os.writeInt(Command.SetValueType);
        os.writeUTF(key);
        os.writeUTF(value);
    }

    public static SetValueCommand deserialize(InputStream is) {
        try {
            var dataInputStream = new DataInputStream(is);
            return new SetValueCommand(dataInputStream.readUTF(),
                    dataInputStream.readUTF());
        } catch (IOException e) {
            throw new RuntimeException(e);
        }
    }
}
```

This makes sure that once the put method returns successfully, even if the process holding the KVStore crashes, its state can be restored by reading the log file at startup.

class KVStore...

```
    public KVStore(Config config) {
        this.config = config;
        this.wal = WriteAheadLog.openWAL(config);
        this.applyLog();
    }

    public void applyLog() {
        List<WALEntry> walEntries = wal.readAll();
        applyEntries(walEntries);
        applyBatchLogEntries(walEntries);
    }

    private void applyEntries(List<WALEntry> walEntries) {
        for (WALEntry walEntry : walEntries) {
            Command command = deserialize(walEntry);
            if (command instanceof SetValueCommand) {
                SetValueCommand setValueCommand = (SetValueCommand)command;
                kv.put(setValueCommand.key, setValueCommand.value);
            }
        }
    }
```

Implementation Considerations

It's important to make sure that entries written to the log file are actually persisted on the physical media. File handling libraries in all programming languages provide a mechanism to force the operating system to flush the file changes to physical media. There is a tradeoff, however, to be considered when using flushing.

Flushing every log write to the disk gives a strong durability guarantee (which is the main purpose of having logs in the first place), but this severely limits performance and can quickly become a bottleneck. If flushing is delayed or done asynchronously, it improves performance but there is a risk of losing entries from the log if the server crashes before entries are flushed. Most implementations use techniques, such as batching, to limit the impact of the flush operation.

Another consideration is to make sure that corrupted log entries are detected while reading the log. To handle this, log entries are usually written with CRC records, which then can be validated when the files are read. While CRC allows detecting corrupted entries at a modest compute cost, even a simple technique like having an end-of-entry marker can be useful. If that marker isn't present, the log entry wasn't written and can be discarded on recovery.

Single log files can become difficult to manage and can quickly consume all the storage. To handle this issue, techniques like *Segmented Log* and *Low-Water Mark* are used.

The write-ahead log is append-only. Because of this behavior, in case of client communication failure and retries, logs can contain duplicate entries. When the log entries are applied, you need to make sure that the duplicates are ignored. If the final state is something like a HashMap, where the updates to the same key are idempotent, no special mechanism is needed. If they're not, there needs to be some mechanism to mark each request with a unique identifier and detect duplicates.

It is important to note that write-ahead logging assumes the presence of stable storage. In the event of a media failure, the write-ahead log itself can be lost. To tolerate such failures, it is necessary to use the *Replicated Log* pattern instead.

Write-ahead logging is a commonly used pattern, particularly due to the characteristics of storage systems used today. It is employed because data is modified in volatile memory (RAM) and then made persistent by storing it on a hard disk. However, in the future, with the emergence of persistent memory products like Intel Optane,[21] the need for write-ahead logging may diminish. Instead, techniques such as write-behind logging [Arulraj2016] can be utilized.

Usage in Transactional Storage

Write-ahead log is often used to implement transactional storage. The concept of a transaction guarantees that changes made within a single transaction are done as one atomic operation. Either all the changes are done or none at all. They also ensure that, once done, the changes are durable. Multiple transactions do not interfere with each other, and when the transaction completes, the data store is in a consistent state.

---

21. www.intel.in/content/www/in/en/products/docs/memory-storage/optane-persistent-memory/overview.html

The basic usage of a write-ahead log provides a way to do durable atomic updates. The other two properties of transactions, consistency and isolation, need to be provided by concurrency control mechanism using locks. It can be implemented as discussed in the section "Locks and Transaction Isolation" of the *Two-Phase Commit* pattern.

RocksDB[22] is a good example of how a write-ahead log is used to provide atomic updates. In RocksDB, the key and values, which need to be atomically stored, are written to a batch. The whole batch is then written to the data store. The data store writes a single entry in the write-ahead log for the entire batch. Once the entry is successfully written to the log, it is added to the key-value store.

For example, if two key-value records need to be added atomically for the keys "author" and "title", it is done as follows. A write batch is created with both key-value records.

```
KVStore kv = new KVStore(config);
WriteBatch batch = new WriteBatch();
batch.put("title", "Microservices");
batch.put("author", "Martin");

kv.put(batch);
```

The whole batch is written into the key-value store. The batch is appended to the write-ahead log as a single entry.

```
public void put(WriteBatch batch) {
    appendLog(batch);
    kv.putAll(batch.kv);
}
```

At restart, when the batch entry is read, the whole batch is applied to restore the keys and values.

```
private void applyBatchLogEntries(List<WALEntry> walEntries) {
    for (WALEntry walEntry : walEntries) {
        Command command = deserialize(walEntry);
        if (command instanceof WriteBatchCommand) {
            WriteBatchCommand batchCommand = (WriteBatchCommand)command;
            WriteBatch batch = batchCommand.getBatch();
            kv.putAll(batch.kv);
        }
    }
}
```

This makes sure that, in the event of a crash, either the whole batch is available or none of it is available.

---

22. https://rocksdb.org

Compared to Event Sourcing

A log of changes is similar to the log of events in event sourcing [Fowler2005]. Indeed, when an event-sourced system uses its log to synchronize multiple systems, it is using its log as a write-ahead log. However, an event-sourced system uses its log for more than just that—for example, to be able to reconstruct a state at previous points in history. For this, an event sourcing log is the persistent source of truth and log entries are kept for a long time, often indefinitely.

The entries for a write-ahead log, however, are only needed for state recovery. Thus they can be discarded when all the nodes have acknowledged an update—that is, below the *Low-Water Mark*.

Examples

- The log implementation in all consensus algorithms, such as Zab [Reed2008] and Raft [Ongaro2014] is similar to a write-ahead log.

- The storage implementation in Apache Kafka uses a structure similar to that of commit logs in databases.

- All the databases, including the nosql databases such as Cassandra, use the write-ahead log technique to guarantee durability.

Chapter 4

Segmented Log

Split log into multiple smaller files instead of a single large file for easier operations.

Problem

A single log file can grow and become a performance bottleneck as it is read at startup. Older logs are cleaned up periodically, but doing cleanup operations on a single huge file is difficult to implement.

Solution

Single log is split into multiple segments. Log files are rolled after a specified size limit.

```
class WriteAheadLog...

  public Long writeEntry(WALEntry entry) {
      maybeRoll();
      return openSegment.writeEntry(entry);
  }

  private void maybeRoll() {
      if (openSegment.
              size() >= config.getMaxLogSize()) {
          openSegment.flush();
          sortedSavedSegments.add(openSegment);
          long lastId = openSegment.getLastLogEntryIndex();
          openSegment = WALSegment.open(lastId, config.getWalDir());
      }
  }
```

With log segmentation, there needs to be an easy way to map logical log offsets (or log sequence numbers) to the log segment files. This can be done in two ways:

- Each log segment name is generated by some known prefix and a base offset (or a log sequence number).

- Each log sequence number is divided into two parts, the name of the file and the transaction offset.

class WALSegment...

```
public static String createFileName(Long startIndex) {
    return logPrefix + "_" + startIndex + logSuffix;
}

public static Long getBaseOffsetFromFileName(String fileName) {
    String[] nameAndSuffix = fileName.split(logSuffix);
    String[] prefixAndOffset = nameAndSuffix[0].split("_");
    if (prefixAndOffset[0].equals(logPrefix))
        return Long.parseLong(prefixAndOffset[1]);

    return -1l;
}
```

With this information, the read operation is two steps. For a given offset (or transaction ID), the log segment is identified and all the log records are read from subsequent log segments.

class WriteAheadLog...

```
public List<WALEntry> readFrom(Long startIndex) {
    List<WALSegment> segments
            = getAllSegmentsContainingLogGreaterThan(startIndex);
    return readWalEntriesFrom(startIndex, segments);
}

private List<WALSegment>
            getAllSegmentsContainingLogGreaterThan(Long startIndex) {

    List<WALSegment> segments = new ArrayList<>();

    //Start from the last segment to the first segment
    // with starting offset less than startIndex
    //This will get all the segments which have log entries
    // more than the startIndex
    for (int i = sortedSavedSegments.size() - 1; i >= 0; i--) {
        WALSegment walSegment = sortedSavedSegments.get(i);
        segments.add(walSegment);

        if (walSegment.getBaseOffset() <= startIndex) {
            // break for the first segment with
            // baseoffset less than startIndex
```

```
            break;
        }
    }

    if (openSegment.getBaseOffset() <= startIndex) {
        segments.add(openSegment);
    }

    return segments;
}
```

Examples

- All consensus implementations, such as Raft, use log segmentation.

- The storage implementation in Apache Kafka uses log segmentation.

- All the databases, including the nosql databases such as Cassandra, use rollover strategy based on some preconfigured log size.

Chapter 5

Low-Water Mark

An index in the write-ahead log showing which portion of the log can be discarded.

Problem

A write-ahead log maintains every update to the persistent store. It can grow indefinitely over time. *Segmented Log* ensures smaller files, but the total disk storage can grow indefinitely if not checked.

Solution

Have a mechanism to tell logging machinery which portion of the log can be safely discarded. The mechanism gives the lowest offset, or low-water mark, before which the logs can be discarded. Have a task running in the background, in a separate thread, which continuously checks which portion of the log can be discarded and deletes the files on the disk.

```
class WriteAheadLog...

  this.logCleaner = newLogCleaner(config);
  this.logCleaner.startup();
```

The log cleaner can be implemented as a scheduled task:

```
class LogCleaner...

  public void startup() {
      scheduleLogCleaning();
  }
```

```
private void scheduleLogCleaning() {
    singleThreadedExecutor.schedule(() -> {
        cleanLogs();
    }, config.getCleanTaskIntervalMs(), TimeUnit.MILLISECONDS);
}

public void cleanLogs() {
    List<WALSegment> segmentsTobeDeleted = getSegmentsToBeDeleted();
    for (WALSegment walSegment : segmentsTobeDeleted) {
        wal.removeAndDeleteSegment(walSegment);
    }
    scheduleLogCleaning();
}
```

Snapshot-Based Low-Water Mark

Most consensus implementations, such as ZooKeeper or etcd (as defined in Raft [Ongaro2014]), use snapshot mechanisms. In this implementation, the storage engine takes periodic snapshots. Along with a snapshot, it also stores the log index which was successfully applied. Referring to the simple key-value store implementation in the *Write-Ahead Log* pattern, the snapshot can be taken as following:

```
class KVStore...

    public SnapShot takeSnapshot() {
        Long snapShotTakenAtLogIndex = wal.getLastLogIndex();
        return new SnapShot(serializeState(kv), snapShotTakenAtLogIndex);
    }
```

Once a snapshot is successfully persisted on the disk, the log manager is given the low-water mark to discard older logs:

```
class SnapshotBasedLogCleaner...

    @Override
    List<WALSegment> getSegmentsToBeDeleted() {
        return getSegmentsBefore(this.snapshotIndex);
    }

    List<WALSegment> getSegmentsBefore(Long snapshotIndex) {
        List<WALSegment> markedForDeletion = new ArrayList<>();
        List<WALSegment> sortedSavedSegments = wal.sortedSavedSegments;
        for (WALSegment sortedSavedSegment : sortedSavedSegments) {
            if (sortedSavedSegment.getLastLogEntryIndex() < snapshotIndex) {
                markedForDeletion.add(sortedSavedSegment);
            }
        }
        return markedForDeletion;
    }
```

Time-Based Low-Water Mark

In some systems, where logs are not used to update the state of the system, logs can be discarded after a given time window without waiting for any other subsystem to share the lowest log index that can be removed. For example, in systems like Kafka, logs are maintained for seven weeks; all the log segments that have messages older than seven weeks are discarded. For this implementation, each log entry also includes the timestamp when it was created. The log cleaner can then check the last entry of each log segment and discard segments that are older than the configured time window.

```
class TimeBasedLogCleaner...

  private List<WALSegment> getSegmentsPast(Long logMaxDurationMs) {
      long now = System.currentTimeMillis();
      List<WALSegment> markedForDeletion = new ArrayList<>();
      List<WALSegment> sortedSavedSegments = wal.sortedSavedSegments;
      for (WALSegment sortedSavedSegment : sortedSavedSegments) {
          Long lastTimestamp = sortedSavedSegment.getLastLogEntryTimestamp();
          if (timeElaspedSince(now, lastTimestamp) > logMaxDurationMs) {
              markedForDeletion.add(sortedSavedSegment);
          }
      }
      return markedForDeletion;
  }

  private long timeElaspedSince(long now, long lastLogEntryTimestamp) {
      return now - lastLogEntryTimestamp;
  }
```

Apart from these techniques, the log can also be cleaned based on its size. Once a configured maximum size is reached, older log entries are automatically removed.

Examples

- All consensus implementations, such as ZooKeeper or Raft, implement snapshot-based log cleaning.

- The storage implementation in Apache Kafka uses time-based log cleaning.

Chapter 6

Leader and Followers

Have a single server to coordinate replication across a set of servers.

Problem

To achieve fault tolerance in systems that manage data, the data needs to be replicated on multiple servers.

It's also important to give some guarantee about consistency to clients. When data is updated on multiple servers, you need to decide when to make it visible to clients. Write and read *Majority Quorum* is not sufficient, as some failure scenarios can cause clients to see data inconsistently. Each individual server does not know about the state of data on the other servers in the quorum. It's only when data is read from multiple servers, the inconsistencies can be resolved. In some cases, this is not enough. Stronger guarantees are needed about the data sent to clients.

Solution

Select one server in the cluster as a leader. The leader is responsible for taking decisions on behalf of the entire cluster and propagating the decisions to all the other servers.

Every server at startup looks for an existing leader. If no leader is found, it triggers a leader election. The servers accept requests only after a leader is elected successfully. Only the leader handles the client requests. If a request is sent directly to a follower server, the follower can forward it to the leader server.

Leader Election

In smaller clusters of three to five nodes, like those systems that implement consensus, leader election can be done within the data cluster itself without depending on any external system. Leader election happens at server startup. Every server starts a leader election at startup and tries to elect a leader. The system does not accept any client requests unless a leader is elected. As explained in the *Generation Clock* pattern, every leader election also needs to update the generation number. A server can only be in one of the three states: Leader, Follower, or Looking For Leader (sometimes referred to as Candidate).

```
public enum ServerRole {
    LOOKING_FOR_LEADER,
    FOLLOWING,
    LEADING;
}
```

HeartBeat mechanism is used to detect when an existing leader has failed, so that a new leader election can be started.

Concurrency, Locks, and State Updates

State updates can be done without any hassle of manipulating synchronization and locking by using *Singular Update Queue*.

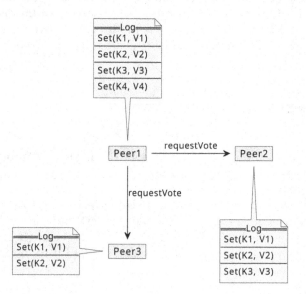

Figure 6.1 *Nodes trigger election at startup.*

New leader election is started by sending each of the peer servers a message requesting a vote (Figure 6.1).

```
class ReplicatedLog...

  private void startLeaderElection() {
      replicationState.setGeneration(replicationState.getGeneration() + 1);
      registerSelfVote();
      requestVoteFrom(followers);
  }
```

Election Algorithm

Zab and Raft

There are two popular mainstream implementations with leader election algorithms that have a few subtle differences: Zab [Reed2008], a part of ZooKeeper implementation, and the leader election algorithm in Raft [Ongaro2014].

Their differences include the point at which the generation number is incremented, the default state the server starts in, and how to make sure there are no split votes. In Zab, each server looks for the leader at startup, generation number is incremented only by a leader when it's elected, and split vote is avoided by making sure each server runs the same logic to choose a leader when multiple servers are equally up-to-date. In the case of Raft, servers start in the follower state by default, expecting to get heartbeats from the existing leader. If no heartbeat is received, they start election by incrementing the generation number. The split vote is avoided by using randomized timeouts before starting the election.

There are two factors to be considered when electing a leader.

- Since these systems are mostly used for data replication, that puts some extra restrictions on which servers can win the election. Only a server that is "the most up-to-date" can be a legitimate leader. For example, in typical consensus-based systems, the "most up-to-date" is defined by two things:

  - The latest *Generation Clock*

  - The latest log index in *Write-Ahead Log*

- If all the servers are equally up-to-date, then the leader is chosen based on:

  - Some implementation-specific criteria, such as which server is ranked better or has higher ID (for example, Zab).

- If care is taken to make sure only one server asks for a vote at a time, then whichever server starts the election before others (for example, Raft).

Once a server is voted for in a given Generation Clock, the same vote is returned for that generation always. This makes sure that some other server requesting a vote for the same generation is not elected, if a successful election has already happened. This is how vote requests are handled (Figure 6.2):

```
class ReplicatedLog...

    VoteResponse handleVoteRequest(VoteRequest voteRequest) {
        //for a higher generation, requester becomes follower.
        // But we do not know who the leader is yet.
        if (voteRequest.getGeneration() > replicationState.getGeneration()) {
            becomeFollower(LEADER_NOT_KNOWN, voteRequest.getGeneration());
        }

        VoteTracker voteTracker = replicationState.getVoteTracker();
        if (voteRequest.getGeneration() == replicationState.getGeneration()
                && !replicationState.hasLeader()) {

            if (isUptoDate(voteRequest) && !voteTracker.alreadyVoted()) {
                voteTracker.registerVote(voteRequest.getServerId());
                return grantVote();
            }
            if (voteTracker.alreadyVoted()) {
                return voteTracker.votedFor == voteRequest.getServerId() ?
                        grantVote() : rejectVote();
            }
        }
        return rejectVote();
    }

    private boolean isUptoDate(VoteRequest voteRequest) {
        Long lastLogEntryGeneration = voteRequest.getLastLogEntryGeneration();
        Long lastLogEntryIndex = voteRequest.getLastLogEntryIndex();
        return lastLogEntryGeneration > wal.getLastLogEntryGeneration()
                || (lastLogEntryGeneration == wal.getLastLogEntryGeneration() &&
                    lastLogEntryIndex >= wal.getLastLogIndex());
    }
```

The server that receives votes from the majority of the servers transitions to the leader state. The majority is determined as discussed in *Majority Quorum*. Once elected, the leader continuously sends *HeartBeat* to all the followers (Figure 6.3). If followers do not get a heartbeat in a specified time interval, a new leader election is triggered.

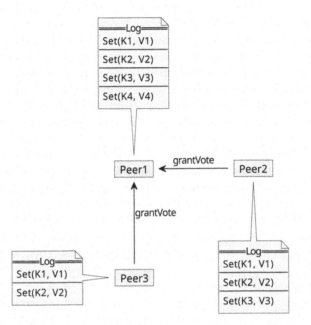

Figure 6.2 *Nodes grant votes.*

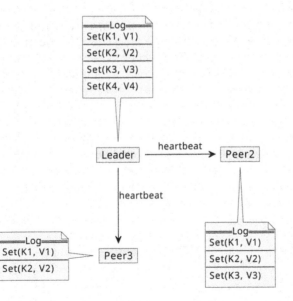

Figure 6.3 *Elected leader sends heartbeats.*

Leader Election Using a Consistent Core

Running a leader election in a data cluster works well for smaller clusters. For large data clusters with thousands of nodes, it's easier to use a *Consistent Core*, such as ZooKeeper or etcd, which internally use consensus and provide linearizability guarantees. Such large clusters typically have a server, marked as a master or a controller node, which makes all decisions on behalf of the entire cluster. You need three things for implementing a leader election:

- A compareAndSwap instruction to set a key atomically

- A heartbeat implementation to expire the key if no heartbeat is received from the elected leader, so that a new election can be triggered

- A notification mechanism to notify all the interested servers if a key expires

For electing the leader, each server uses the compareAndSwap instruction to try and create a key in the external store. Whichever server succeeds first is elected as a leader. Depending on the external store used, the key is created with a small time to live. The elected leader repeatedly updates the key before the time to live expires. Every server can set a watch on this key and get notified if the key expires without getting updated from the existing leader. For example, etcd allows a compareAndSwap operation by allowing a set key operation only if the key does not exist previously. In Apache ZooKeeper, there is no explicit compareAndSwap operation supported, but it can be implemented by trying to create a node and expecting an exception if the node already exists. There is no explicit time-to-live either, but ZooKeeper has a concept of ephemeral node. The node exists while the server has an active session with ZooKeeper, otherwise it is removed and everyone who is watching that node is notified. For example, ZooKeeper can be used to elect leader as following:

```
class Server...

  public void startup() {
      zookeeperClient.subscribeLeaderChangeListener(this);
      elect();
  }

  public void elect() {
      var leaderId = serverId;
      try {
          zookeeperClient.tryCreatingLeaderPath(leaderId);
          this.currentLeader = serverId;
          onBecomingLeader();
      } catch (ZkNodeExistsException e) {
          //back off
          this.currentLeader = zookeeperClient.getLeaderId();
      }
  }
```

All other servers watch for the liveness of the existing leader. When it is detected that the existing leader is down, a new leader election is triggered. The failure detection happens using the same Consistent Core used for the leader election. This Consistent Core also has facilities to implement group membership and failure detection mechanisms. For example, extending the above ZooKeeper-based implementation, a change listener can be configured with ZooKeeper which is triggered when a change in the existing leader node happens.

```
class ZookeeperClient...

    public void subscribeLeaderChangeListener(IZkDataListener listener) {
        zkClient.subscribeDataChanges(LeaderPath, listener);
    }
```

Every server in the cluster subscribes for this change. Whenever the callback is called, a new election is triggered again in the same way shown above, as Figure 6.4 demonstrates.

```
class Server...

    @Override
    public void handleDataDeleted(String dataPath) {
        elect();
    }
```

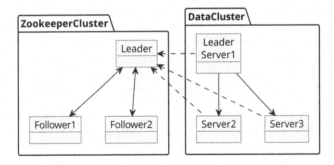

Figure 6.4 *ZooKeeper-based election*

Systems like etcd or Consul can be used in the same way to implement leader election.

Why Quorum Read/Writes Are Not Enough for Strong Consistency Guarantees

You might think that quorum read/write, provided by Dynamo-style databases like Cassandra, is enough for getting strong consistency in case of server failures.

But that is not the case. Consider the following example. Let's say we have a cluster with three servers. Variable x is stored on all three servers. (It has a replication factor of 3.) Value of x is 1 at startup.

- Let's say writer1 writes $x = 2$, with replication factor of 3. The write request is sent to all three servers. The write is successful on server1 but fails for server2 and server3 (either a network glitch or writer1 just went into a long garbage collection pause after sending the write request to server1).

- Client c1 reads the value of x from server1 and server2. It gets the latest value of $x = 2$ because server1 has the latest value.

- Client c2 triggers a read for x. But server1 goes down temporarily. So c1 reads it from server2 or server3, which have the old value of $x = 1$. So c2 gets the old value even though it read it after c1 read the latest value.

Here, two consecutive reads show the latest value disappearing. Once server1 comes back up, subsequent reads will again give the latest value. And, assuming a read repair or anti-entropy process is running, the rest of the servers will eventually get the latest value as well. But there is no guarantee provided by the storage cluster that once a particular value is visible to any client, all subsequent reads will continue to get that value.

Examples

- For systems which implement consensus, it's important that only one server coordinates activities for the replication process. As noted in the paper "Paxos Made Simple" [Lamport2001], it's important for the liveness of the system.

- In Raft and Zab consensus algorithms, leader election is an explicit phase that happens at startup or on leader failure.

- The Viewstamped Replication [Liskov2012] algorithm has a concept of a primary, similar to the leader in other algorithms.

- Apache Kafka has a controller [Rao2014] which is responsible for taking all decisions on behalf of the rest of the cluster. It reacts to events from ZooKeeper. For each partition in Kafka, there is a designated leader broker and follower brokers. The leader and follower selection is done by the controller broker.

Chapter 7

HeartBeat

Show a server is available by periodically sending a message to all the other servers.

Problem

When multiple servers form a cluster, each server is responsible for storing some portion of the data, based on the partitioning and replication schemes used. Timely detection of server failures is important for taking corrective actions by making some other server responsible for handling requests for the data on a failed server.

Solution

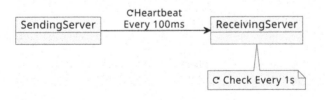

Figure 7.1 *Heartbeat*

Periodically send a request to all the other servers indicating liveness of the sending server (Figure 7.1). Select the request interval to be more than the network round trip time between the servers. All the listening servers wait for the timeout interval, which is a multiple of the request interval. In general,

timeout interval > request interval > network round trip time between the servers

It is useful to know the network round trip times within and between data-centers when choosing values for the heartbeat interval and timeout. For example, if the network round trip time between the servers is 20 ms, heartbeats can be sent every 100 ms, and servers can check after 1 second to give enough time for multiple heartbeats to be sent without getting false negatives. If a server receives no heartbeat within this interval, it declares that the sending server has failed.

Both servers, the one sending the heartbeat and the one receiving it, have a scheduler defined as follows. The scheduler is given a method to be executed at a regular interval. When started, the task is scheduled to execute the given method.

class HeartBeatScheduler...

```
public class HeartBeatScheduler {
    private ScheduledThreadPoolExecutor executor
            = new ScheduledThreadPoolExecutor(1);

    private Runnable action;
    private Long heartBeatInterval;

    public HeartBeatScheduler(Runnable action, Long heartBeatIntervalMs) {
        this.action = action;
        this.heartBeatInterval = heartBeatIntervalMs;
    }

    private ScheduledFuture<?> scheduledTask;

    public void start() {
        scheduledTask = executor
                .scheduleWithFixedDelay(new HeartBeatTask(action),
                    heartBeatInterval, heartBeatInterval,
                    TimeUnit.MILLISECONDS);
    }
```

On the sending server, the scheduler executes a method to send heartbeat messages.

class SendingServer...

```
private void sendHeartbeat() throws IOException {
    socketChannel.blockingSend(newHeartbeatRequest(serverId));
}
```

On the receiving server, the failure detection mechanism has a similar scheduler started. At regular intervals, it checks if a heartbeat was received.

```
class AbstractFailureDetector...

  private HeartBeatScheduler heartbeatScheduler = new HeartBeatScheduler(this::heartBeatCheck, 100l);

  abstract void heartBeatCheck();
  abstract void heartBeatReceived(T serverId);
```

The failure detector needs to have two methods:

- A method to be called whenever the receiving server receives the heartbeat, to tell the failure detector that everything is OK:

  ```
  class ReceivingServer...

    private void handleRequest(Message<RequestOrResponse> request,
                               ClientConnection clientConnection) {
      RequestOrResponse clientRequest = request.getRequest();
      if (isHeartbeatRequest(clientRequest)) {
        HeartbeatRequest heartbeatRequest = deserialize(clientRequest);
        failureDetector.heartBeatReceived(heartbeatRequest.getServerId());
        sendResponse(clientConnection, request.getRequest().getCorrelationId());
      } else {
        //processes other requests
      }
    }
  ```

- A method to periodically check the heartbeat status and detect possible failures

Deciding when to mark a server as failed uses various criteria and needs to address a number of tradeoffs. The smaller the heartbeat interval, the quicker the failures are detected, but there is also a higher probability of false failure detections. So the heartbeat intervals and the interpretation of missing heartbeats is implemented as per the requirements of the cluster. There are two broad categories: small clusters and large clusters.

Small Clusters: Consensus-Based Systems

Consensus-based systems include Raft or ZooKeeper. In all consensus implementations, heartbeats are sent from the leader server to all follower servers. Every time a heartbeat is received, the timestamp of the heartbeat arrival is recorded:

```
class TimeoutBasedFailureDetector...

  @Override
  public void heartBeatReceived(T serverId) {
    Long currentTime = System.nanoTime();
    heartbeatReceivedTimes.put(serverId, currentTime);
    markUp(serverId);
  }
```

If no heartbeat is received in a fixed time window, the leader is considered crashed, and a new server is elected as a leader. There are chances of false failure detection because of slow processes or network delays, so *Generation Clock* needs to be used to detect the stale leader. This improves the availability of the system, as crashes are detected in shorter time periods. This is suitable for smaller clusters—typically three to five nodes, as used in most consensus implementations.

```
class TimeoutBasedFailureDetector...

    @Override
    void heartBeatCheck() {
        Long now = System.nanoTime();
        Set<T> serverIds = heartbeatReceivedTimes.keySet();
        for (T serverId : serverIds) {
            Long lastHeartbeatReceivedTime = heartbeatReceivedTimes.get(serverId);
            Long timeSinceLastHeartbeat = now - lastHeartbeatReceivedTime;
            if (timeSinceLastHeartbeat >= timeoutNanos) {
                markDown(serverId);
            }
        }
    }
```

Technical Considerations

When *Single-Socket Channel* is used to communicate between servers, you need to make sure that the *head-of-line blocking* does not prevent heartbeat messages from being processed. Head-of-line blocking is caused when the requests are blocked because of slow processing of requests ahead of them. This blocking can cause delays long enough to falsely detect the sending server to be down even though it's sending heartbeats normally. *Request Pipeline* can be used to make sure servers do not wait for the response to previous requests before sending heartbeats. When using *Singular Update Queue*, some tasks, such as disk writes, can cause delays in processing of timing interrupts and sending heartbeats.

These issues can be solved by using a separate thread for sending heartbeats asynchronously. Frameworks such as HashiCorp Consul and Akka send heartbeats asynchronously. This can be an issue on receiving servers as well. A receiving server that's doing a disk write can only check the heartbeat after the write is complete, potentially causing false failure detection. So the receiving server using Singular Update Queue can reset its heartbeat-checking mechanism to incorporate those delays. A reference implementation of Raft, LogCabin,[23] does this.

Sometimes, a local pause caused by runtime-specific events, such as garbage collection, can delay the processing of heartbeats. There needs to be a mechanism to check if the processing is happening after a possible local pause. A simple workaround is to check if the processing is happening after a long enough time

---

23. https://github.com/logcabin/logcabin

window—for example, 5 seconds. In that case, nothing is marked as failed based on the time window, and it's deferred to the next cycle. Implementation in Cassandra[24] is a good example of this.

Large Clusters: Gossip-Based Protocols

Heartbeating, as described in the previous section, does not scale to larger clusters with hundreds or thousands of servers spanning across wide-area networks. In large clusters, two things need to be considered:

- There is a fixed limit on the number of messages generated per server.

- The total bandwidth consumed by the heartbeat messages cannot consume too much network bandwidth. There should be an upper bound of a few hundred kilobytes so that the heartbeat messages do not affect actual data transfer across the cluster.

For these reasons, all-to-all heartbeating is avoided in large clusters. Failure detectors, along with *Gossip Dissemination* protocols for propagating failure information across the cluster, are typically used in these situations. These clusters typically move data across nodes in case of failures, so they prefer correct detection and tolerate longer (although bounded) delays. The main challenge is to avoid incorrectly detecting a node as faulty because of network delays or slow processes. A common mechanism is for each process to be assigned a suspicion number, which increments if there is no gossip including that process within a bounded time. The suspicion number is calculated based on past statistics, and only when it reaches a configured upper limit, the node is marked as failed.

There are two mainstream implementations:

- Phi Accrual failure detector, used in Akka and Cassandra

- SWIM with Lifeguard enhancement, used in HashiCorp Consul and memberlist

These implementations scale over a wide-area network with thousands of machines. Akka is known to have been tried for 2400[25] servers. HashiCorp Consul is routinely deployed with several thousand consul servers in a group. Having a reliable failure detector—which works efficiently for large cluster deployments while providing some consistency guarantees—remains an area of active research. Some recent developments in frameworks such as Rapid[26] look promising.

It is important to note that heartbeat does not necessarily require a distinct message type. When cluster nodes are already engaged in communication,

---

24. https://issues.apache.org/jira/browse/CASSANDRA-9183
25. https://www.lightbend.com/blog/running-a-2400-akka-nodes-cluster-on-google-compute-engine
26. https://github.com/lalithsuresh/rapid

such as when replicating data, the existing messages can serve the purpose of heartbeats.

Examples

- Consensus implementations (Zab, Raft), which work with small 3-to-5-node clusters, implement a fixed-time-window failure detection.

- Akka Actors and Cassandra use Phi Accrual failure detector [Hayashibara2004].

- HashiCorp Consul uses a gossip-based failure detector based on SWIM [Das2002].

Chapter 8

Majority Quorum

Avoid two groups of servers making independent decisions by requiring majority for taking every decision.

Problem

Safety and Liveness

Liveness is the property of a system that says that the system always makes progress. Safety is the property that says that the system is always in the correct state. If we focus only on safety, then the system as a whole might not make progress. If we focus only on liveness, then safety might be compromised.

In a distributed system, whenever a server takes any action, it needs to ensure that in the event of a crash the results of the actions are available to the clients. This can be achieved by replicating the result to other servers in the cluster. But that leads to the question: How many other servers need to confirm the replication before the original server can be confident that the update is fully recognized? If the original server waits for too many replications, then it will respond slowly—reducing liveness. But if it doesn't have enough replications, then the update could be lost—a failure of safety. It's critical to balance between the overall system performance and system integrity.

Solution

A cluster agrees that it's received an update when a majority of the nodes in the cluster have acknowledged the update. We call this number a quorum. So if we have a cluster of five nodes, we need a quorum of 3. For a cluster of n nodes, the quorum is $n / 2 + 1$.

The need for a quorum indicates how many failures can be tolerated—which is the size of the cluster minus the quorum. A cluster of five nodes can tolerate two of them failing. In general, if we want to tolerate f failures we need a cluster size of $2f + 1$.

Consider two examples that need a quorum:

- **Updating data in a cluster of servers.** *High-Water Mark* is used to ensure that only data guaranteed to be available on the majority of servers is visible to clients.

- **Leader election.** In *Leader and Followers*, a leader is selected only if it gets votes from a majority of the servers.

Deciding on Number of Servers in a Cluster

- In his book *Guide to Reliable Distributed Systems* [Birman2012], Dr. Kenneth Birman builds on the analysis done by Dr. Jim Gray for the world of relational databases. Dr. Birman states that the throughput of quorum-based systems can go down as $O(1 / n ** 2)$, where n is the number of servers in a cluster.

- ZooKeeper [Hunt2010] and other consensus-based systems are known to have lower write throughput when the number of servers in a cluster goes beyond five.

- In his talk "Applying The Universal Scalability Law to Distributed Systems,"[27] Dr. Neil Gunther shows how the throughput of the system goes down with the number of coordinating servers in a cluster.

The cluster can function only if the majority of servers are up and running. In systems doing data replication, there are two things to consider:

---

27. https://speakerdeck.com/drqz/applying-the-universal-scalability-law-to-distributed-systems?slide=68

- **The throughput of write operations.** Every time data is written to the cluster, it needs to be copied to multiple servers. Every additional server adds some overhead to complete this write. The latency of data write is directly proportional to the number of servers forming the quorum. As we will see below, doubling the number of servers in a cluster will reduce throughput to half of the value for the original cluster.

- **The number of failures which need to be tolerated.** The number of server failures tolerated depends on the size of the cluster. But just adding one more server to an existing cluster doesn't always give you more fault tolerance: With a three-server cluster, adding one server doesn't increase failure tolerance.

Considering these two factors, most practical quorum-based systems have cluster sizes of three or five. A five-server cluster tolerates two server failures and has tolerable data write throughput of a few thousand requests per second.

Table 8.1 shows an example of how to choose the number of servers, based on the number of tolerated failures and the approximate impact on the throughput. The throughput column shows the approximate relative throughput to highlight how throughput degrades with the number of servers. The number will vary from system to system. As an example, readers can refer to the actual throughput data published in Raft Ph.D. thesis and the original ZooKeeper paper.

Table 8.1 *Impact of Quorum Size on Tolerated Failures and Throughput*

Number of Servers	Quorum	Number of Tolerated Failures	Representative Throughput
1	1	0	100
2	2	0	85
3	2	1	82
4	3	1	57
5	3	2	48
6	4	2	41
7	4	3	36

Flexible Quorums

With majority quorums, two quorums always overlap in at least one node. This quorum intersection is the key. It can be achieved even if operations use different quorum sizes, as long as there is an intersection. One of the main advantages of using quorums of different sizes is that operations that are more frequent can use a smaller quorum size. For example, in a five-node cluster where 90% of the interactions involve reads and only 10% involve writes, reads can use a quorum size of 2 while writes can use a quorum size of 4. This ensures that the quorum intersection is still maintained. The use of a smaller quorum size for the majority of operations allows for higher throughput and lower latency.

As discussed in the quorum usage of *Paxos* and *Replicated Log*, quorum intersection is required across two phases of execution. In typical implementations of Replicated Log, where phase 1 involves leader election and is less frequent, a larger quorum size can be used for that phase. All other client operations can use a smaller quorum size, thereby improving overall throughput and latency.

Examples

- All the consensus implementations (Zab [Reed2008], Raft [Ongaro2014], Paxos [Lamport2001]) use majority quorum.

- Even in systems that don't use consensus, quorum is used to make sure the latest update is available to at least one server in case of failures or network partition. For instance, in databases like Apache Cassandra, a database update can be configured to return success only after a majority of the servers have updated the record successfully.

Chapter 9

Generation Clock

A monotonically increasing number indicating the generation of the server.
Also known as: Term
Also known as: Epoch
Also known as: Generation

Problem

In *Leader and Followers* setup, there is a possibility of the leader being temporarily disconnected from the followers. There might be a garbage collection pause in the leader process, or a temporary network disruption which disconnects the leader from the follower. In this case the leader process is still running, and after the pause or the network disruption is over, it will try sending replication requests to the followers. This is dangerous, as meanwhile the rest of the cluster might have selected a new leader and accepted requests from the client. It is important for the rest of the cluster to detect any requests from the old leader. The old leader itself should also be able to detect that it was temporarily disconnected from the cluster and take necessary corrective action to step down from leadership.

Solution

> Generation Clock pattern is an example of a *Lamport Clock*: a simple technique used to determine ordering of events across a set of processes, without depending on a system clock. Each process maintains an integer counter, which is incremented after every action the process performs. Each process also sends this integer to other processes along with the messages processes exchange. The process receiving the message sets its integer counter by choosing the maximum between its own counter and the integer value of the message. This way, any process can figure out which action happened before the other by comparing the associated integers. The comparison is possible for actions across multiple processes as well, if the messages were exchanged between the processes. Actions which can be compared this way are said to be *causally related*.

Maintain a monotonically increasing number indicating the generation of the server. Every time a new leader election happens, it should be marked by incrementing the generation. The generation needs to be available beyond a server reboot, so it is stored with every entry in the *Write-Ahead Log*. As discussed in *High-Water Mark*, followers use this information to find conflicting entries in their log.

At startup, the server reads the last known generation from the log.

class ReplicatedLog...

```
  this.replicationState = new ReplicationState(config, wal.getLastLogEntryGeneration());
```

With Leader and Followers, servers increment the generation every time there's a new leader election.

class ReplicatedLog...

```
  private void startLeaderElection() {
      replicationState.setGeneration(replicationState.getGeneration() + 1);
      registerSelfVote();
      requestVoteFrom(followers);
  }
```

Servers send the generation to other servers as part of the vote requests. This way, after a successful leader election, all the servers have the same generation. Once the leader is elected, followers are told about the new generation:

follower (class ReplicatedLog...)

```
  private void becomeFollower(int leaderId, Long generation) {
      replicationState.reset();
```

```
        replicationState.setGeneration(generation);
        replicationState.setLeaderId(leaderId);
        transitionTo(ServerRole.FOLLOWING);
    }
```

Thereafter, the leader includes the generation in each request it sends to the followers. It includes it in every *HeartBeat* message as well as the replication requests sent to followers.

Leader persists the generation along with every entry in its Write-Ahead Log:

leader (class ReplicatedLog...)

```
Long appendToLocalLog(byte[] data) {
    Long generation = replicationState.getGeneration();
    return appendToLocalLog(data, generation);
}

Long appendToLocalLog(byte[] data, Long generation) {
    var logEntryId = wal.getLastLogIndex() + 1;
    var logEntry = new WALEntry(logEntryId, data, EntryType.DATA, generation);
    return wal.writeEntry(logEntry);
}
```

This way, it is also persisted in the follower log as part of the replication mechanism of Leader and Followers.

If a follower gets a message from a deposed leader, the follower can tell because its generation is too low. The follower then replies with a failure response.

follower (class ReplicatedLog...)

```
Long currentGeneration = replicationState.getGeneration();
if (currentGeneration > request.getGeneration()) {
    return new ReplicationResponse(FAILED, serverId(),
            currentGeneration, wal.getLastLogIndex());
}
```

When a leader gets such a failure response, it becomes a follower and expects communication from the new leader.

Old leader (class ReplicatedLog...)

```
if (!response.isSucceeded()) {
    if (response.getGeneration() > replicationState.getGeneration()) {
        becomeFollower(LEADER_NOT_KNOWN, response.getGeneration());
        return;
    }
```

Consider the following example. In a three server cluster, Leader1 is the existing leader. All the servers in the cluster have the generation as 1. Leader1 sends continuous heartbeats to the followers (Figure 9.1). Then, Leader1 is having a long garbage collection pause—say, 5 seconds. The followers stop getting heartbeats, so after a timeout they elect a new leader (Figure 9.2). The new leader increments the generation to 2. After the garbage collection pause is over, Leader1 continues sending requests to other servers. The followers and the new leader, which are at generation 2, reject the requests and send a failure response with generation 2 (Figure 9.3). Leader1 handles the failure response and steps down to be a follower, with generation updated to 2 (Figure 9.4).

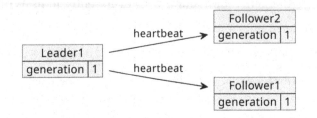

Figure 9.1 *Leader heartbeats*

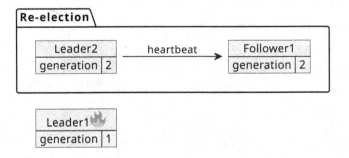

Figure 9.2 *New leader is elected.*

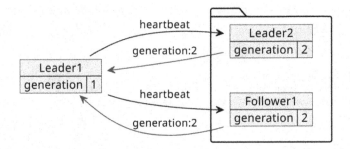

Figure 9.3 *Old leader reconnects.*

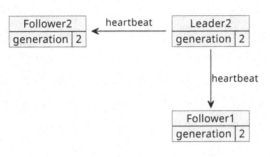

Figure 9.4 *Old leader steps down.*

Examples

- Raft uses the concept of a term for marking the leader generation.

- In ZooKeeper [Hunt2010], an epoch number is maintained as part of every transaction ID. So every transaction persisted in ZooKeeper has a generation marked by epoch.

- In Apache Cassandra, each server stores a generation number which is incremented every time a server restarts. The generation information is persisted in the system keyspace and propagated as part of the gossip messages to other servers. A server receiving a gossip message can then compare the generation value it knows about and the generation value in the gossip message. If the generation in the gossip message is higher, it knows that the server was restarted, so it discards all the state it has maintained for that server and asks for the new state.

- In Apache Kafka, an epoch number is created and stored in ZooKeeper every time a new controller is elected for a Kafka cluster. The epoch is included in every request that is sent from the controller to other servers in the cluster. Another epoch called Leader Epoch [Stopford2021] is maintained to detect if the followers of a partition are lagging behind in their High-Water Mark.

Chapter 10

High-Water Mark

An index in the write-ahead log showing the last successful replication.
Also known as: CommitIndex

Problem

The *Write-Ahead Log* pattern is used to recover state after a server crashes and restarts. But a write-ahead log is not enough to provide availability in case of server failure. If a single server fails, then clients won't be able to function until the server restarts. To get a more available system, we can replicate the log on multiple servers. Using *Leader and Followers* the leader replicates all its log entries to a *Majority Quorum* of followers. Now, should the leader fail, a new leader can be elected, and clients can mostly continue to work with the cluster as before. But there are still a couple things that can go wrong:

- The leader can fail before sending its log entries to any followers.

- The leader can fail after sending log entries to some followers, but before sending it to the majority of followers.

In these error scenarios, some followers can be missing entries in their logs, and some followers can have more entries than others. So it becomes important for each follower to know what part of the log is safe to be made available to the clients.

Solution

The high-water mark is an index into the log file that records the last log entry known to have successfully replicated to a Majority Quorum of followers. The leader also passes on the high-water mark to its followers during its replication. All servers in the cluster should only transmit to clients the data that reflects updates below the high-water mark.

Figure 10.1 shows the sequence of operations.

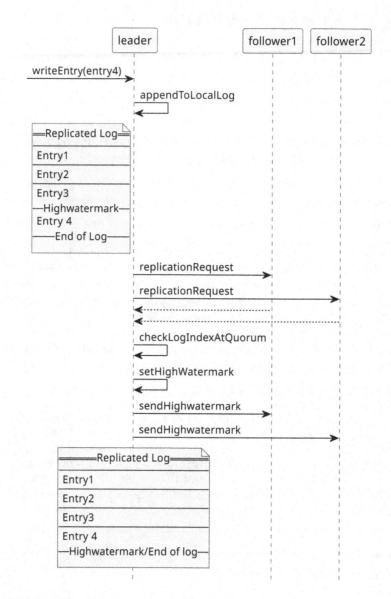

Figure 10.1 *High-Water Mark*

For each log entry, the leader appends it to its local write-ahead log and then sends it to all the followers.

leader (class ReplicatedLog...)

```java
private Long appendAndReplicate(byte[] data) {
    Long lastLogEntryIndex = appendToLocalLog(data);
    replicateOnFollowers(lastLogEntryIndex);
    return lastLogEntryIndex;
}

private void replicateOnFollowers(Long entryAtIndex) {
    for (final FollowerHandler follower : followers) {
        replicateOn(follower, entryAtIndex); //send replication requests to followers
    }
}
```

The followers handle the replication request and append the log entries to their local logs. After successfully appending the log entries, they respond to the leader with the index of the latest log entry they have. The response also includes the current *Generation Clock* of the server.

follower (class ReplicatedLog...)

```java
private ReplicationResponse appendEntries(ReplicationRequest replicationRequest) {
    var entries = replicationRequest.getEntries();

    entries.stream()
            .filter(e -> !wal.exists(e))
            .forEach(e -> wal.writeEntry(e));

    return new ReplicationResponse(SUCCEEDED, serverId(),
            replicationState.getGeneration(), wal.getLastLogIndex());
}
```

When responses are received, the leader keeps track of log indexes replicated at each server.

class ReplicatedLog...

```java
logger.info("Updating matchIndex for "
        + response.getServerId()
        + " to "
        + response.getReplicatedLogIndex());

updateMatchingLogIndex(response.getServerId(),
        response.getReplicatedLogIndex());

var logIndexAtQuorum = computeHighwaterMark(logIndexesAtAllServers(),
        config.numberOfServers());

var currentHighWaterMark = replicationState.getHighWaterMark();
```

```
if (logIndexAtQuorum > currentHighWaterMark && logIndexAtQuorum != 0) {
    applyLogEntries(currentHighWaterMark, logIndexAtQuorum);
    replicationState.setHighWaterMark(logIndexAtQuorum);
}
```

The high-water mark can be calculated by looking at the log indexes of all the followers and the log of the leader itself, and picking up the index which is available on the majority of the servers.

```
class ReplicatedLog...

    Long computeHighwaterMark(List<Long> serverLogIndexes, int noOfServers) {
        serverLogIndexes.sort(Long::compareTo);
        return serverLogIndexes.get(noOfServers / 2);
    }
```

A subtle problem can come up with a leader election. We must ensure all the servers in the cluster have an up-to-date log before any server sends data to clients.

There is a problem if the existing leader fails before propagating the high-water mark to all the followers. Raft solves this by appending a no-op entry to the leader's log after a successful leader election, and only serves clients once this is confirmed by its followers. In Zab, the new leader explicitly tries to push all its entries to all the followers before starting to serve the clients.

The leader propagates the high-water mark to the followers either as part of the regular *HeartBeat* or as separate requests. The followers then set their high-water mark accordingly.

Any client can read the log entries only till the high-water mark. Log entries beyond the high-water mark are not visible to clients because there is no confirmation that the entries are replicated, so they might not be available if the leader fails and some other server is elected as a leader.

```
class ReplicatedLog...

    public WALEntry readEntry(long index) {
        if (index > replicationState.getHighWaterMark()) {
            throw new IllegalArgumentException("Log entry not available");
        }
        return wal.readAt(index);
    }
```

Log Truncation

When a server joins the cluster after crash/restart, there is always a possibility of having some conflicting entries in its log. So whenever a server joins the cluster, it checks with the leader of the cluster to know which entries in the log are potentially conflicting. It then truncates the log to the point where entries match with the leader, and then updates the log with the subsequent entries to ensure its log matches the rest of the cluster.

Consider the following example. The client sends requests to add four entries in the log (Figure 10.2). The leader successfully replicates three entries, but fails after adding entry 4 to its own log. One of the followers is elected as a new leader and accepts more entries from the client (Figure 10.3). When the failed leader joins the cluster again, it has entry 4 which is conflicting. So it needs to truncate its log till entry 3, and then add entry 5 to match the log with the rest of the cluster (Figure 10.4).

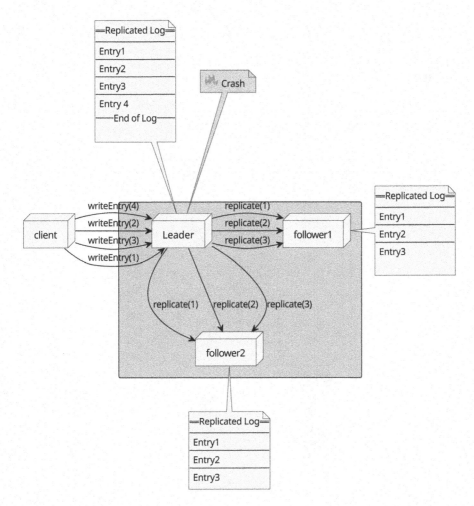

Figure 10.2 *Leader failure*

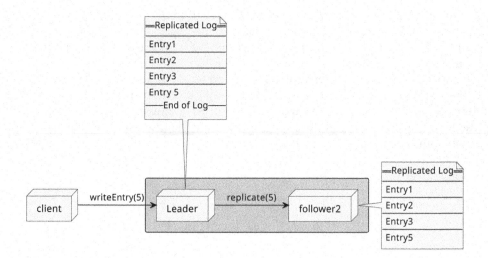

Figure 10.3 *New leader*

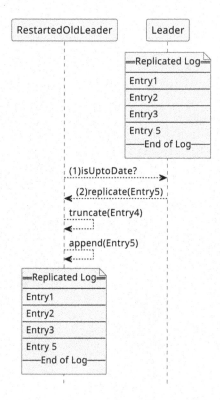

Figure 10.4 *Log truncation*

Any server which restarts or rejoins the cluster after a pause finds the new leader. It then explicitly asks for the current high-water mark, truncates its log to the high-water mark, and then gets all the entries beyond high-water mark from the leader. Replication algorithms like Raft have ways to find out conflicting entries by checking log entries in its own log against the log entries in the request. The entries with the same log index, but at a lower *Generation Clock*, are removed.

class ReplicatedLog...

```java
void maybeTruncate(ReplicationRequest replicationRequest) {
    replicationRequest.getEntries().stream()
            .filter(this::isConflicting)
            .forEach(this::truncate);
}

private boolean isConflicting(WALEntry requestEntry) {
    return wal.getLastLogIndex() >= requestEntry.getEntryIndex()
            && requestEntry.getGeneration()
            != wal.getGeneration(requestEntry.getEntryIndex());
}
```

A simple implementation to support log truncation is to keep a map of log indexes and file position. Then the log can be truncated at a given index:

class WALSegment...

```java
public synchronized  void truncate(Long logIndex) throws IOException {
    var filePosition = entryOffsets.get(logIndex);
    if (filePosition == null) {
        throw new IllegalArgumentException(
                "No file position available for logIndex=" + logIndex);
    }

    fileChannel.truncate(filePosition);
    truncateIndex(logIndex);
}

private void truncateIndex(Long logIndex) {
    entryOffsets.entrySet().removeIf(entry -> entry.getKey() >= logIndex);
}
```

Examples

- All the consensus algorithms use the concept of high-water mark to know when to apply the proposed state mutations. In the Raft consensus algorithm, high-water mark is called `commitIndex`.

- In the Apache Kafka replication protocol, there is a separate index maintained called high-water mark. Consumers can see entries only until the high-water mark.

- Apache BookKeeper[28] has a concept of *last add confirmed*,[29] which is the entry that was successfully replicated on a quorum of bookies.

---

28. https://bookkeeper.apache.org
29. https://bookkeeper.apache.org/archives/docs/r4.4.0/bookkeeperProtocol.html

Chapter 11

Paxos

by Unmesh Joshi and Martin Fowler

> *Use two consensus-building phases to reach safe consensus even when nodes disconnect.*

Problem

When multiple nodes share state, they often need to agree between themselves on a particular value. With *Leader and Followers*, the leader decides and passes its value to the followers. But if there is no leader, then the nodes need to determine a value themselves. (Even with a leader-follower, they may need to do this to elect a leader.)

A leader can ensure that replicas safely acquire an update by using *Two-Phase Commit*, but without a leader we can have competing nodes attempt to gather a *Majority Quorum*. This process is further complicated because any node may fail or disconnect. A node may achieve majority quorum on a value, but disconnect before it is able to communicate this value to the entire cluster.

Solution

The Paxos algorithm was developed by Leslie Lamport, published in his 1998 paper "The Part-Time Parliament" [Lamport1998]. Paxos works in three phases to make sure multiple nodes agree on the same value in spite of partial network or node failures. The first two phases act to build consensus around a value and the last phase then communicates that consensus to the remaining replicas.

- Prepare phase: Establish the latest *Generation Clock* and gather any already accepted values.

- Accept phase: Propose a value for this generation for replicas to accept.

- Commit phase: Let all the replicas know that a value has been chosen.

In the first phase (called **prepare phase**), the node proposing a value (called a **proposer**) contacts all the nodes in the cluster (called **acceptors**) and asks them if they will promise to consider its value. Once a majority quorum of acceptors returns such a promise, the proposer moves onto the second phase. In the second phase (called the **accept phase**), the proposer sends out a proposed value. If a majority quorum of nodes accepts this value then the value is **chosen**. In the final phase (called the **commit phase**), the proposer can then commit the chosen value to all the nodes in the cluster.

Flow of the Protocol

Paxos is a difficult protocol to understand. We'll start by showing an example of a typical flow of the protocol (Table 11.1), and then dig into some of the details of how it works. This brief explanation aims to provide an intuitive sense of how the protocol works, but it's not a comprehensive description to base an implementation upon.

In the original Paxos papers (1998 and 2001 [Lamport2001]), there is no mention of the commit phase, as the focus of the algorithm is to prove that only a single value is chosen and that is enough even if only the proposer cluster node knows about the chosen value. But in practice, all of the cluster nodes need to know about the chosen value, so there is a need for a commit phase where the proposer communicates the decision to all of the cluster nodes.

Those are the basic rules for Paxos, but it's hard to understand how they combine for an effective behavior. Figure 11.1 shows an example of how this works.

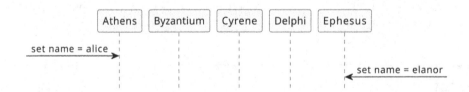

Figure 11.1   *Athens and Ephesus get client requests.*

Consider a cluster of five nodes: Athens, Byzantium, Cyrene, Delphi, and Ephesus. A client contacts the Athens node, requesting to set the cluster's name to "alice". The Athens node now needs to initiate a Paxos interaction to see if all

Table 11.1 *Paxos Summary—the Flow of the Protocol*

Proposer	Acceptor
Obtains the next generation number from a *Generation Clock*. Sends a prepare request with this generation number to all acceptors.	
	If the generation number of the prepare request is later than its promised generation variable, it updates its promise generation with this later value and returns a promise response. If it has already accepted a proposal, it returns this proposal.
When it receives promises from a majority quorum of acceptors, it checks if any of these responses contain accepted values. If so, it changes its own proposed value to that of the returned proposal with the highest generation number. It sends accept requests to all acceptors with its generation number and proposed value.	
	If the generation number of the accept request is later than or equal to its promised generation variable, it stores the proposal as its accepted proposal and responds that it has accepted the request.
When it receives a successful response from a majority quorum of acceptors, it records the value as chosen and sends commit messages to all nodes.	

the nodes will agree to this change. Athens is called the proposer, in that Athens will propose to all the other nodes that the name of the cluster become "alice". All the nodes in the cluster (including Athens) are acceptors, meaning they are capable of accepting proposals.

At the same time that Athens is proposing "alice", the node Ephesus gets a request to set the cluster's name to "elanor". This makes Ephesus another proposer (Figure 11.2).

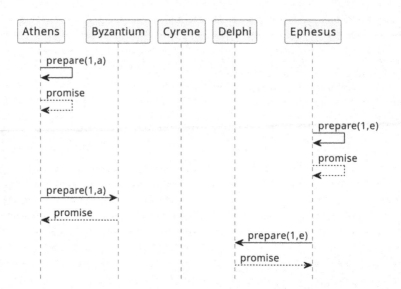

Figure 11.2   *Both Athens and Ephesus initiate the prepare phase.*

In the prepare phase, the proposers begin by sending prepare requests which include a generation number. Since Paxos is intended to avoid single points of failure, we don't take this from a single generation clock. Instead, each node maintains its own generation clock where it combines a generation number with a node ID. The node ID is used to break ties, so [2,a] > [1,e] > [1,a]. Each acceptor records the latest promise it has seen so far.

Node	Athens	Byzantium	Cyrene	Delphi	Ephesus
Promised generation	1,a	1,a	0	1,e	1,e
Accepted value	none	none	none	none	none

Since they haven't seen any requests before this, they all return a promise to the calling proposer. We call the returned value a "promise" because it indicates that the acceptor promises to not consider any messages with an earlier generation clock than the promised one.

Athens sends its prepare message to Cyrene (Figure 11.3). When it receives a promise in return, this means it now has promises from three of the five nodes, which represents a *Majority Quorum*. Athens now shifts from sending prepare messages to sending accept messages.

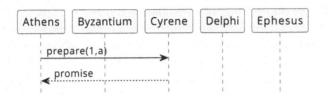

Figure 11.3   *Athens gets Majority Quorum promises with Cyrene's response.*

It is possible that Athens fails to receive a promise from a majority of the cluster nodes. In that case, Athens retries the prepare request by incrementing the generation clock.

Node	Athens	Byzantium	Cyrene	Delphi	Ephesus
Promised generation	1,a	1,a	1,a	1,e	1,e
Accepted value	none	none	none	none	none

Athens now starts sending accept messages, containing the generation and the proposed value (Figure 11.4). Athens and Byzantium accept the proposal.

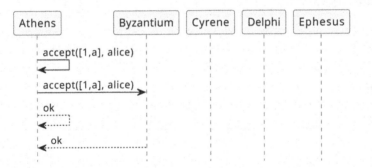

Figure 11.4   *Athens initiates the accept phase.*

Node	Athens	Byzantium	Cyrene	Delphi	Ephesus
Promised generation	1,a	1,a	1,a	1,e	1,e
Accepted value	alice	alice	none	none	none

Ephesus now sends a prepare message to Cyrene (Figure 11.5). Cyrene had sent a promise to Athens, but Ephesus's request has a higher generation, so it takes precedence. Cyrene sends back a promise to Ephesus.

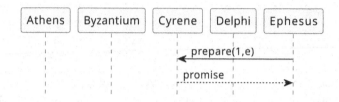

Figure 11.5 *Ephesus gets Majority Quorum promises with Cyrene's response.*

Cyrene now gets an accept request from Athens but rejects it as the generation number is behind its promise to Ephesus (Figure 11.6).

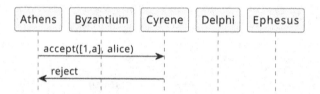

Figure 11.6 *Cyrene rejects Athens' accept request.*

Node	Athens	Byzantium	Cyrene	Delphi	Ephesus
Promised generation	1,a	1,a	1,e	1,e	1,e
Accepted value	alice	alice	none	none	none

Ephesus has now got a majority quorum from its prepare messages, so it can move on to sending accepts (Figure 11.7). It sends accepts to itself and to Delphi but then crashes before it can send any more accepts.

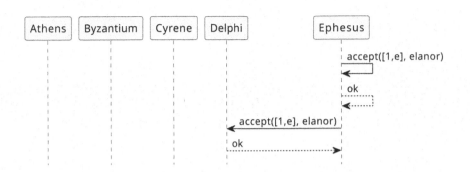

Figure 11.7   *Ephesus initiates the accept phase.*

Node	Athens	Byzantium	Cyrene	Delphi	Ephesus
Promised generation	1,a	1,a	1,e	1,e	1,e
Accepted value	alice	alice	none	elanor	elanor

Meanwhile, Athens has to deal with the rejection of its accept request from Cyrene. This indicates that a majority quorum is no longer promised to it and thus its proposal will fail. This will always happen to a proposer who loses its initial majority quorum like this; for another proposer to achieve quorum, at least one member of the first proposer's majority quorum will defect.

With a simple two-phase commit, we would now expect Ephesus to just go on and get its value chosen—but such a scheme is now in trouble since Ephesus has crashed. If it had a lock on a majority quorum of acceptors, its crash would deadlock the whole proposal process. Paxos, however, expects this kind of thing to happen, so Athens will make another try, this time with a higher generation (Figure 11.8).

It sends prepare messages again, but this time with a higher generation number. As with the first round, it gets back a trio of promises, but with an important difference. Athens already accepted "alice" earlier, and Delphi had accepted "elanor". Both of these acceptors return a promise, but also the value they had already accepted, together with the generation number of that accepted proposal. When they return that value, they update their promised generation to [2,a] to reflect the promise they made to Athens.

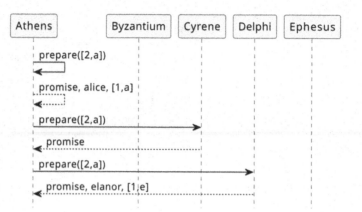

Figure 11.8   *Athens initiates the prepare phase with a higher generation.*

Node	Athens	Byzantium	Cyrene	Delphi	Ephesus
Promised generation	2,a	1,a	2,a	2,a	1,e
Accepted value	alice	alice	none	elanor	elanor

Athens, with a quorum, must now move onto the accept phase, but it must propose the already accepted value, "elanor", with the highest generation. It was accepted by Delphi with a generation of [1,e], which is greater than Athens's acceptance of "alice" with [1,a] (Figure 11.9).

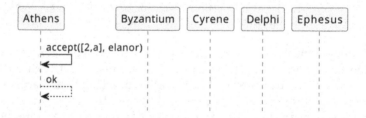

Figure 11.9   *Athens proposes the already accepted value, "elanor".*

Athens starts to send out accept requests, but now with "elanor" and its current generation. Athens sends an accept request to itself, which is accepted. This is a crucial acceptance because now there are three nodes accepting "elanor", which is a quorum, therefore we can consider "elanor" to be the chosen value.

Node	Athens	Byzantium	Cyrene	Delphi	Ephesus
Promised generation	2,a	1,a	2,a	2,a	1,e
Accepted value	elanor	alice	none	elanor	elanor

But although "elanor" is now the chosen value, nobody is yet aware of it. Within the accept stage, Athens only knows of itself having "elanor" as the value, which isn't a quorum, and Ephesus is offline. All Athens needs to do is have a couple more accept requests accepted and it will be able to commit. But now Athens crashes.

At this point, Athens and Ephesus have both crashed. But the cluster still has a majority quorum of nodes operating, so they should be able to keep working. Indeed, by following the protocol they can discover that "elanor" is the chosen value (Figure 11.10).

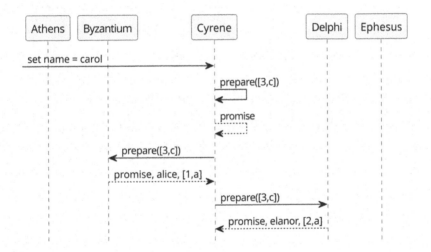

Figure 11.10   *Cyrene initiates the prepare phase.*

Cyrene gets a request to set the name to "carol", so it becomes a proposer. It has seen generation [2,a] so it kicks off a prepare phase with generation [3,c]. While it wishes to propose "carol" as the name, for the moment it's just issuing prepare requests.

Cyrene sends prepare messages to the remaining nodes in the cluster. As with Athens's earlier prepare phase, Cyrene gets accepted values back, so "carol" never gets proposed as a value. As before, Delphi's "elanor" is later than Byzantium's "alice", so Cyrene starts an accept phase with "elanor" and [3,c] (Figure 11.11).

Node	Athens	Byzantium	Cyrene	Delphi	Ephesus
Promised generation	2,a	3,c	3,c	3,c	1,e
Accepted value	elanor	alice	none	elanor	elanor

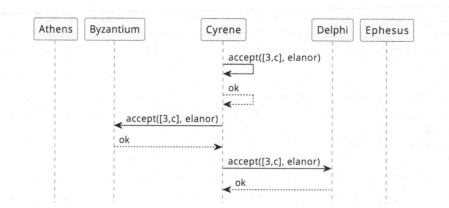

Figure 11.11 *Cyrene proposes the already accepted value, "*elanor*".*

While I could continue to crash and wake up nodes, it's clear now that "elanor" will win out. As long as a majority quorum of nodes are up, at least one of them will have "elanor" as its value, and any node attempting a prepare will have to contact one node that's accepted "elanor" in order to get a quorum for its prepare phase. So we'll finish with Cyrene sending out commits (Figure 11.12).

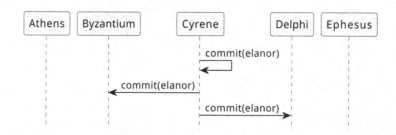

Figure 11.12 *Cyrene commits the value "*elanor*".*

At some point, Athens and Ephesus will come back online and discover what the majority majority quorum has chosen.

Requests Don't Need to Be Rejected

In the example above, we saw acceptors rejecting requests with an aged generation. But the protocol does not require an explicit rejection like this. As formulated, an acceptor may just ignore an out-of-date request. In that case, the protocol will still converge on a single consensus value. This is an important feature of the protocol because, as this is a distributed system, connections can be lost at any time, so it's better to not be dependent on rejections to ensure the safety of the protocol. (*Safety* here means that the protocol will choose only one value, and once chosen, it won't be overwritten.)

Sending rejections, however, is still useful as it improves performance. The quicker proposers find out they are old, the sooner they can start another round with a higher generation.

Competing Proposers May Fail to Choose

One way this protocol can go wrong is if two (or more) proposers get into a cycle. This situation is called a livelock.

- "alice" is accepted by Athens and Byzantium.

- "elanor" is prepared by all nodes, preventing "alice" from gaining quorum.

- "elanor" is accepted by Delphi and Ephesus.

- "alice" is prepared by all nodes, preventing elanor from gaining quorum.

- "alice" is accepted by Athens and Byzantium.

- . . . and so on.

The FLP impossibility result [Fischer1985] shows that even a single faulty node can stop a cluster from ever choosing a value.

We can reduce the chances of a livelock happening by ensuring that whenever a proposer needs to choose a new generation, it must wait a random period of time. This randomness makes it likely that one proposer will be able to get a majority quorum accepted before the other sends a prepare request to the full quorum.

But we can never ensure that livelock can't happen. This is a fundamental tradeoff: We can ensure either safety or liveness, but not both. Paxos ensures safety first.

An Example Key-Value Store

The Paxos protocol, as explained here, builds consensus on a single value (often called single-decree Paxos). Most practical implementations used in mainstream products like Azure Cosmos DB[30] or Google Spanner use a modification of Paxos called Multi-Paxos which is implemented as a *Replicated Log*.

But a simple key-value store can be built using basic Paxos. Apache Cassandra uses basic Paxos to implement its lightweight transactions.

The key-value store maintains a Paxos instance per key.

class PaxosPerKeyStore...

```
int serverId;
public PaxosPerKeyStore(int serverId) {
    this.serverId = serverId;
}

Map<String, Acceptor> key2Acceptors = new HashMap<String, Acceptor>();
List<PaxosPerKeyStore> peers;
```

The Acceptor stores the promisedGeneration, acceptedGeneration, and acceptedValue.

class Acceptor...

```
public class Acceptor {
    MonotonicId promisedGeneration = MonotonicId.empty();

    Optional<MonotonicId> acceptedGeneration = Optional.empty();
    Optional<Command> acceptedValue = Optional.empty();

    Optional<Command> committedValue = Optional.empty();
    Optional<MonotonicId> committedGeneration = Optional.empty();

    public AcceptorState state = AcceptorState.NEW;
    private BiConsumer<Acceptor, Command> kvStore;
```

When the key-and-value is put in the kvStore, it runs the Paxos protocol.

class PaxosPerKeyStore...

```
int maxKnownPaxosRoundId = 1;
int maxAttempts = 4;
public void put(String key, String defaultProposal) {
    int attempts = 0;
    while(attempts <= maxAttempts) {
        attempts++;
        var requestId = new MonotonicId(maxKnownPaxosRoundId++, serverId);
        var setValueCommand = new SetValueCommand(key, defaultProposal);

        if (runPaxos(key, requestId, setValueCommand)) {
            return;
        }
```

---

30. https://azure.microsoft.com/en-in/products/cosmos-db

```
        Uninterruptibles
                .sleepUninterruptibly(ThreadLocalRandom
                        .current().nextInt(100), MILLISECONDS);
        logger.warn("Experienced Paxos contention. " +
                "Attempting with higher generation");
    }
    throw new WriteTimeoutException(attempts);
}

private boolean runPaxos(String key,
                         MonotonicId generation,
                         Command initialValue) {
    var allAcceptors = getAcceptorInstancesFor(key);
    var prepareResponses = sendPrepare(generation, allAcceptors);
    if (isQuorumPrepared(prepareResponses)) {
        Command proposedValue = getValue(prepareResponses, initialValue);
        if (sendAccept(generation, proposedValue, allAcceptors)) {
            sendCommit(generation, proposedValue, allAcceptors);
        }
        if (proposedValue == initialValue) {
            return true;
        }
    }
    return false;
}

public Command getValue(List<PrepareResponse> prepareResponses,
                        Command initialValue) {
    var mostRecentAcceptedValue =
            getMostRecentAcceptedValue(prepareResponses);
    var proposedValue
            = mostRecentAcceptedValue.acceptedValue.isEmpty()
            ? initialValue
            : mostRecentAcceptedValue.acceptedValue.get();
    return proposedValue;
}

private PrepareResponse getMostRecentAcceptedValue(List<PrepareResponse>
                                                        prepareResponses) {
    return prepareResponses
            .stream()
            .max(Comparator
                    .comparing(r ->
                            r.acceptedGeneration
                                    .orElse(MonotonicId.empty())))).get();
}

class Acceptor...

public PrepareResponse prepare(MonotonicId generation) {

    if (promisedGeneration.isAfter(generation)) {
```

```
                    return new PrepareResponse(false,
                            acceptedValue,
                            acceptedGeneration,
                            committedGeneration,
                            committedValue);
            }
            promisedGeneration = generation;
            state = AcceptorState.PROMISED;
            return new PrepareResponse(true,
                    acceptedValue,
                    acceptedGeneration,
                    committedGeneration,
                    committedValue);

        }
```

class Acceptor...

```
    public boolean accept(MonotonicId generation, Command value) {
        if (generation.equals(promisedGeneration)
                || generation.isAfter(promisedGeneration)) {
            this.promisedGeneration = generation;
            this.acceptedGeneration = Optional.of(generation);
            this.acceptedValue = Optional.of(value);
            return true;
        }
        state = AcceptorState.ACCEPTED;
        return false;
    }
```

The value is stored in the kvStore only when it can be successfully committed.

class Acceptor...

```
    public void commit(MonotonicId generation, Command value) {
        committedGeneration = Optional.of(generation);
        committedValue = Optional.of(value);
        state = AcceptorState.COMMITTED;
        kvStore.accept(this, value);
    }
```

class PaxosPerKeyStore...

```
    private void accept(Acceptor acceptor, Command command) {
        if (command instanceof SetValueCommand) {
            var setValueCommand = (SetValueCommand) command;
            kv.put(setValueCommand.getKey(), setValueCommand.getValue());
        }
        acceptor.resetPaxosState();
    }
```

The Paxos state needs to be persisted. That can be easily done by using a *Write-Ahead Log*.

Handling Multiple Values

It is important to note that Paxos is specified and proven to work on a single value. Therefore, handling multiple values with the single-value Paxos protocol needs to be done outside of the protocol specification. One alternative is to reset the state and store committed values separately to make sure they are not lost.

class Acceptor...

```
public void resetPaxosState() {
    //This implementation has issues if committed values are not stored
    //and handled separately in the prepare phase.
    //See Apache Cassandra implementation as a reference.
    promisedGeneration = MonotonicId.empty();
    acceptedGeneration = Optional.empty();
    acceptedValue = Optional.empty();
}
```

There is an alternative, described in CASPaxos [Rystsov2018], which slightly modifies the basic Paxos to allow setting multiple values. This need for executing steps beyond the basic algorithm is the reason why, in practice, *Replicated Log* is preferred.

Reading the Values

Paxos relies on the prepare phase to detect any uncommitted values. So if basic Paxos is used to implement a key-value store as shown above, the read operation also needs to run the full Paxos algorithm.

class PaxosPerKeyStore...

```
public String get(String key) {
    int attempts = 0;
    while(attempts <= maxAttempts) {
        attempts++;
        var requestId = new MonotonicId(maxKnownPaxosRoundId++, serverId);
        var getValueCommand = new NoOpCommand(key);
        if (runPaxos(key, requestId, getValueCommand)) {
            return kv.get(key);
        }

        Uninterruptibles
                .sleepUninterruptibly(ThreadLocalRandom
                        .current()
                        .nextInt(100), MILLISECONDS);
        logger
                .warn("Experienced Paxos contention. " +
                        "Attempting with higher generation");
    }
    throw new WriteTimeoutException(attempts);
}
```

Flexible Paxos

The original description of Paxos requires *Majority Quorum* in both the prepare and the accept phases. Some recent work by Heidi Howard and others [Howard2016] shows that the main requirement of Paxos is to have an overlap in the quorums of the prepare and the accept phase. As long as this requirement is fulfilled, it does not require a Majority Quorum in both phases.

Examples

- Apache Cassandra uses Paxos to implement lightweight transactions.
- All the consensus algorithms such as Raft use concepts similar to the basic Paxos. *Two-Phase Commit*, *Majority Quorum*, and *Generation Clock* are used in a similar manner.

Chapter 12

Replicated Log

Keep the state of multiple nodes synchronized by using a write-ahead
log that is replicated to all the cluster nodes.

Problem

When multiple nodes share a state, that state needs to be synchronized. All
cluster nodes need to agree on the same state, even when some nodes crash or
get disconnected. This requires achieving consensus for each state change request.

But achieving consensus on individual requests is not enough. Each replica
also needs to execute requests in the same order, otherwise different replicas can
get into a different final state, even if they have consensus on an individual
request.

Solution

Cluster nodes maintain a *Write-Ahead Log*. Each log entry stores the state required
for consensus along with the user request. They coordinate to build consensus
over the log entries, so that all cluster nodes have exactly the same write-ahead
log. The requests are then executed sequentially as per the log. Because all cluster
nodes agree on each log entry, they execute the same requests in the same order.
This ensures that all the cluster nodes share the same state.

A fault-tolerant consensus-building mechanism using *Majority Quorum* needs
two phases.

- A phase to establish a *Generation Clock* and to know about the log entries
  replicated in the previous Majority Quorum.

- A phase to replicate requests on all the cluster nodes.

Executing two phases for each state change request is inefficient. Therefore, cluster nodes elect a leader at startup. The leader election phase establishes the Generation Clock and detects all the log entries in the previous Majority Quorum (the entries the previous leader might have copied to the majority of the cluster nodes). Once there is a stable leader, only the leader coordinates the replication. Clients communicate with the leader. The leader adds each request to the log and makes sure it's replicated on all the followers. Consensus is reached once a log entry is successfully replicated to the majority of the followers. This way, when there is a stable leader, only a single phase to reach consensus is needed for each state change operation.

Failure Assumptions

Depending on the failure assumptions, different algorithms are used to build consensus over log entries. The most commonly used assumption is that of crash fault. With crash fault, when a cluster node is faulty, it stops working. A more complex failure assumption is that of Byzantine fault. With Byzantine faults, faulty cluster nodes can behave arbitrarily. They might be controlled by an adversary which keeps the node functional but deliberately sends requests or responses with wrong data—for example, a fraudulent transaction to steal money.

Most enterprise systems, such as databases, message brokers, or even enterprise blockchain products like Hyperledger Fabric,[31] assume crash faults. So, consensus algorithms like Raft and *Paxos*, which are built with crash fault assumptions, are almost always used.

Algorithms like PBFT [Castro1999] are used for systems which need to allow Byzantine failures. The PBFT algorithm uses log in a similar way, but to tolerate a Byzantine failure, it needs three-phased execution and a quorum of $3f + 1$, where f is the number of tolerated failures.

Multi-Paxos and Raft

Multi-Paxos [Lamport2001] and Raft [Ongaro2014] are the most popular algorithms to implement replicated log. Multi-Paxos is only vaguely described in academic papers. Cloud databases such as Google Spanner and Azure Cosmos DB use Multi-Paxos, but the implementation details are not well-documented. Raft very clearly documents all the implementation details, and is a preferred implementation choice in most open source systems, even though Paxos and its variants are discussed a lot more in academia.

The following sections describe how Raft implements a replicated log.

---

31. https://github.com/hyperledger/fabric

Replicating Client Requests

For each log entry, the leader appends it to its local write-ahead log and then sends it to all the followers (Figure 12.1).

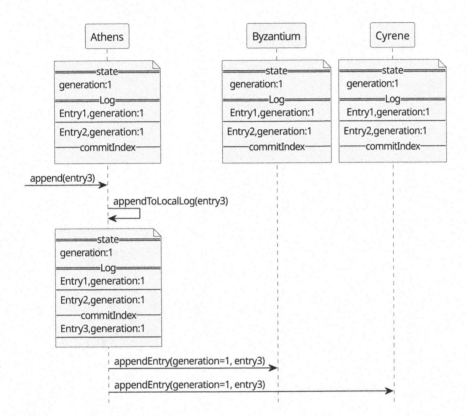

Figure 12.1 *Leader appends to its own log.*

```
leader (class ReplicatedLog...)

  private Long appendAndReplicate(byte[] data) {
      Long lastLogEntryIndex = appendToLocalLog(data);
      replicateOnFollowers(lastLogEntryIndex);
      return lastLogEntryIndex;
  }

  private void replicateOnFollowers(Long entryAtIndex) {
      for (final FollowerHandler follower : followers) {
          replicateOn(follower, entryAtIndex); //send replication requests to followers
      }
  }
```

The followers handle the replication request and append the log entries to their local logs. After successfully appending the log entries, they respond to the leader with the index of the latest log entry they have (Figure 12.2).

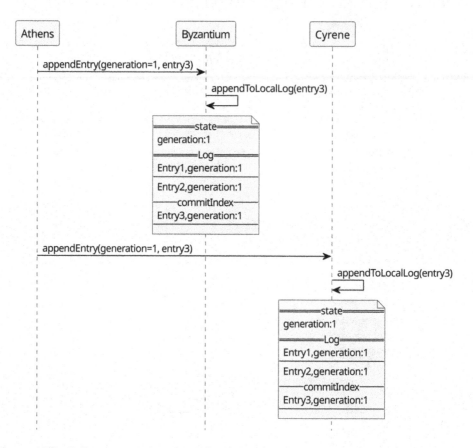

Figure 12.2 *Followers append to their logs.*

The response also includes the current *Generation Clock* of the server.

Each follower also checks if the entries already exist or there are entries beyond the ones being replicated. It ignores entries which are already present. But if there are entries from different generations, it removes the conflicting entries.

follower (class ReplicatedLog...)

```
void maybeTruncate(ReplicationRequest replicationRequest) {
    replicationRequest.getEntries().stream()
            .filter(this::isConflicting)
            .forEach(this::truncate);
}
```

```
private boolean isConflicting(WALEntry requestEntry) {
    return wal.getLastLogIndex() >= requestEntry.getEntryIndex()
            && requestEntry.getGeneration()
            != wal.getGeneration(requestEntry.getEntryIndex());
}

private void truncate(WALEntry entry) {
    wal.truncate(entry.getEntryIndex());
}
```

follower (class ReplicatedLog...)

```
private ReplicationResponse appendEntries(ReplicationRequest replicationRequest) {
    var entries = replicationRequest.getEntries();

    entries.stream()
            .filter(e -> !wal.exists(e))
            .forEach(e -> wal.writeEntry(e));

    return new ReplicationResponse(SUCCEEDED, serverId(),
            replicationState.getGeneration(), wal.getLastLogIndex());
}
```

The follower rejects the replication request when the generation number in the request is lower than the latest generation this follower server knows about. This rejection notifies the leader to step down and become a follower.

follower (class ReplicatedLog...)

```
Long currentGeneration = replicationState.getGeneration();
if (currentGeneration > request.getGeneration()) {
    return new ReplicationResponse(FAILED, serverId(),
            currentGeneration, wal.getLastLogIndex());
}
```

As it receives the responses, the leader keeps track of log indexes replicated at each server. It tracks the log entries which are successfully copied to the *Majority Quorum* and records that index as a commitIndex, which is the *High-Water Mark* in the log (Figure 12.3).

leader (class ReplicatedLog...)

```
logger.info("Updating matchIndex for "
        + response.getServerId()
        + " to "
        + response.getReplicatedLogIndex());

updateMatchingLogIndex(response.getServerId(),
        response.getReplicatedLogIndex());

var logIndexAtQuorum = computeHighwaterMark(logIndexesAtAllServers(),
        config.numberOfServers());
```

```
var currentHighWaterMark = replicationState.getHighWaterMark();

if (logIndexAtQuorum > currentHighWaterMark && logIndexAtQuorum != 0) {
    applyLogEntries(currentHighWaterMark, logIndexAtQuorum);
    replicationState.setHighWaterMark(logIndexAtQuorum);
}
```

leader (class ReplicatedLog...)

```
Long computeHighwaterMark(List<Long> serverLogIndexes, int noOfServers) {
    serverLogIndexes.sort(Long::compareTo);
    return serverLogIndexes.get(noOfServers / 2);
}
```

leader (class ReplicatedLog...)

```
private void updateMatchingLogIndex(int serverId, long replicatedLogIndex) {
    FollowerHandler follower = getFollowerHandler(serverId);
    follower.updateLastReplicationIndex(replicatedLogIndex);
}
```

leader (class ReplicatedLog...)

```
public void updateLastReplicationIndex(long lastReplicatedLogIndex) {
    this.matchIndex = lastReplicatedLogIndex;
}
```

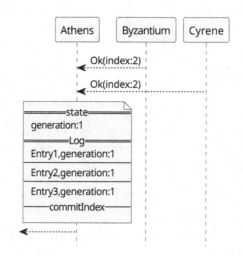

Figure 12.3 *Leader updates* commitIndex.

Full Replication

It is important to ensure that all the cluster nodes receive all the log entries from the leader, even when they are disconnected or crash and come back up. Raft has a mechanism to make sure all the cluster nodes receive all the log entries from the leader.

In Raft, with every replication request, the leader also sends the log index and generation of the log entries which immediately precede the new entries getting replicated. If the previous log index and term do not match with a follower's local log, the follower rejects the request. This indicates to the leader that the follower log needs to be synced for some of the older entries.

follower (class ReplicatedLog...)

```
if (!wal.isEmpty()
        && request.getPrevLogIndex() >= wal.getLogStartIndex()
        && isPreviousEntryGenerationMismatched(request)) {
    return new ReplicationResponse(FAILED, serverId(),
            replicationState.getGeneration(), wal.getLastLogIndex());
}
```

follower (class ReplicatedLog...)

```
private boolean isPreviousEntryGenerationMismatched(ReplicationRequest request) {
    return generationAt(request.getPrevLogIndex())
            != request.getPrevLogGeneration();
}

private Long generationAt(long prevLogIndex) {
    WALEntry walEntry = wal.readAt(prevLogIndex);

    return walEntry.getGeneration();
}
```

So the leader maintains another index, called matchIndex. This is the index up to which the follower log is known to be in sync. If a replication request is rejected indicating that some previous log entries need to be synced, the leader decrements the matchIndex and tries sending log entries at the lower index. This continues until the followers accept the replication request.

leader (class ReplicatedLog...)

```
//rejected because of conflicting entries, decrement matchIndex
FollowerHandler peer = getFollowerHandler(response.getServerId());
logger.info("decrementing nextIndex for peer "
        + peer.getId() + " from " + peer.getNextIndex());
peer.decrementNextIndex();
replicateOn(peer, peer.getNextIndex());
```

This check on the previous log index and generation allows the leader to detect two things.

- If a follower's log has missing entries. For example, if the follower log has only one entry and the leader starts replicating the third entry, the requests will be rejected until the leader replicates the second entry.

- If the previous entries in a follower's log are from a different generation, higher or lower than the corresponding entries in the leader log. The leader will try replicating entries from lower indexes until the requests get accepted. The followers truncate the entries for which the generation does not match.

This way, the leader tries to push its own log to all the followers continuously, using the previous index to detect missing entries or conflicting entries. This makes sure that all the cluster nodes eventually receive all the log entries from the leader even if they were disconnected for some time.

Raft does not have a separate commit message, but sends the commitIndex as part of its normal replication requests. Empty replication requests are also sent as heartbeats, so commitIndex is sent to followers as part of the heartbeat messages.

Log Entries Are Executed in the Log Order

Once the leader updates its commitIndex, it executes the log entries in order, from the last value of the commitIndex to its latest value. The client requests are completed and the response is returned to the client once the log entries are executed.

class ReplicatedLog...

```
private void applyLogEntries(Long previousCommitIndex, Long commitIndex) {
    for (long index = previousCommitIndex + 1; index <= commitIndex; index++) {
        WALEntry walEntry = wal.readAt(index);
        logger.info("Applying entry at " + index + " on server " + serverId());
        var responses = stateMachine.applyEntry(walEntry);
        completeActiveProposals(index, responses);
    }
}
```

The leader also includes the commitIndex with the heartbeat messages it sends to the followers. The followers update the commitIndex and apply the entries the same way. commitIndex is an example of *High-Water Mark*.

class ReplicatedLog...

```
private void updateHighWaterMark(ReplicationRequest request) {
    if (request.getHighWaterMark() > replicationState.getHighWaterMark()) {
        var previousHighWaterMark = replicationState.getHighWaterMark();
        replicationState.setHighWaterMark(request.getHighWaterMark());
        applyLogEntries(previousHighWaterMark, request.getHighWaterMark());
    }
}
```

Leader Election

It is possible that multiple cluster nodes start leader election at the same time. To reduce the possibility of this happening, each cluster node waits for a random amount of time before triggering the election. This way, at most one cluster node starts the election and wins it.

Leader election is also a problem that needs all of the cluster nodes to reach an agreement. The approach taken by Raft and other consensus algorithms is to allow not having an agreement in the worst case. In such cases, consistency is preferred over availability. An incident at Cloudflare[32] is a good example of that. Stale leaders are also tolerated. In such cases, *Generation Clock* makes sure that only one leader succeeds in getting its requests accepted by the followers.

Leader election is the phase where log entries committed in the previous quorum are detected. Every cluster node operates in three states: candidate, leader, or follower. The cluster nodes start in a follower state expecting a *HeartBeat* from an existing leader. If a follower doesn't hear from any leader in a predetermined time period, it moves on to the candidate state and starts leader election. The leader election algorithm establishes a new Generation Clock value. Raft refers to the Generation Clock as **term**.

The leader election mechanism also makes sure the elected leader has as many up-to-date log entries as stipulated by the *Majority Quorum*. This is an optimization done by Raft which avoids log entries from previous Majority Quorum being transferred to the new leader.

New leader election is started by sending each of the peer servers a message requesting a vote.

```
class ReplicatedLog...

  private void startLeaderElection() {
      replicationState.setGeneration(replicationState.getGeneration() + 1);
      registerSelfVote();
      requestVoteFrom(followers);
  }
```

Once a server is voted for in a given generation, the same vote is returned for that generation always. This ensures that some other server requesting a vote for the same generation is not elected after a successful election has already happened. The handling of the vote request happens as follows:

---

32. https://blog.cloudflare.com/a-byzantine-failure-in-the-real-world

```
class ReplicatedLog...

    VoteResponse handleVoteRequest(VoteRequest voteRequest) {
        //for a higher generation, requester becomes follower.
        // But we do not know who the leader is yet.
        if (voteRequest.getGeneration() > replicationState.getGeneration()) {
            becomeFollower(LEADER_NOT_KNOWN, voteRequest.getGeneration());
        }

        VoteTracker voteTracker = replicationState.getVoteTracker();
        if (voteRequest.getGeneration() == replicationState.getGeneration()
                && !replicationState.hasLeader()) {

            if (isUptoDate(voteRequest) && !voteTracker.alreadyVoted()) {
                voteTracker.registerVote(voteRequest.getServerId());
                return grantVote();
            }
            if (voteTracker.alreadyVoted()) {
                return voteTracker.votedFor == voteRequest.getServerId() ?
                        grantVote() : rejectVote();
            }
        }
        return rejectVote();
    }

    private boolean isUptoDate(VoteRequest voteRequest) {
        Long lastLogEntryGeneration = voteRequest.getLastLogEntryGeneration();
        Long lastLogEntryIndex = voteRequest.getLastLogEntryIndex();
        return lastLogEntryGeneration > wal.getLastLogEntryGeneration()
                || (lastLogEntryGeneration == wal.getLastLogEntryGeneration() &&
                    lastLogEntryIndex >= wal.getLastLogIndex());
    }
```

The server receiving votes from the majority of the servers transitions to the leader state. The majority is determined as discussed in Majority Quorum. Once elected, the leader continuously sends a HeartBeat to all of the followers. If the followers don't receive a HeartBeat in a specified time interval, a new leader election is triggered.

Log Entries from Previous Generation

As discussed in the previous section, the first phase of a consensus algorithm detects the existing values which had been copied on the previous runs of the algorithm. The other key aspect is that these values are proposed as the values with the latest generation of the leader. The second phase decides that the value is committed only if the values are proposed for the current generation. Raft never updates generation numbers for the existing entries in the log. So if the leader has log entries from an older generation which are missing from some of the followers, it cannot mark those entries as committed just based on the majority quorum. That is because some other server, which may not be available now, can have an entry at the same index with a higher generation. If the leader goes down without replicating an entry from its current generation, those entries can get overwritten by the new leader. So in Raft, the new leader must commit at least one entry in its term. It can then safely commit all the previous entries. Most practical implementations of Raft try to commit a no-op entry immediately after a leader election, before the leader is considered ready to serve client requests. Refer to Raft thesis, Section 3.6.1 for details.

An Example Leader Election

Consider five servers: Athens, Byzantium, Cyrene, Delphi, and Ephesus. Ephesus is the leader for generation 1. It has replicated entries to itself, Delphi and Athens (Figure 12.4).

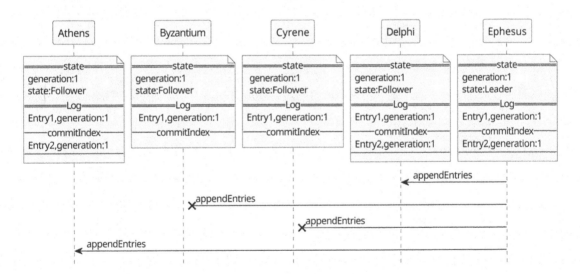

Figure 12.4 *Lost heartbeat triggers an election.*

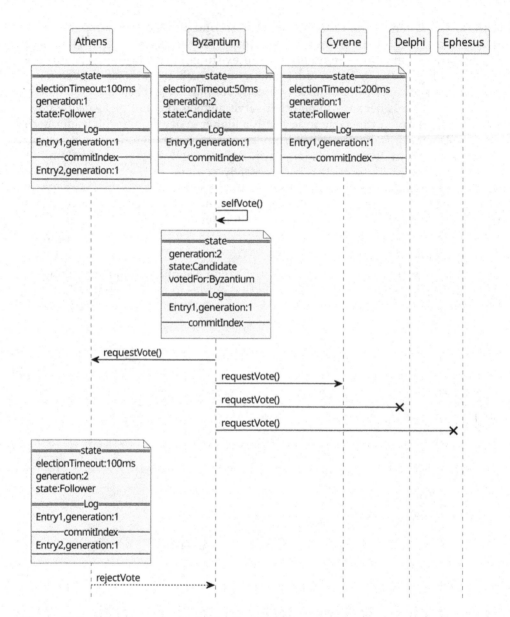

Figure 12.5 *Byzantium cannot get votes from majority quorum.*

At this point, Ephesus and Delphi get disconnected from the rest of the cluster.

Byzantium has the least election timeout, so it triggers the election by incrementing its *Generation Clock* to 2. Cyrene has its generation less than 2 and it also has the same log entry as Byzantium, so it grants the vote. But Athens has an extra entry in its log, so it rejects the vote.

Since Byzantium can't get a majority of three votes (Figure 12.5), it loses the election and moves back to follower state (Figure 12.6).

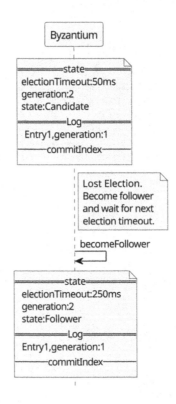

Figure 12.6 *Byzantium loses election.*

Athens times out and triggers the election next (Figure 12.7). It increments the Generation Clock to 3 and sends vote requests to Byzantium and Cyrene. Because both Byzantium and Cyrene have a lower generation number and less log entries than Athens, they both grant the vote to Athens. Once Athens gets majority of the votes, it becomes the leader and starts sending heartbeats to Byzantium and Cyrene (Figure 12.8). Once Byzantium and Cyrene receive a heartbeat from the leader at a higher generation, this confirms the leadership of Athens. Athens then replicates its own log to Byzantium and Cyrene.

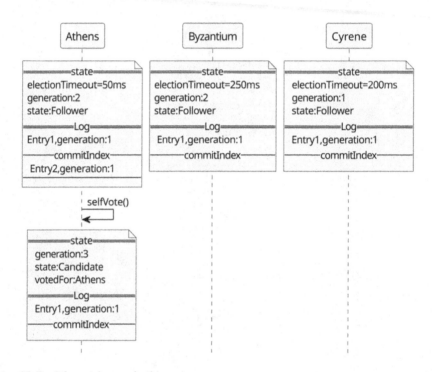

Figure 12.7 *Athens triggers election.*

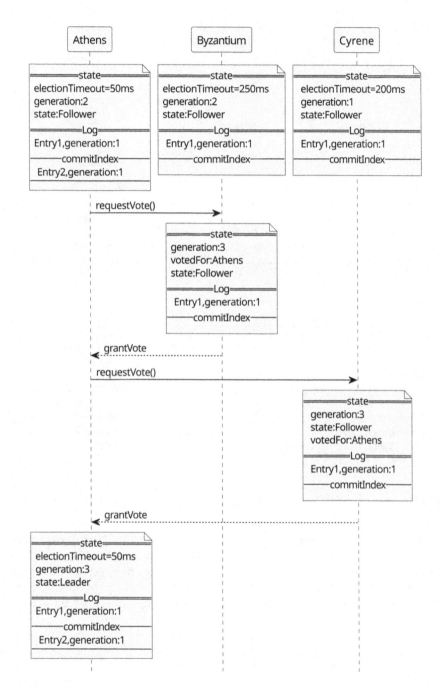

Figure 12.8 *Athens wins election.*

Athens now replicates Entry2 from generation 1 to Byzantium and Cyrene. But because it's an entry from the previous generation, it does not update the commitIndex even when Entry2 is successfully replicated on the majority quorum, as shown in Figure 12.9.

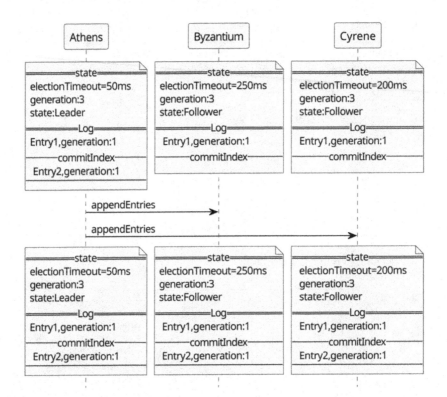

Figure 12.9 *Athens replicates previous generation entry.*

Athens appends a no-op entry to its local log. After this new entry in generation 3 is successfully replicated, it updates the commitIndex (Figure 12.10).

If Ephesus comes back up or restores network connectivity, it sends request to Cyrene. But Cyrene is now at generation 3, so it rejects the requests. Ephesus gets the new term in the rejection response, and steps down to be a follower (Figure 12.11).

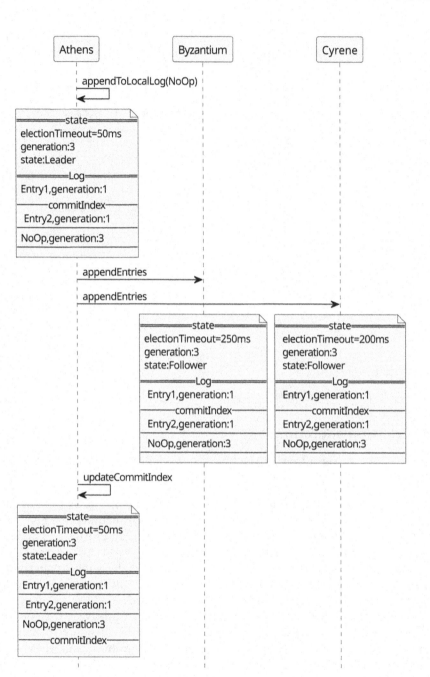

Figure 12.10 *Athens replicates a no-op entry.*

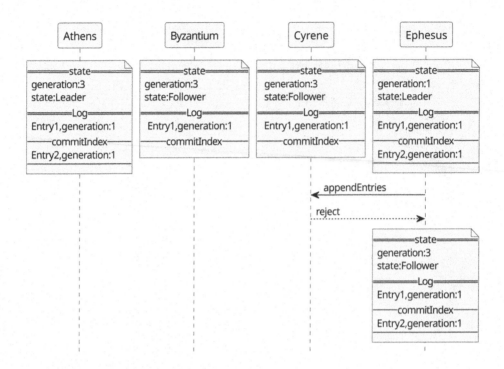

Figure 12.11 *Ephesus steps down.*

Technical Considerations

Here are some of the important technical considerations for any replicated log mechanism:

- The first phase of any consensus-building mechanism needs to know about the log entries that might have been replicated on the previous *Majority Quorum*. The leader needs to know about all such log entries and make sure they are replicated on each cluster node.

    Raft makes sure that the node with as up-to-date a log as the majority quorum of the servers is elected a leader, so log entries do not need to be passed from other cluster nodes to the new leader.

    It is possible that some entries are conflicting. In this case, the conflicting entries from the follower log are overwritten. This is considered safe because these entries were only appended and not committed, and clients never received acknowledgment for these entries.

- It is possible that some cluster nodes in the cluster lag behind, either because they crash and restart or get disconnected from the leader. The leader needs to track each cluster node and make sure that it sends all the missing entries.

Raft maintains a state-per-cluster node to know the log index to which the log entries are successfully copied to each node. The replication requests to each cluster node are sent with all the entries from that log index, making sure that each cluster node gets all the log entries.

- The client needs to find the leader to send the requests. This is required as the leader is the one which makes sure the the requests are ordered and executed only when they are replicated on the Majority Quorum. How a client interacts with the replicated log to find the leader is discussed in the section "Finding the Leader" of the *Consistent Core* pattern. Detecting duplicate requests caused by client retries is handled by the *Idempotent Receiver*.

- The logs are generally compacted by using *Low-Water Mark*. A snapshot of the store backed by replicated log is taken periodically, say after a few thousand entries are applied. The log is then discarded to the index at which the snapshot is taken. Slow followers or newly added servers, which need the full log to be sent, are sent the snapshot instead of individual log entries.

- One of the key assumptions here is that all the requests are strictly ordered. This might not be the requirement always. For example, a key-value store might not require ordering across requests for different keys. In such situations, it is possible to run a different consensus instance per key. This also removes the need to have a single leader for all the requests.

  EPaxos [Moraru2013] is an algorithm which does not rely on a single leader for ordering of requests.

  In partitioned databases like MongoDB, a replicated log is maintained per partition. So, requests are ordered per partition, but not across partitions.

Push vs. Pull

In the Raft replication mechanism explained here, the leader pushes all the log entries to followers. It is also possible to have followers pull the log entries. The Raft implementation [Gustafson2023] in Apache Kafka uses pull-based replication.

What Goes in the Log?

The replicated log mechanism is used for a wide variety of applications, from a key-value store to a blockchain.

For a key-value store, the entries in the log are about setting key-value records. For a *Lease*, the entries are about setting up named leases. For a blockchain, the entries are the blocks in a blockchain which need to be served to all the peers in the same order. For databases like MongoDB, the entries are the data that needs to be consistently replicated.

More generally, any requests which make state changes are placed in the log.

Bypassing the Log for Read Requests

Replicated log generally acts as a *Write-Ahead Log* for a data store. Data stores are expected to handle a lot more read requests than write requests. Read requests are more latency-sensitive. So, most replicated-log implementations, such as etcd which uses Raft or Apache ZooKeeper, serve read requests directly from the key-value stores without going through the replicated log. This avoids the log replication overhead.

One of the key issues with this is that the read requests can return older values if the leader was disconnected from the rest of the cluster. With the standard log replication, the leader won't be able to execute any request which are put in the log unilaterally. This provides safety because:

- Leader won't be able to execute a request unless it can replicate that request on the *Majority Quorum* nodes.

- Majority Quorum makes sure that requests which reach quorum are not lost.

- Log provides strict ordering of the requests. So when a request is executed, it is guaranteed to see the result of the preceding request.

When this mechanism is not used, you can run into subtle issues. For read requests on a key-value store, this can result in getting older values and missing on latest updates even when the client reads from the node that it thinks is the leader.

Consider three nodes as before, Athens, Byzantium, and Cyrene. Athens is the leader. All three nodes have an existing value of "Nitroservices" for title (Figure 12.12).

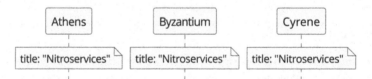

Figure 12.12   *Initial value on three nodes implementing a Replicated Log.*

Let's say Athens gets disconnected from the rest of the cluster. Byzantium and Cyrene then run an election and Cyrene is the new leader. Athens won't know that it got disconnected unless it receives some communication—either a heartbeat or a response from the new leader asking it to step down. Alice communicates with Cyrene and updates the title to "Microservices". After some time, Bob communicates with Athens to read the latest value of title. Athens still thinks that it is the leader, so it returns what it thinks is the latest value. Bob ends up reading the old value, after Alice has successfully updated the value, even though Bob thinks that the value came from a legitimate leader (Figure 12.13).

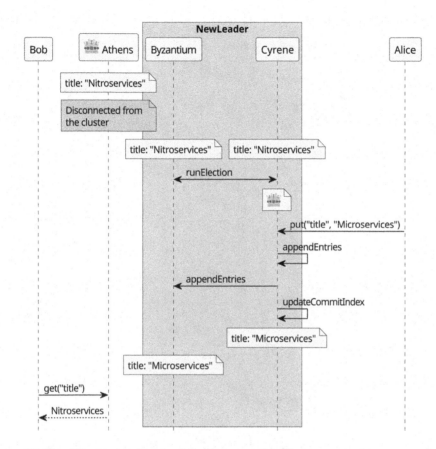

Figure 12.13 *Client gets stale value from disconnected leader.*

Products like etcd and Consul were known to have these issues,[33] which were later fixed. Apache ZooKeeper specifically documents this limitation and provides no guarantee about getting the latest values in the read requests.

There are two solutions for this issue.

- Before serving the read request, the leader can send a heartbeat message to followers. It serves the read request only if it gets a successful response from the Majority Quorum of the followers. This guarantees that this leader is still the valid leader. Raft documents a mechanism which works the same way.

  In the above example, when Bob's request is handled by Athens, it sends the *HeartBeat* to other nodes. If it cannot reach the Majority Quorum, it steps down and returns error to Bob (Figure 12.14).

---

33. https://github.com/etcd-io/etcd/issues/741

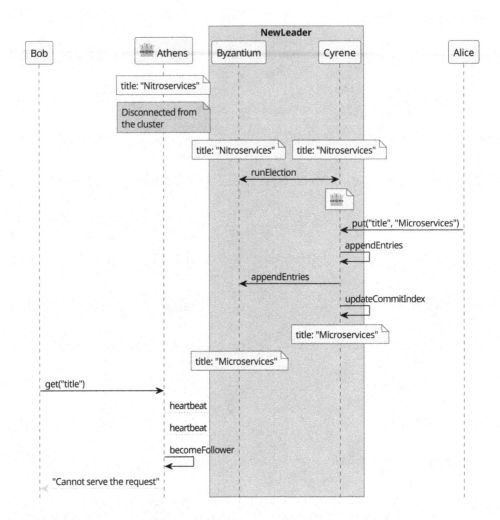

Figure 12.14 *Leader verifies leadership before returning the value.*

- The network round trip for a heartbeat per read request can be too much of a cost to pay, particularly if the cluster is geo-distributed, with servers placed in distant geographic regions. That's why often, another solution is used where the leader implements a leader lease.[34] This solution depends on the monotonic clocks.[35] This makes sure that the old leader steps down if it detects that it is disconnected from the cluster. No other leader is allowed to serve requests while there is a possibility of an older leader still being around.

---

34. https://www.yugabyte.com/blog/low-latency-reads-in-geo-distributed-sql-with-raft-leader-leases
35. https://linux.die.net/man/2/clock_gettime

The leader maintains a time interval called `leaderLeaseTimeout` within which it expects to get a successful response from the followers. When the leader gets a successful response from the followers for its requests, it marks the time at which it got the response from each follower (Figure 12.15).

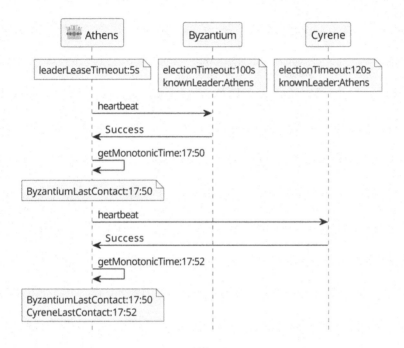

Figure 12.15   *Leader tracks last contacted time for each follower.*

Before serving the read request, it checks if it could contact with the Majority Quorum of the followers within the `leaderLeaseTimeout`. It serves the read request if it received successful response from enough followers. This proves that the cluster does not yet have another leader. Let's say `leaderLeaseTimeout` is 5 seconds. Bob's request is received by Athens at 17:55. It had received responses from Cyrene at 17:52. For a three-node cluster, Athens and Cyrene form a majority quorum. So Athens confirms that it could reach majority quorum within the last 5 seconds (Figure 12.16).

Now, Athens did not receive any response after the response from Cyrene at 17:52. If Bob sends a read request at 18:00, Athens detects that it has not received responses from the Majority Quorum of the servers recently enough. It steps down and rejects the read requests (Figure 12.17).

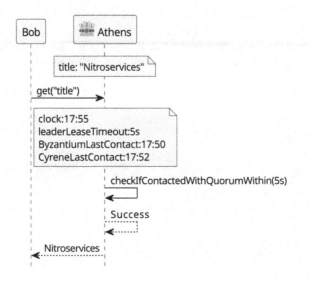

Figure 12.16 *Leader verifies that it could reach Majority Quorum within* `leaderLeaseTimeout`.

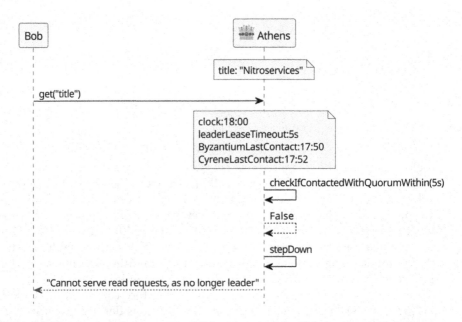

Figure 12.17 *Leader rejects requests if it is not contacted within* `leaderLeaseTimeout`.

As discussed in a Consul post,[36] the electionTimeout is kept higher than the leaderLeaseTimeout. Followers also store the known leader address, which they reset only when electionTimeout period elapses without a HeartBeat from the leader. The followers do not grant vote to any vote requests so long as they have a known leader (Figure 12.18).

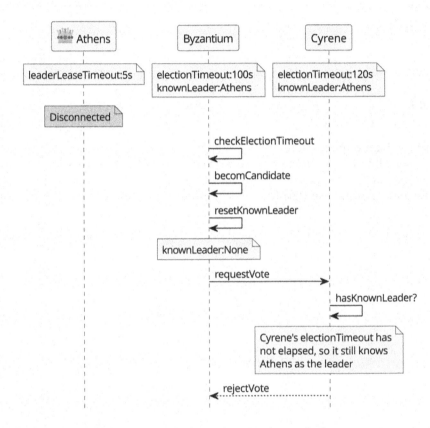

Figure 12.18 *Nodes do not grant vote when there is a known leader.*

These two things make sure that as long as the existing leader thinks that it has a leader lease, no other node can win an election, and there can be no other leader.

This implementation assumes that clock drift across monotonic clocks[37] in a cluster is bounded and that electionTimeout on followers will not elapse faster than the leaderLeaseTimeout elapses on the leader.

---

36. https://github.com/hashicorp/raft/issues/108
37. https://linux.die.net/man/2/clock_gettime

Products like YugabyteDB, etcd, and HashiCorp Consul implement a leader lease[38] to ensure that there are never two leaders serving the read and write requests.

Examples

- Replicated log is the mechanism used by Raft, Multi-Paxos, Zab [Reed2008], and Viewstamped Replication [Liskov2012] protocols. The technique where replicas execute the same commands in the same order is called state machine replication [Schneider1990]. *Consistent Core* is often built with state machine replication.

- Blockchain implementations like Hyperledger Fabric have an ordering component based on a replicated log mechanism. Previous versions of Hyperledger Fabric used Apache Kafka for ordering of the blocks in the blockchain. Recent versions use Raft for the same purpose.

---

38. https://www.yugabyte.com/blog/low-latency-reads-in-geo-distributed-sql-with-raft-leader-leases

Chapter 13

Singular Update Queue

*Use a single thread to process requests asynchronously to maintain
order without blocking the caller.*

Problem

When the state needs to be updated by multiple concurrent clients, we need it
to be safely updated with one-at-a-time changes. Consider the example of the
Write-Ahead Log pattern. We need entries to be processed one at a time, even if
several concurrent clients are trying to write. Generally, locks are used to protect
against concurrent modifications. But if the tasks being performed are time-
consuming, such as writing to a file, blocking all the other calling threads until
the task is completed can have severe impact on the overall system throughput
and latency. It is important to make effective use of compute resources, while
still maintaining the guarantee of one-at-a-time execution.

Solution

Implement a work queue and a single thread working off the queue (Figure 13.1).
Multiple concurrent clients can submit state changes to the queue—but a single
thread works on state changes. This can be naturally implemented with goroutines
and channels in languages like Go.

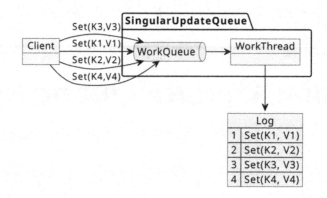

Figure 13.1 *Single thread backed by a work queue*

A typical Java implementation is shown in Figure 13.2.

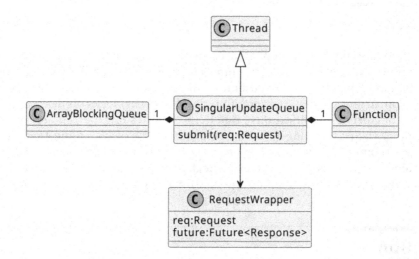

Figure 13.2 SingularUpdateQueue *in Java*

The implementation shown here uses Java's Thread class, just to demonstrate basic code structure. It is possible to use Java's ExecutorService with a single thread to achieve the same. Refer to *Java Concurrency in Practice* [Goetz2006] to learn more about using ExecutorService.

A `SingularUpdateQueue` has a queue and a function to be applied for work items in the queue. It extends from `java.lang.Thread` to make sure that it has its own single thread of execution.

```
public class SingularUpdateQueue<Req, Res> extends Thread {
    private ArrayBlockingQueue<RequestWrapper<Req, Res>> workQueue
            = new ArrayBlockingQueue<RequestWrapper<Req, Res>>(100);
    private Function<Req, Res> handler;
    private volatile boolean isRunning = false;
```

Clients submit requests to the queue on their own threads. The queue wraps each request in a simple wrapper to combine it with a future, returning the future to the client so that the client can react once the request is eventually completed.

class SingularUpdateQueue...

```
public CompletableFuture<Res> submit(Req request) {
    try {
        var requestWrapper = new RequestWrapper<Req, Res>(request);
        workQueue.put(requestWrapper);
        return requestWrapper.getFuture();

    } catch (InterruptedException e) {
        throw new RuntimeException(e);
    }
}
```

class RequestWrapper...

```
private final CompletableFuture<Res> future;
private final Req request;

public RequestWrapper(Req request) {
    this.request = request;
    this.future = new CompletableFuture<Res>();
}

public CompletableFuture<Res> getFuture() { return future; }
public Req getRequest()                   { return request; }
```

The elements in the queue are processed by the single dedicated thread that `SingularUpdateQueue` inherits from `Thread`. The queue allows multiple concurrent producers to add tasks for execution. The queue implementation should be thread-safe and should not add a lot of overhead under contention. The execution thread picks up requests from the queue and processes them one at a time. The `CompletableFuture` is completed with the response of the task execution.

class SingularUpdateQueue...

```
@Override
public void run() {
    isRunning = true;
```

```java
        while(isRunning) {
            Optional<RequestWrapper<Req, Res>> item = take();
            item.ifPresent(requestWrapper -> {
                try {
                    Res response = handler.apply(requestWrapper.getRequest());
                    requestWrapper.complete(response);

                } catch (Exception e) {
                    requestWrapper.completeExceptionally(e);
                }
            });
        }
    }
```

```java
class RequestWrapper...

    public void complete(Res response) {
        future.complete(response);
    }

    public void completeExceptionally(Exception e) {
        future.completeExceptionally(e);
    }
```

Note that we can put a timeout while reading items from the queue, instead of blocking it indefinitely. It allows us to exit the thread if needed, with isRunning set to false, and the queue will not block indefinitely, blocking the execution thread, if it's empty. So we use the poll method with a timeout, instead of the take method, which blocks indefinitely. This gives us the ability to shut down the thread of execution cleanly.

```java
class SingularUpdateQueue...

    private Optional<RequestWrapper<Req, Res>> take() {
        try {
            return Optional.ofNullable(workQueue.poll(2, TimeUnit.MILLISECONDS));

        } catch (InterruptedException e) {
            return Optional.empty();
        }
    }

    public void shutdown() {
        this.isRunning = false;
    }
```

For example, a server processing requests from multiple clients and updating write-ahead log can use a SingularUpdateQueue, as Figure 13.3 demonstrates.

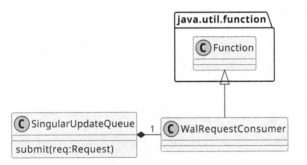

Figure 13.3 *A* SingularUpdateQueue *to update write-ahead log*

A client of the SingularUpdateQueue would set it up by specifying its parameterized types and the function to run when processing the message from the queue. For this example, we're using a consumer of requests for a write-ahead log. There is a single instance of this consumer, which will control access to the log data structure. The consumer needs to put each request into a log and then return a response. That response message can only be sent after the message has been put into the log. We use a SingularUpdateQueue to ensure there's a reliable ordering for these actions.

```
public class WalRequestConsumer
        implements Function<Message<RequestOrResponse>,
                CompletableFuture<Message<RequestOrResponse>>> {

    private final SingularUpdateQueue<Message<RequestOrResponse>,
            Message<RequestOrResponse>> walWriterQueue;
    private final WriteAheadLog wal;

    public WalRequestConsumer(Config config) {
        this.wal = WriteAheadLog.openWAL(config);
        walWriterQueue = new SingularUpdateQueue<>((message) -> {
            wal.writeEntry(serialize(message));
            return responseMessage(message);
        });
        startHandling();
    }

    private void startHandling() { this.walWriterQueue.start(); }
```

The consumer's accept method takes a message, puts it on the queue, and, after each message is processed, sends a response. This method is run on the caller's thread, allowing many callers to invoke apply at the same time.

```
class WalRequestConsumer...

  @Override
  public CompletableFuture<Message<RequestOrResponse>> apply(Message message) {
      return walWriterQueue.submit(message);
  }
```

Choice of the Queue

Which queue data structure to use is an important choice. In the concurrent collection library of the JDK, there is a wide range of data structures to select from:

- ArrayBlockingQueue (used in Kafka request queue)

    As the name suggests, this is an array-backed blocking queue. It is used when a fixed-bound queue needs to be created. Once the queue fills up, the producer will block. This provides blocking backpressure and is helpful when we have slow consumers and fast producers.

- ConcurrentLinkedQueue along with ForkJoinPool (used in Akka Actors mailbox implementation)

    ConcurrentLinkedQueue can be used when we do not have consumers waiting for the producer, but there is some coordinator that schedules consumers only after tasks are queued onto the ConcurrentLinkedQueue.

- LinkedBlockingDeque (used by ZooKeeper and Kafka response queue)

    It is mostly used for unbounded queues that don't block the producer. We need to be careful with this choice, as the queue might fill up quickly and consume all the memory if no backpressure is implemented.

- Ring buffer (used in LMAX Disruptor)

    As discussed in *LMAX Disruptor* [Thomson2011b], task processing is sometimes latency-sensitive—so much so that copying tasks between processing stages with an ArrayBlockingQueue can add to latencies making them unacceptable. Ring buffer can be used in these cases to pass tasks between stages.

Using Channels and Lightweight Threads

This can be a natural fit for languages or libraries supporting lightweight threads along with the concept of channels (such as Go or Kotlin). All the requests are passed to a single channel to be processed. In Go, there is a single goroutine which processes all the messages to update state. The response is then written to a separate channel and processed by a separate goroutine to send it back to clients. As seen in the following code, the requests to update key value are passed onto a single shared request channel:

```
func (s *server) putKv(w http.ResponseWriter, r *http.Request)  {
  kv, err := s.readRequest(r, w)
```

```
    if err != nil {
      log.Panic(err)
      return
    }

    request := &requestResponse{
      request:         kv,
      responseChannel: make(chan string),
    }

    s.requestChannel <- request
    response := s.waitForResponse(request)
    w.Write([]byte(response))
}
```

The requests are processed in a single goroutine to update all the states:

```
func (s* server) Start() error {
  go s.serveHttp()

  go s.singularUpdateQueue()

  return nil
}

func (s *server) singularUpdateQueue() {
  for {
    select {
    case e := <-s.requestChannel:
      s.updateState(e)
      e.responseChannel <- buildResponse(e);
    }
  }
}
```

Backpressure

Backpressure can be an important concern when a work queue is used to communicate between threads. If the consumer is slow and the producer is fast, the queue might fill up fast. Unless some precautions are taken, it might run out of memory with a large number of tasks filling up the queue. Generally, the queue is kept bounded with sender blocking if the queue is full. For example, java.util.concurrent.ArrayBlockingQueue has two methods to add elements. The put method blocks the producer if the array is full. The add method throws IllegalStateException if the queue is full, but doesn't block the producer. It's important to know the semantics of the methods available for adding tasks to the queue. In the case of ArrayBlockingQueue, the put method should be used to block the sender and provide backpressure by blocking. Frameworks like Reactive Streams can help implement a more sophisticated backpressure mechanism from consumer to the producer.

Other Considerations

- **Task chaining.** Most of the time, processing needs to be done with chaining multiple tasks together. The results of a SingularUpdateQueue execution need to be passed to other stages. For example, in the WalRequestConsumer above, after the records are written to the write-ahead log, the response needs to be sent over the socket connection. This can be done by executing the future returned by SingularUpdateQueue on a separate thread. It can submit the task to other SingularUpdateQueue as well.

- **Making external service calls.** Sometimes, as part of the task execution in the SingularUpdateQueue, external service calls need to be made so that the state of the SingularUpdateQueue is updated by responses to the service calls. In this scenario, it's important that no blocking network calls are made, or it blocks the only thread which is processing all the tasks. The calls are made asynchronously. Care must be taken to not access the SingularUpdateQueue state in the future callback of the asynchronous service call because this can happen in a separate thread, defeating the purpose of doing all state changes in the SingularUpdateQueue by a single thread. The result of the call should be added to the work queue similar to other events or requests.

Examples

All the consensus implementations, such as ZooKeeper (Zab) or etcd (Raft), need requests to be processed in strict order, one at a time. They use a similar code structure.

- The ZooKeeper implementation of request processing pipeline is done with single-threaded request processors.

- Controller [Qin2015] in Apache Kafka, which needs to update state based on multiple concurrent events from ZooKeeper, handles them in a single thread with all the event handlers submitting the events in a queue.

- Apache Cassandra, which uses SEDA [Welsh2001] architecture, uses single-threaded stages to update its gossip state.

- etcd and other Go-based implementations have a single goroutine working off a request channel to update its state.

- LMAX Disruptor architecture follows Single Writer Principle [Thomson2011a] to avoid mutual exclusion while updating the local state.

Chapter 14

Request Waiting List

*Track client requests which require responses after the criteria to respond
is met based on responses from other cluster nodes.*

Problem

A cluster node needs to communicate with other cluster nodes to replicate data
while processing a client request. A response from all other cluster nodes or a
Majority Quorum is needed before responding to clients.

Communication to other cluster nodes is done asynchronously. Asynchronous
communication allows patterns like *Request Pipeline* and *Request Batch* to be used.

So the cluster node receives and processes responses from multiple other
cluster nodes asynchronously. It then needs to correlate them to check if the
Majority Quorum for a particular client request is reached.

Solution

The cluster node maintains a waiting list which maps a key and a callback function. The key is chosen depending on the specific criteria to invoke the callback.
For example, if it needs to be invoked whenever a message from other cluster
node is received, it can be the correlation ID[39] of the message. In the case of
Replicated Log, it is the *High-Water Mark*. The callback handles the response and
decides if the client request can be fulfilled.

Consider the example of a key-value store where data is replicated on multiple
servers. Here, Majority Quorum can be used to decide when a replication can
be considered successful to initiate a response to the client. The cluster node

---

39. https://www.enterpriseintegrationpatterns.com/CorrelationIdentifier.html

then tracks the requests sent to other cluster nodes, and a callback is registered with each request. Each request is marked with a Correlation ID, which is used to map response to the request. The waiting list is then notified to invoke the callback when responses from other cluster nodes are received.

Let's look at an example with three cluster nodes, Athens, Byzantium, and Cyrene (Figure 14.1). The client connects with Athens to store "title" as "Microservices". Athens needs to replicate it on Byzantium and Cyrene, so it sends a request to itself to store the key-value and sends requests to both Byzantium and Cyrene concurrently. To track responses, Athens creates a `WriteQuorumResponseCallback` and adds it to the waiting list for each of the requests sent.

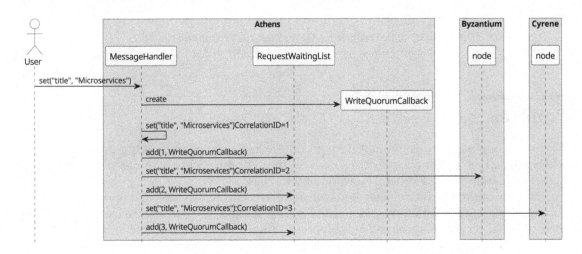

Figure 14.1 *Caller adds callback with correlation ID to Request Waiting List.*

For every response received, the `WriteQuorumResponseCallback` is invoked to handle the response. It checks whether the required number of responses have been received. Once the response is received from Byzantium, the quorum is reached and the pending client request is completed. Cyrene can respond later, but the response can be sent to the client without waiting for it (Figure 14.2).

The code looks like the sample below. Note that every cluster node maintains its own instance of a waiting list. The waiting list tracks the keys and the associated callbacks and stores the timestamps at which each callback was registered. The timestamp is used to check whether the callbacks need to be expired if responses haven't been received within the expected time.

```
public class RequestWaitingList<Key, Response> {
    private Map<Key, CallbackDetails> pendingRequests
        = new ConcurrentHashMap<>();

    public void add(Key key, RequestCallback<Response> callback) {
```

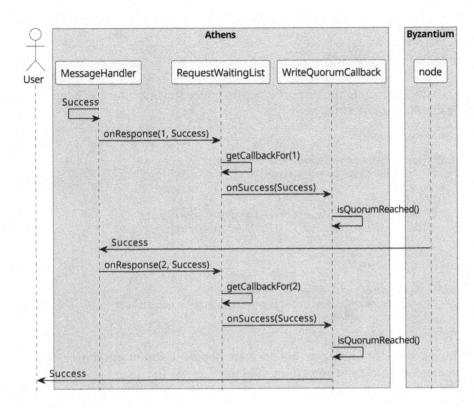

Figure 14.2 *Callback verifies quorum and responds to client.*

```
        pendingRequests.put(key, new CallbackDetails(callback,
                                      clock.nanoTime())));
    }

class CallbackDetails {
    RequestCallback requestCallback;
    long createTime;

    public CallbackDetails(RequestCallback requestCallback, long createTime) {
        this.requestCallback = requestCallback;
        this.createTime = createTime;
    }

    public RequestCallback getRequestCallback() {
        return requestCallback;
    }

    public long elapsedTime(long now) {
        return now - createTime;
    }
}
```

```
public interface RequestCallback<T> {
    void onResponse(T r);
    void onError(Throwable e);
}
```

It is asked to handle the response or error once the response has been received from the other cluster node.

class RequestWaitingList...

```
public void handleResponse(Key key, Response response) {
    if (!pendingRequests.containsKey(key)) {
        return;
    }
    CallbackDetails callbackDetails = pendingRequests.remove(key);
    callbackDetails.getRequestCallback().onResponse(response);
}
```

class RequestWaitingList...

```
public void handleError(int requestId, Throwable e) {
    CallbackDetails callbackDetails = pendingRequests.remove(requestId);
    callbackDetails.getRequestCallback().onError(e);
}
```

The waiting list can then be used to handle quorum responses, with the implementation looking something like this:

```
static class WriteQuorumCallback
        implements RequestCallback<RequestOrResponse> {

    private final int quorum;
    private volatile int expectedNumberOfResponses;
    private volatile int receivedResponses;
    private volatile int receivedErrors;
    private volatile boolean done;

    private final RequestOrResponse request;
    private final ClientConnection clientConnection;

    public WriteQuorumCallback(int totalExpectedResponses,
                               RequestOrResponse clientRequest,
                               ClientConnection clientConnection) {

        this.expectedNumberOfResponses = totalExpectedResponses;
        this.quorum = expectedNumberOfResponses / 2 + 1;
        this.request = clientRequest;
        this.clientConnection = clientConnection;
    }

    @Override
    public void onResponse(RequestOrResponse response) {
        receivedResponses++;
```

```
            if (receivedResponses == quorum && !done) {
                respondToClient("Success");
                done = true;
            }
        }

        @Override
        public void onError(Throwable t) {
            receivedErrors++;
            if (receivedErrors == quorum && !done) {
                respondToClient("Error");
                done = true;
            }
        }

        private void respondToClient(String response) {
            clientConnection
                    .write(new RequestOrResponse(
                            new StringRequest(
                                        RequestId.SetValueResponse,
                                        response.getBytes()),
                                        request.getCorrelationId()));
        }
    }
```

Whenever a cluster node sends requests to other nodes, it adds a callback to the waiting list, mapping it with the Correlation ID of the request sent.

class ClusterNode...

```
    private void handleSetValueClientRequestRequiringQuorum(
            List<InetAddressAndPort> replicas,
            RequestOrResponse request, ClientConnection clientConnection) {

        SetValueRequest setValueRequest = deserialize(request);

        var totalExpectedResponses = replicas.size();
        var requestCallback = new WriteQuorumCallback(totalExpectedResponses,
                request, clientConnection);

        for (InetAddressAndPort replica : replicas) {
            var correlationId = nextRequestId();
            requestWaitingList.add(correlationId, requestCallback);
            sendRequestToReplica(replica, setValueRequest, correlationId);
        }
    }

    private void sendRequestToReplica(InetAddressAndPort replica,
                                      SetValueRequest setValueRequest,
                                      int correlationId) {
        try {
            var client = new SocketClient(replica);
```

```
        var requestOrResponse = new RequestOrResponse(setValueRequest,
                correlationId, listenAddress);
        client.sendOneway(requestOrResponse);

    } catch (IOException e) {
        requestWaitingList.handleError(correlationId, e);
    }
}
```

Once the response is received, the waiting list is asked to handle it:

class ClusterNode...

```
private void handleSetValueResponse(RequestOrResponse response) {
    requestWaitingList.handleResponse(response.getCorrelationId(), response);
}
```

The waiting list will then invoke the associated `WriteQuorumCallback`. The `WriteQuorumCallback` instance verifies if the quorum responses have been received and invokes the callback to respond to the client.

Expiring Long Pending Requests

Sometimes, responses from the other cluster nodes are delayed. For these cases, the waiting list needs a mechanism to expire requests after a timeout:

class RequestWaitingList...

```
private SystemClock clock;
private ScheduledExecutorService executor
        = Executors.newSingleThreadScheduledExecutor();
private long expirationIntervalMillis = 2000;

public RequestWaitingList(SystemClock clock) {
    this.clock = clock;
    executor
            .scheduleWithFixedDelay(this::expire,
                    expirationIntervalMillis,
                    expirationIntervalMillis, MILLISECONDS);
}

private void expire() {
    long now = clock.nanoTime();
    List<Key> expiredRequestKeys = getExpiredRequestKeys(now);

    expiredRequestKeys.stream().forEach(expiredRequestKey -> {
        CallbackDetails request = pendingRequests.remove(expiredRequestKey);
        request.requestCallback
                .onError(new TimeoutException("Request expired"));
    });
}
```

```
private List<Key> getExpiredRequestKeys(long now) {
    return pendingRequests
            .entrySet()
            .stream()
            .filter(entry -> entry.getValue()
                            .elapsedTime(now) > expirationIntervalMillis)
            .map(e -> e.getKey()).collect(Collectors.toList());
}
```

Examples

- Apache Cassandra uses asynchronous message passing for internode communication. It uses *Majority Quorum* and processes response messages asynchronously the same way.

- Apache Kafka tracks the pending requests using a data structure called *purgatory*.[40]

- etcd maintains a waiting list to respond to client requests in a similar way.

---

40. https://www.confluent.io/blog/apache-kafka-purgatory-hierarchical-timing-wheels

Chapter 15

Idempotent Receiver

Identify requests from clients uniquely so you can ignore duplicate requests when client retries.

Problem

Clients send requests to servers but might not get a response. It's impossible for clients to know if the response was lost or the server crashed before processing the request. To make sure its request is processed, the client has to resend the request.

If a server had already processed the request and crashed after that, servers will get duplicate requests from the client when it retries.

Solution

Identify a client uniquely by assigning a unique ID to each client. Before sending any requests, the client registers itself with the server.

```
class ConsistentCoreClient...

  private void registerWithLeader() {
      RequestOrResponse request
            = new RequestOrResponse(RequestId.RegisterClientRequest,
            correlationId.incrementAndGet());

      //blockingSend will attempt to create a new connection
      //if there is a network error.
      RequestOrResponse response = blockingSend(request);
      RegisterClientResponse registerClientResponse
            = deserialize(response.getMessageBody(),
            RegisterClientResponse.class);
```

```
        this.clientId = registerClientResponse.getClientId();
    }
```

When the server receives a client registration request, it assigns a unique ID to the client. If the server is a *Consistent Core*, it can assign the *Write-Ahead Log* index as a client identifier.

class ReplicatedKVStore...

```
  private Map<Long, Session> clientSessions = new ConcurrentHashMap<>();

  private RegisterClientResponse registerClient(WALEntry walEntry) {
      Long clientId = walEntry.getEntryIndex();
      //clientId to store client responses.
      clientSessions.put(clientId, new Session(clock.nanoTime()));
      return new RegisterClientResponse(clientId);
  }
```

The server creates a session to store responses for the requests for the registered client. It also tracks the time at which the session was created, so that inactive sessions can be discarded as explained in later sections.

```
public class Session {
    long lastAccessTimestamp;
    Queue<Response> clientResponses = new ArrayDeque<>();

    public Session(long lastAccessTimestamp) {
        this.lastAccessTimestamp = lastAccessTimestamp;
    }

    public long getLastAccessTimestamp() {
        return lastAccessTimestamp;
    }

    public Optional<Response> getResponse(int requestNumber) {
        return clientResponses.stream().
                filter(r -> requestNumber == r.getRequestNumber()).findFirst();
    }

    private static final int MAX_SAVED_RESPONSES = 5;

    public void addResponse(Response response) {
        if (clientResponses.size() == MAX_SAVED_RESPONSES) {
            clientResponses.remove(); //remove the oldest request
        }
        clientResponses.add(response);
    }

    public void refresh(long nanoTime) {
        this.lastAccessTimestamp = nanoTime;
    }
}
```

For a Consistent Core, the client registration request is also replicated as part of the consensus algorithm. So the client registration is available even if the existing leader fails. The server then also stores the responses sent to the client for subsequent requests.

Idempotent and Non-Idempotent Requests

It is important to note that some of the requests are by nature idempotent. For example, setting a key and a value in a key-value store is naturally idempotent. Even if the same key-value is set multiple times, it doesn't create a problem.

On the other hand, creating a *Lease* is not idempotent. If a lease is already created, a retried request to create a lease will fail. This is a problem. Consider the following scenario. A client sends a request to create a lease. The server creates a lease successfully, but then crashes, or the connection fails before the response is sent to the client. The client creates the connection again, and retries creating the lease. Since the server already has a lease with the given name, it returns an error. So the client thinks that it doesn't have a lease. This is clearly not the behavior we expect to have.

With an idempotent receiver, the client will send the lease request with the same request number. Since the response from the already processed request is saved on the server, the same response is returned. This way, if the client could successfully create a lease before the connection failed, it will get the same response after it retries the same request.

For every non-idempotent request (see sidebar) that the server receives, it stores the response in the client session after successful execution.

class ReplicatedKVStore...

```
    private Response applyRegisterLeaseCommand(WALEntry walEntry,
                                            RegisterLeaseCommand command) {
        logger.info("Creating lease with id " + command.getName()
                + "with timeout " + command.getTimeout()
                + " on server " + getReplicatedLog().getServerId());
        try {
            leaseTracker.addLease(command.getName(),
                    command.getTimeout());
            Response success =
                    Response.success(RequestId.RegisterLeaseResponse,
                            walEntry.getEntryIndex());

            if (command.hasClientId()) {
                Session session = clientSessions.get(command.getClientId());
                session.addResponse(success
                        .withRequestNumber(command.getRequestNumber()));
            }
```

```
            return success;

        } catch (DuplicateLeaseException e) {
            logger.error("lease with id " + command.getName()
                    + " on server " + getReplicatedLog().getServerId()
                    + " already exists.");

            return Response
                    .error(RequestId.RegisterLeaseResponse,
                            DUPLICATE_LEASE_ERROR,
                            e.getMessage(),
                            walEntry.getEntryIndex());
        }
    }
```

The client sends the client identifier with each request that is sent to the server. The client also keeps a counter to assign request numbers to each request sent to the server.

class ConsistentCoreClient...

```
    AtomicInteger nextRequestNumber = new AtomicInteger(1);

    public void registerLease(String name, Duration ttl)
            throws DuplicateLeaseException {
        var registerLeaseRequest
            = new RegisterLeaseRequest(clientId,
                                        nextRequestNumber.getAndIncrement(),
                                        name, ttl.toNanos());

        var serializedRequest = new RequestOrResponse(
                registerLeaseRequest,
                correlationId.getAndIncrement());

        logger.info("Sending RegisterLeaseRequest for " + name);
        var serializedResponse = sendWithRetries(serializedRequest);
        Response response = deserialize(serializedResponse.getMessageBody(),
                Response.class);

        if (response.error == Errors.DUPLICATE_LEASE_ERROR) {
            throw new DuplicateLeaseException(name);
        }
    }

    private static final int MAX_RETRIES = 3;

    private RequestOrResponse blockingSendWithRetries(RequestOrResponse request)
    {
        for (int i = 0; i <= MAX_RETRIES; i++) {
            try {
                //blockingSend will attempt to create a new connection
                // if there is no connection.
```

```
            logger.info("ConsistentCoreClient Attempt " + i);
            return blockingSend(request);

        } catch (NetworkException e) {
            resetConnectionToLeader();
            logger.error("ConsistentCoreClient Failed sending request  "
                    + request + ". Try " + i, e);
        }
    }

    throw new NetworkException("Timed out after " + MAX_RETRIES
            + " retries");
}
```

When the server receives a request, it checks if the request with the given request number from the same client is already processed. If it finds a saved response, it returns the same response to the client, without processing the request again.

class ReplicatedKVStore...

```
private Response applyWalEntry(WALEntry walEntry) {
    Command command = deserialize(walEntry);
    if (command.hasClientId()) {
        var session = clientSessions.get(command.getClientId());
        var savedResponse = session.getResponse(command.getRequestNumber());
        if(savedResponse.isPresent()) {
            return savedResponse.get();
        } //else continue and execute this command.
    }
}
```

Expiring the Saved Client Requests

The requests stored per client cannot be stored forever. There are multiple ways the requests can be expired. In the reference implementation for Raft, the client keeps a separate number to note the request number for which the response is successfully received. This number is then sent with each request to the server. The server can safely discard any requests with the request number less than this number.

If a client is guaranteed to send the next request only after receiving the response for the previous request, the server can safely remove all previous requests once it gets a new request from the client. There is a problem when *Request Pipeline* is used, as there can be multiple in-flight requests for which the client might not have received the response. If the server knows the maximum number of in-flight requests a client can have, it can store only that many responses and remove all the rest. For example, Apache Kafka can have a maximum of five in-flight requests for its producer, so it stores a maximum of five previous responses.

class Session...

```
private static final int MAX_SAVED_RESPONSES = 5;

public void addResponse(Response response) {
    if (clientResponses.size() == MAX_SAVED_RESPONSES) {
        clientResponses.remove(); //remove the oldest request
    }
    clientResponses.add(response);
}
```

Removing the Registered Clients

It is important to note that this mechanism to detect duplicate messages is only applicable for client retries on connection failures. If a client fails and is restarted, it will be registered again, so no deduplication is achieved across client restarts.

It is also not aware of any application-level logic. So, if an application sends multiple requests which are considered duplicate at the application level, there is no way for the storage server implementation to know about it. The application needs to handle it independently.

The client's session is not kept on the server forever. A server can have a maximum-time-to-live for the client sessions it stores. Clients send a *HeartBeat* periodically. If there are no heartbeats from the client during this time to live, the client's state on the server can be removed.

The server starts a scheduled task to periodically check for expired sessions and remove the sessions which are expired.

class ReplicatedKVStore...

```
private long sessionCheckingIntervalMs = TimeUnit.SECONDS.toMillis(10);
private long sessionTimeoutNanos = TimeUnit.SECONDS.toNanos(30);

private void startSessionCheckerTask() {
    scheduledTask = executor.scheduleWithFixedDelay(() -> {
        removeExpiredSession();
    }, sessionCheckingIntervalMs, sessionCheckingIntervalMs, TimeUnit.MILLISECONDS);
}

private void removeExpiredSession() {
    long now = System.nanoTime();
    for (Long clientId : clientSessions.keySet()) {
        Session session = clientSessions.get(clientId);
        long elapsedNanosSinceLastAccess
                = now - session.getLastAccessTimestamp();
```

```
        if (elapsedNanosSinceLastAccess > sessionTimeoutNanos) {
            clientSessions.remove(clientId);
        }
    }
}
```

At-Most-Once, At-Least-Once, and Exactly-Once Actions

Depending on how the client interacts with the server, the guarantee of whether the server will do a certain action is predetermined. If a client experiences a failure after the request is sent and before receiving the response, there can be three possibilities.

If the client doesn't retry the request in case of failure, the server might have processed the request or it might have failed before processing the request. So the request is processed at most once on the server.

If the client retries the request, and the server had processed it before the communication failure, it might process it again. So the request is processed at least once, but can be processed multiple times.

With an idempotent receiver, even with multiple client retries, the server processes the request only once. So, to achieve the exactly-once guarantee, you need idempotent receivers.

Examples

- Raft's reference implementation, LogCabin, has idempotency for providing linearizable actions.

- Apache Kafka allows idempotent producer[41] which allows clients to retry requests and ignores duplicate requests.

- ZooKeeper has the concept of sessions and a zxid which allows clients to recover.

- HBase has a wrapper[42] that implements idempotent actions following the guidelines of error handling in ZooKeeper.[43]

---

41. https://cwiki.apache.org/confluence/display/KAFKA/Idempotent+Producer
42. https://docs.cloudera.com/HDPDocuments/HDP2/HDP-2.4.0/bk_hbase_java_api/org/apache/hadoop/hbase/zookeeper/RecoverableZooKeeper.html
43. https://cwiki.apache.org/confluence/display/ZOOKEEPER/ErrorHandling

Chapter 16

Follower Reads

*Serve read requests from followers to achieve better throughput and
lower latency.*

Problem

When using the *Leader and Followers* pattern, it's possible that the leader may get
overloaded if too many requests are sent to it. Furthermore, in a multi-datacenter
setup where the client is in a remote datacenter, requests to the leader will be
subject to additional latency.

Solution

While the write requests need to go to the leader to maintain consistency, the
read-only requests can instead go to the nearest follower. This is particularly
useful when clients are mostly read-only.

It is important to remember that clients reading from followers can get old
values. There will always be a replication lag between the leader and the followers,
even in systems implementing consensus algorithms like Raft. That's because even
when the leader knows which values are committed, it needs another message
to communicate it to a follower. So, reading from a follower server is used only
in situations where slightly older values are tolerated, as shown in Figure 16.1.

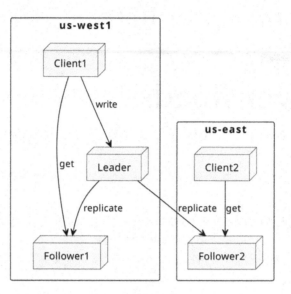

Figure 16.1 *Reading from the nearest follower*

Finding the Nearest Replica

Cluster nodes maintain additional metadata about their location.

```
class ReplicaDescriptor...

  public class ReplicaDescriptor {
      private InetAddressAndPort address;
      private String region;

      public ReplicaDescriptor(InetAddressAndPort address, String region) {
          this.address = address;
          this.region = region;
      }

      public InetAddressAndPort getAddress() {
          return address;
      }

      public String getRegion() {
          return region;
      }
  }
```

A client of the cluster can then pick up the local replica based on its own region.

```
class ClusterClient...

    public List<String> get(String key) {
        var allReplicas = allFollowerReplicas(key);
        var nearestFollower = findNearestFollowerBasedOnLocality(allReplicas,
                clientRegion);
        var getValueResponse = sendGetRequest(nearestFollower.getAddress(),
                new GetValueRequest(key));
        return getValueResponse.getValue();
    }


    ReplicaDescriptor findNearestFollowerBasedOnLocality(
                                    List<ReplicaDescriptor> followers,
                                    String clientRegion) {

        var sameRegionFollowers = matchLocality(followers, clientRegion);
        var finalList = sameRegionFollowers.isEmpty()
                ? followers
                : sameRegionFollowers;
        return finalList.get(0);
    }

    private List<ReplicaDescriptor> matchLocality(
                                    List<ReplicaDescriptor> followers,
                                    String clientRegion) {
        return followers
                .stream()
                .filter(rd -> clientRegion.equals(rd.getRegion()))
                .collect(Collectors.toList());
    }
```

For example, suppose there are two follower replicas, one in the region US-west and the other in the region US-east. The client from US-east region will be connected to the US-east replica:

```
class CausalKVStoreTest...

    @Test
    public void getFollowersInSameRegion() {
        var followers = createReplicas("us-west", "us-east");
        var nearestFollower =
                new ClusterClient(followers, "us-east")
                        .findNearestFollower(followers);
        assertEquals(nearestFollower.getRegion(), "us-east");
    }
```

A client or a coordinating cluster node can also track latencies observed with cluster nodes. It can send periodic heartbeats to capture the latencies, and use that to pick up a follower with minimum latency. To do a more fair selection, products like MongoDB or CockroachDB calculate latencies as a moving average. Cluster nodes generally maintain a *Single-Socket Channel* to communicate with other cluster nodes. A single-socket channel needs a *HeartBeat* to keep the connection alive, so capturing latencies and calculating the moving average can be easily implemented.

```
class WeightedAverage...

    public class WeightedAverage {
        long averageLatencyMs = 0;

        public void update(long heartbeatRequestLatency) {
            //Example implementation of weighted average as used in Mongodb
            //The running, weighted average round trip time for heartbeat
            // messages to the target node. Weighted 80% to the old round trip time,
            // and 20% to the new round trip time.
            averageLatencyMs = averageLatencyMs == 0
                    ? heartbeatRequestLatency
                    : (averageLatencyMs * 4 + heartbeatRequestLatency) / 5;
        }

        public long getAverageLatency() {
            return averageLatencyMs;
        }
    }

class ClusterClient...

    private Map<InetAddressAndPort, WeightedAverage> latencyMap
            = new HashMap<>();

    private void sendHeartbeat(InetAddressAndPort clusterNodeAddress) {
        try {
            long startTimeNanos = System.nanoTime();
            sendHeartbeatRequest(clusterNodeAddress);
            long endTimeNanos = System.nanoTime();

            WeightedAverage heartbeatStats = latencyMap.get(clusterNodeAddress);
            if (heartbeatStats == null) {
                heartbeatStats = new WeightedAverage();
                latencyMap.put(clusterNodeAddress, new WeightedAverage());
            }
            heartbeatStats
                    .update(endTimeNanos - startTimeNanos);

        } catch (NetworkException e) {
            logger.error(e);
        }
    }
```

This latency information can then be used to pick up the follower with the least network latency.

```
class ClusterClient...

    ReplicaDescriptor findNearestFollower(List<ReplicaDescriptor> allFollowers) {

        var sameRegionFollowers = matchLocality(allFollowers, clientRegion);
        var finalList
                = sameRegionFollowers.isEmpty() ? allFollowers
                                                :sameRegionFollowers;

        return finalList.stream().sorted((r1, r2) -> {
            if (!latenciesAvailableFor(r1, r2)) {
                return 0;
            }

            return Long.compare(latencyMap.get(r1).getAverageLatency(),
                                latencyMap.get(r2).getAverageLatency());

        }).findFirst().get();
    }

    private boolean latenciesAvailableFor(ReplicaDescriptor r1,
                                          ReplicaDescriptor r2) {

        return latencyMap.containsKey(r1) && latencyMap.containsKey(r2);
    }
```

Disconnected or Slow Followers

A follower might get disconnected from the leader and stop getting updates. In some cases, followers can suffer from slow disks impeding the replication process, which causes them to lag behind the leader. A follower can track if it has not heard from the leader in a while, and then stop serving user requests.

For example, products like MongoDB allow selecting a replica with a maximum allowed lag time.[44] If the replica lags behind the leader beyond this maximum time, it's not selected to serve requests. In Apache Kafka, if the follower detects that the offset asked by the consumer is too large, it responds with OFFSET_OUT_OF_RANGE error. The consumer is then expected to communicate with the leader [Gustafson2018].

---

44. https://docs.mongodb.com/manual/core/read-preference-staleness/#std-label-replica-set-read-preference-max-staleness

Read Your Own Writes

Causal Consistency

When an event A in a system happens before another event B, they are said to have causal relationship. This means that A might have some role in causing B.

For a data storage system, the events are writing and reading values. To provide causal consistency, the storage system needs to track the happens-before relationship between read and write events. *Lamport Clock* and its variants are used for this purpose.

Reading from follower servers can be problematic as it can give surprising results in common scenarios where a client writes something and then immediately tries to read it.

Consider a client who notices that some book data erroneously has "title": "Nitroservices". It corrects this by a write, "title": "Microservices", which goes to the leader. It then immediately reads back the value—but the read request goes to a follower, which may not have been updated yet (Figure 16.2).

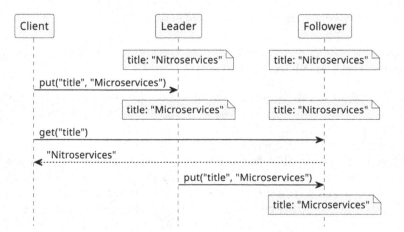

Figure 16.2 *Reading stale value from follower*

This is a common problem. For example, until very recently Amazon S3 did not prevent this.[45]

---

45. https://aws.amazon.com/about-aws/whats-new/2020/12/amazon-s3-now-delivers-strong-read-after-write-consistency-automatically-for-all-applications

To fix this issue, with each write, the server stores not just the new value but also a monotonically increasing version stamp. The stamp can be a *High-Water Mark* or a *Hybrid Clock*. The server returns this version stamp of the stored value in the response to the write request. Then, should the client wish to read the value later, it includes the version stamp as part of its read request. Should the read request go to a follower, it checks its stored value to see if it is equal or later than the requested version stamp. If it isn't, it waits until it has an up-to-date version before returning the value. This way, clients will always read a value that's consistent with a value they write—this is often referred to as **read-your-writes consistency**.

The flow of requests is shown in Figure 16.3. To correct a wrong value, "title": "Microservices" is written to the leader. The leader returns version 2 to the client in the response. When the client tries to read the value for "title", it passes the version number 2 in the request. The follower server that receives the request checks if its own version number is up-to-date. As the version number at the follower server is still 1, it waits till it gets that version from the leader. Once it has the matching (or later) version, it completes the read request and returns the value "Microservices".

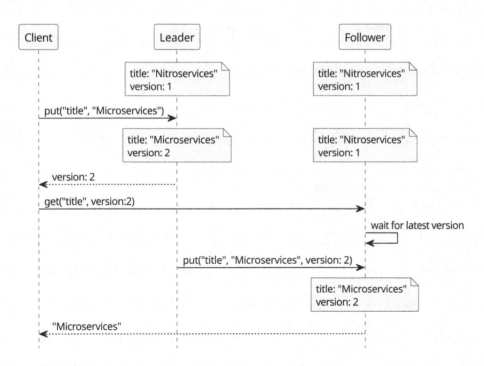

Figure 16.3 *Read-your-own-writes at follower*

The code for the key-value store looks as follows. It is important to note that the follower can be lagging behind too much or be disconnected from the leader. So it does not wait indefinitely—there is a configured timeout value. If the follower server cannot get the update within timeout, an error response is returned to the client. The client can then retry reading from other followers.

class ReplicatedKVStore...

```
Map<Integer, CompletableFuture> waitingRequests = new ConcurrentHashMap<>();
public CompletableFuture<Optional<String>> get(String key, int atVersion) {
    if(this.replicatedLog.getRole() == ServerRole.FOLLOWING) {
        //check if we have the version with us;
        if (!isVersionUptoDate(atVersion)) {
            //wait till we get the latest version.
            var future = new CompletableFuture<Optional<String>>();
            //Timeout if version does not progress to required version
            //before followerWaitTimeout ms.
            future.orTimeout(config.getFollowerWaitTimeoutMs(),
                    TimeUnit.MILLISECONDS);
            waitingRequests.put(atVersion, future);
            return future;
        }
    }
    return CompletableFuture.completedFuture(mvccStore.get(key, atVersion));
}

private boolean isVersionUptoDate(int atVersion) {
    return version >= atVersion;
}
```

Once the key-value store progresses to the version the client requested, it can send the response to the client.

class ReplicatedKVStore...

```
private Response applyWalEntry(WALEntry walEntry) {
    Command command = deserialize(walEntry);
    if (command instanceof SetValueCommand) {
        return applySetValueCommandsAndCompleteClientRequests(
                (SetValueCommand) command);
    }
    throw new IllegalArgumentException("Unknown command type " + command);
}

private Response
    applySetValueCommandsAndCompleteClientRequests(SetValueCommand
                                                        setValueCommand) {
    version = version + 1;
    getLogger()
            .info(replicatedLog.getServerId() + " Setting key value "
                    + setValueCommand.getKey()
                    + " =" + setValueCommand.getValue() + " at " + version);
```

```
mvccStore.put(new VersionedKey(setValueCommand.getKey(), version),
        setValueCommand.getValue());

completeWaitingFuturesIfFollower(version, setValueCommand.getValue());

var response = Response.success(RequestId.SetValueResponse, version);
return response;
}

private void completeWaitingFuturesIfFollower(int version, String value) {
    CompletableFuture completableFuture = waitingRequests.remove(version);

    if (completableFuture != null) {
        logger.info("Completing pending requests for version "
                + version + " with " + value);
        completableFuture.complete(Optional.of(value));
    }
}
```

Linearizable Reads

Sometimes read requests need to get the latest available data, and the replication lag cannot be tolerated. In these cases, the read requests need to be redirected to the leader. The leader must take additional precautions to ensure its leadership status before responding to user queries, as explained in the section "Bypassing the Log for Read Requests" of the *Replicated Log* pattern. This is a common design issue tackled by the *Consistent Core*.

Examples

- Neo4j[46] allows causal clusters[47] to be set up. Every write operation returns a bookmark, which can be passed when executing queries against read replicas. The bookmark ensures that the client will always get the values written at the bookmark.

- MongoDB maintains causal consistency[48] in its replica sets. The write operations return an operationTime that is passed in the subsequent read requests to make sure read requests return the writes which happened before the read request.

---

46. https://neo4j.com
47. https://neo4j.com/developer/kb/when-to-use-bookmarks
48. https://docs.mongodb.com/manual/core/causal-consistency-read-write-concerns

- CockroachDB allows clients to read from follower servers.[49] The leader servers publish the latest timestamps at which the writes are completed on the leader, called closed timestamps. A follower allows reading the values if it has values at the closed timestamp.

- Apache Kafka allows consuming the messages from the follower brokers. The followers know about the *High-Water Mark* at the leader. In Kafka's design, instead of waiting for the latest updates, the broker returns an OFFSET_NOT_AVAILABLE error to the consumers and expects consumers to retry.

---

49. https://www.cockroachlabs.com/docs/v20.2/follower-reads.html

Chapter 17

Versioned Value

Store every update to a value with a new version, to allow reading historical values.

Problem

In a distributed system, nodes need to be able to tell which value for a key is the most recent. Sometimes they need to know past values so they can react properly to changes in a value.

Solution

Store a version number with each value. The version number is incremented for every update. This allows every update to be converted to a new write without blocking a read. Clients can read historical values at a specific version number.

Consider a simple example of a replicated key-value store. The leader of the cluster handles all the writes to the key-value store. It saves the write requests in a *Write-Ahead Log*. The write-ahead log is replicated using *Leader and Followers*. The leader applies entries from the write-ahead log at *High-Water Mark* to the key-value store. This is a standard replication method called state machine replication [Schneider1990]. Most data systems backed by the consensus algorithm (such as Raft) are implemented this way. In this case, the key-value store keeps an integer version counter. It increments the version counter every time the key-value write command is applied from the write-ahead log. It then constructs the new key with the incremented version counter. This way, no existing value is updated, but every write request keeps on appending new values to the backing store.

```
class ReplicatedKVStore...

  int version = 0;
  MVCCStore mvccStore = new MVCCStore();

  @Override
  public CompletableFuture<Response> put(String key, String value) {
      return replicatedLog.propose(new SetValueCommand(key, value));
  }
```

Ordering of Versioned Keys

Embedded data stores, such as RocksDB or Bolt, are commonly used as storage layers of databases. In these data stores, all data is logically arranged in sorted order of keys, similar to the implementation shown here. Since these storages use byte-array-based keys and values, it's important to have the order maintained when the keys are serialized to byte arrays.

Navigating quickly to the best matching versions is an important implementation concern, therefore the versioned keys are arranged in such a way as to form a natural ordering by using version number as a suffix to the key. This maintains an order that fits well with the underlying data structure. For example, if there are two versions of a key, key1 and key2, key1 will be ordered before key2.

To store versioned key values, a data structure that allows quick navigation to the nearest matching version is used, such as a skip list. In Java, a MVCC (multiversion concurrency control) storage can be built as following:

```
class MVCCStore...

  public class MVCCStore {
      NavigableMap<VersionedKey, String> kv = new ConcurrentSkipListMap<>();

      public void put(VersionedKey key, String value) {
          kv.put(key, value);
      }
```

To work with the navigable map, the versioned key is implemented as follows. It includes a comparator to allow natural ordering of keys.

```
class VersionedKey...

  public class VersionedKey implements Comparable<VersionedKey> {
      private String key;
      private long version;

      public VersionedKey(String key, long version) {
          this.key = key;
          this.version = version;
```

```
        }

        public String getKey() {
            return key;
        }

        public long getVersion() {
            return version;
        }

        @Override
        public int compareTo(VersionedKey other) {
            int keyCompare = this.key.compareTo(other.key);
            if (keyCompare != 0) {
                return keyCompare;
            }
            return Long.compare(this.version, other.version);
        }
    }
}
```

This implementation allows getting values for a specific version using the navigable map API.

class MVCCStore...

```
public Optional<String> get(final String key, final int readAt) {
    var entry = kv.floorEntry(new VersionedKey(key, readAt));
    return Optional
            .ofNullable(entry)
            .filter(e -> e.getKey().getKey().equals(key))
            .map(e -> e.getValue());
}
```

Consider an example where there are four versions of a key stored at version numbers 1, 2, 3, and 5 (Figure 17.1). Depending on the version used by clients to read values, the nearest matching version of the key is returned.

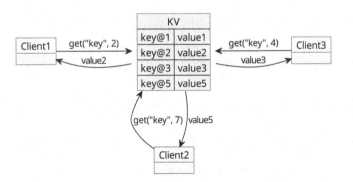

Figure 17.1 *Read request returns the nearest matching version.*

The version at which the specific key value is stored is returned to the client. The client can then use this version to read the values. The overall process is shown in Figures 17.2 and 17.3.

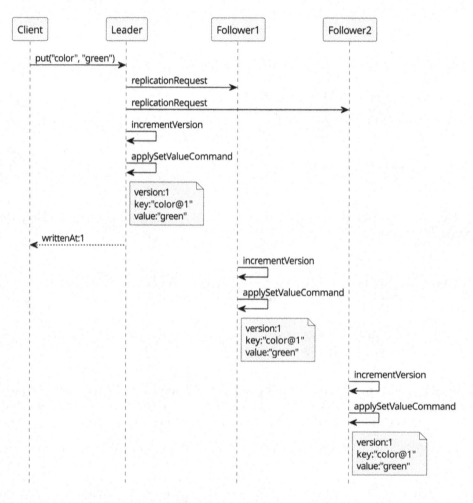

Figure 17.2 *Handling of a* put *request*

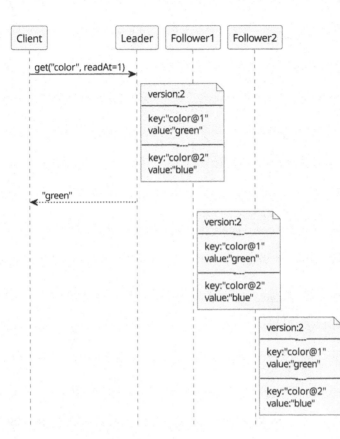

Figure 17.3 *Reading at a specific version*

Reading Multiple Versions

Sometimes clients need to get all the versions from a given version number. For example, in *State Watch*, the client needs to get all the events from a specific version.

The cluster node can use additional index structures to store all the versions for a key.

```
class IndexedMVCCStore...

  public class IndexedMVCCStore {
      NavigableMap<String, List<Integer>> keyVersionIndex = new TreeMap<>();
      NavigableMap<VersionedKey, String> kv = new TreeMap<>();

      ReadWriteLock rwLock = new ReentrantReadWriteLock();

      int version = 0;
```

```java
public int put(String key, String value) {
    rwLock.writeLock().lock();
    try {
        version = version + 1;
        kv.put(new VersionedKey(key, version), value);

        updateVersionIndex(key, version);

        return version;
    } finally {
        rwLock.writeLock().unlock();
    }
}

private void updateVersionIndex(String key, int newVersion) {
    List<Integer> versions = getVersions(key);
    versions.add(newVersion);
    keyVersionIndex.put(key, versions);
}

private List<Integer> getVersions(String key) {
    List<Integer> versions = keyVersionIndex.get(key);
    if (versions == null) {
        versions = new ArrayList<>();
        keyVersionIndex.put(key, versions);
    }
    return versions;
}
```

Then, a client API can be provided to read values from a specific version or from a version range.

class IndexedMVCCStore...

```java
public List<String> getRange(String key, int fromVersion, int toVersion) {
    rwLock.readLock().lock();

    try {
        int maxVersionForKey = getMaxVersionForKey(key);
        int maxVersionToRead = Math.min(maxVersionForKey, toVersion);
        var versionMap = kv.subMap(
                new VersionedKey(key, fromVersion),
                new VersionedKey(key, maxVersionToRead)
        );
        return new ArrayList<>(versionMap.values());
    } finally {
        rwLock.readLock().unlock();
    }
}

private int getMaxVersionForKey(String key) {
    List<Integer> versions = keyVersionIndex.get(key);
```

```
    int maxVersionForKey = versions.stream()
                        .max(Integer::compareTo).orElse(0);
    return maxVersionForKey;
}
```

Care must be taken to use appropriate locking while updating and reading from the index.

There is an alternate implementation that saves a list of all the versioned values with the key. It's used in *Gossip Dissemination* as discussed in the section "Avoiding Unnecessary State Exchange" of that pattern.

MVCC and Transaction Isolation

Databases use versioned values to implement MVCC and transaction isolation.

Concurrency control is about preventing concurrent threads from corrupting data. When locks are used to synchronize access, all the other requests are blocked until a request holding the lock is complete and the lock released. With versioned values, every write request adds a new record. This allows usage of nonblocking data structures to store the values.

Transaction isolation levels, such as snapshot isolation, can be naturally implemented as well, as discussed in the section "Snapshot Isolation" of the *Two-Phase Commit* pattern. When a client starts reading at a particular version (Figure 17.4), it's guaranteed to get the same value every time it reads from the database, even if there are concurrent write transactions that commit a different value in between the read requests.

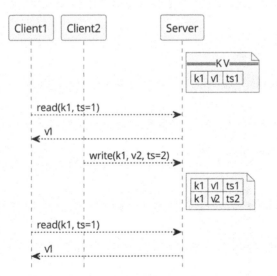

Figure 17.4 *Reading a snapshot*

Using RocksDB-Like Storage Engines

It is very common to use RocksDB or similar embedded storage engines as a storage backend for data stores. For example, etcd uses Bolt,[50] CockroachDB earlier used RocksDB and now uses a Go clone of RocksDB called Pebble.

These storage engines are suitable for storing versioned values. They internally use skip lists the same way described in the above section and rely on the ordering of keys. There is a way to provide custom comparator for ordering keys.

class VersionedKeyComparator...

```
public class VersionedKeyComparator extends Comparator {
    public VersionedKeyComparator() {
        super(new ComparatorOptions());
    }

    @Override
    public String name() {
        return "VersionedKeyComparator";
    }

    @Override
    public int compare(Slice s1, Slice s2) {
        var key1 = VersionedKey.deserialize(ByteBuffer.wrap(s1.data()));
        var key2 = VersionedKey.deserialize(ByteBuffer.wrap(s2.data()));
        return key1.compareTo(key2);
    }
}
```

An implementation using RocksDB can be done as follows:

class RocksDBStore...

```
private final RocksDB db;

public RocksDBStore(File cacheDir) {
    Options options = new Options();
    options.setKeepLogFileNum(30);
    options.setCreateIfMissing(true);
    options.setLogFileTimeToRoll(TimeUnit.DAYS.toSeconds(1));
    options.setComparator(new VersionedKeyComparator());

    try {
        db = RocksDB.open(options, cacheDir.getPath());
    } catch (RocksDBException e) {
        throw new RuntimeException(e);
    }
}
```

---

50. https://github.com/etcd-io/bbolt

```
public void put(String key, int version, String value) throws RocksDBException {
    VersionedKey versionKey = new VersionedKey(key, version);
    db.put(versionKey.serialize(), value.getBytes());
}

public String get(String key, int readAtVersion) {
    RocksIterator rocksIterator = db.newIterator();
    rocksIterator.seekForPrev(new VersionedKey(key, readAtVersion).serialize());

    byte[] valueBytes = rocksIterator.value();
    return new String(valueBytes);
}
```

Examples

- etcd3[51] uses MVCC backend with a single integer representing a version.

- MongoDB and CockroachDB use MVCC backend with a hybrid logical clock.

---

51. https://coreos.com/blog/etcd3-a-new-etcd.html

Chapter 18

Version Vector

Maintain a list of counters, one per cluster node, to detect concurrent updates.

Problem

If multiple servers allow the same key to be updated, it's important to detect when the values are concurrently updated across a set of replicas.

Solution

Each key value is associated with a version vector that maintains a number for each cluster node.

In essence, a version vector is a set of counters, one for each node. A version vector for three nodes (blue, green, black) would look something like [blue: 43, green: 54, black: 12]. Each time a node has an internal update, it updates its own counter, so an update in the green node would change the vector to [blue: 43, green: 55, black: 12]. Whenever two nodes communicate, they synchronize their vector stamps, allowing them to detect any simultaneous updates.

The Difference with Vector Clock

Vector Clock implementation is similar. But vector clocks are used to track every event occurring on the server. In contrast, version vectors are used to detect concurrent updates to the same key across a set of replicas. So an instance of a version vector is stored per key and not per server. Databases like Riak[52] use the term version vector instead of vector clock for their implementation.[53]

A typical version vector implementation is as follows:

class VersionVector...

```
private final TreeMap<String, Long> versions;

public VersionVector() {
    this(new TreeMap<>());
}

public VersionVector(TreeMap<String, Long> versions) {
    this.versions = versions;
}

public VersionVector increment(String nodeId) {
    TreeMap<String, Long> versions = new TreeMap<>();
    versions.putAll(this.versions);
    Long version = versions.get(nodeId);

    if(version == null) {
        version = 1L;
    } else {
        version = version + 1L;
    }
    versions.put(nodeId, version);
    return new VersionVector(versions);
}
```

Each value stored on the server is associated with a version vector:

class VersionedValue...

```
String value;
VersionVector versionVector;

public VersionedValue(String value, VersionVector versionVector) {
    this.value = value;
```

---

52. https://riak.com
53. https://riak.com/posts/technical/vector-clocks-revisited/index.html?p=9545.html

```
            this.versionVector = versionVector;
    }

    @Override
    public boolean equals(Object o) {
        if (this == o) return true;
        if (o == null || getClass() != o.getClass()) return false;
        VersionedValue that = (VersionedValue) o;
        return Objects.equal(value, that.value)
                && Objects.equal(versionVector, that.versionVector);
    }

    @Override
    public int hashCode() {
        return Objects.hashCode(value, versionVector);
    }
}
```

Comparing Version Vectors

Version vectors are compared by comparing version number for each node. A version vector A is considered higher than the version vector B if both have version number for the same cluster nodes and each version number is higher in A than the one in B. If neither vector has all of the version numbers higher, or if they have version numbers for different cluster nodes, they are considered concurrent.

Here are some example comparisons:

{blue:2, green:1}	is greater than	{blue:1, green:1}
{blue:2, green:1}	is concurrent with	{blue:1, green:2}
{blue:1, green:1, red: 1}	is greater than	{blue:1, green:1}
{blue:1, green:1, red: 1}	is concurrent with	{blue:1, green:1, pink: 1}

The comparison in database like Voldemort[54] is implemented as follows:

```
public enum Ordering {
    Before,
    After,
    Concurrent
}
```

---

54. https://www.project-voldemort.com/voldemort

```
class VersionVector...

    public static Ordering compare(VersionVector v1, VersionVector v2) {
        validateNotNull(v1, v2);

        SortedSet<String> v1Nodes = v1.getVersions().navigableKeySet();
        SortedSet<String> v2Nodes = v2.getVersions().navigableKeySet();
        SortedSet<String> commonNodes = getCommonNodes(v1Nodes, v2Nodes);

        // Determine if v1 or v2 has more nodes than common nodes
        boolean v1Bigger = v1Nodes.size() > commonNodes.size();
        boolean v2Bigger = v2Nodes.size() > commonNodes.size();

        // Compare versions for common nodes
        for (String nodeId : commonNodes) {
            if (v1Bigger && v2Bigger) {
                break; // No need to compare further
            }
            long v1Version = v1.getVersions().get(nodeId);
            long v2Version = v2.getVersions().get(nodeId);
            if (v1Version > v2Version) {
                v1Bigger = true;
            } else if (v1Version < v2Version) {
                v2Bigger = true;
            }
        }

        return determineOrdering(v1Bigger, v2Bigger);
    }

    private static Ordering determineOrdering(boolean v1Bigger,
                                              boolean v2Bigger) {
        if (!v1Bigger && !v2Bigger) {
            return Ordering.Before;
        } else if (v1Bigger && !v2Bigger) {
            return Ordering.After;
        } else if (!v1Bigger && v2Bigger) {
            return Ordering.Before;
        } else {
            return Ordering.Concurrent;
        }
    }

    private static void validateNotNull(VersionVector v1, VersionVector v2) {
        if (v1 == null || v2 == null) {
            throw new IllegalArgumentException(
                    "Can't compare null vector clocks!");
        }
    }

    private static SortedSet<String> getCommonNodes(SortedSet<String> v1Nodes,
                                                    SortedSet<String> v2Nodes) {
```

```
    // get clocks(nodeIds) that both v1 and v2 has
    SortedSet<String> commonNodes = Sets.newTreeSet(v1Nodes);
    commonNodes.retainAll(v2Nodes);
    return commonNodes;
}
```

Using Version Vector in a Key-Value Store

The version vector can be used in a key-value storage as follows. A list of versioned values is needed, as there can be multiple values which are concurrent.

class VersionVectorKVStore...

```
public class VersionVectorKVStore {
    Map<String, List<VersionedValue>> kv = new HashMap<>();
```

When a client wants to store a value, it first reads the latest known version for the given key. It then picks up the cluster node to store the value, based on the key. While storing the value, the client passes back the known version. The request flow is shown in Figure 18.1. There are two servers named blue and green. For the key "name", blue is the primary server.

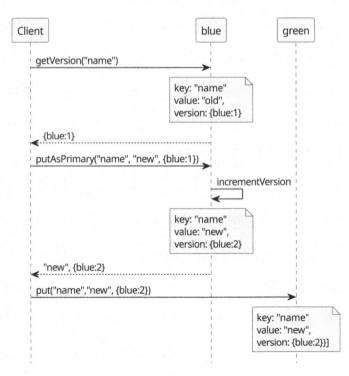

Figure 18.1 *Version counter for the primary node is incremented when value is stored.*

In the leaderless replication scheme, the client or a coordinator node picks up the node to write data based on the key. The version vector is updated based on the primary cluster node that the key maps to. A value with the same version vector is copied on the other cluster nodes for replication. If the cluster node mapping to the key is not available, the next node is chosen. The version vector is only incremented for the first cluster node the value is saved to. All the other nodes save a copy of the data. The code for incrementing version vector in databases like Voldemort looks like this:

```
class ClusterClient...

    public void put(String key, String value, VersionVector existingVersion) {
        List<Integer> allReplicas = findReplicas(key);
        int nodeIndex = 0;
        List<Exception> failures = new ArrayList<>();
        VersionedValue valueWrittenToPrimary = null;

        for (; nodeIndex < allReplicas.size(); nodeIndex++) {
            try {
                ClusterNode node = clusterNodes.get(nodeIndex);
                //the node which is the primary holder of the key value is
                // responsible for incrementing version number.
                valueWrittenToPrimary = node.putAsPrimary(key,
                        value, existingVersion);
                break;

            } catch (Exception e) {
                //if there is exception writing the value to the node,
                // try other replica.
                failures.add(e);
            }
        }

        if (valueWrittenToPrimary == null) {
            throw new NotEnoughNodesAvailable("No node succeeded " +
                    "in writing the value.", failures);
        }

        //Succeeded in writing the first node, copy the same to other nodes.
        nodeIndex++;
        for (; nodeIndex < allReplicas.size(); nodeIndex++) {
            ClusterNode node = clusterNodes.get(nodeIndex);
            node.put(key, valueWrittenToPrimary);
        }
    }
```

The node acting as a primary is the one which increments the version number.

```
public VersionedValue putAsPrimary(String key, String value, VersionVector existingVersion) {
    VersionVector newVersion = existingVersion.increment(nodeId);
    VersionedValue versionedValue = new VersionedValue(value, newVersion);
    put(key, versionedValue);
    return versionedValue;
}

public void put(String key, VersionedValue value) {
    versionVectorKvStore.put(key, value);
}
```

As can be seen in the above code, it is possible for different clients to update the same key on different nodes, for instance when a client cannot reach a specific node. This creates a situation where different nodes have different values which are considered concurrent according to their version vector.

As shown in Figure 18.2, both Client1 and Client2 are trying to write to the key "name". If Client1 cannot write to server green, the green server will be missing the value written by Client1. When Client2 tries to write, but fails to connect to server blue, it will write on server green. The version vector for the key "name" will reflect that the servers blue and green have concurrent writes.

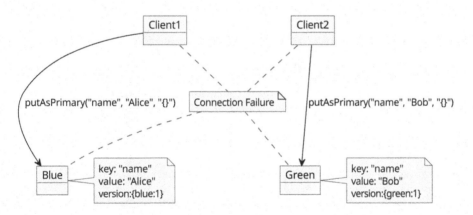

Figure 18.2 *Concurrent updates on different replicas*

Therefore, when the versions are considered concurrent, the version-vector-based storage keeps multiple versions for any key.

```
class VersionVectorKVStore...

    public void put(String key, VersionedValue newValue) {
        List<VersionedValue> existingValues = kv.get(key);
        if (existingValues == null) {
            existingValues = new ArrayList<>();
        }

        rejectIfOldWrite(key, newValue, existingValues);
        List<VersionedValue> newValues = merge(newValue, existingValues);
        kv.put(key, newValues);
    }

    //If the newValue is older than the existing one, reject it.
    private void rejectIfOldWrite(String key,
                                  VersionedValue newValue,
                                  List<VersionedValue> existingValues) {

        for (VersionedValue existingValue : existingValues) {
            if (existingValue.descendsVersion(newValue)) {
                throw new ObsoleteVersionException(
                        "Obsolete version for key '" + key
                        + "': " + newValue.versionVector);
            }
        }
    }

    //Merge new value with existing values. Remove values with
    // lower version than the newValue. If the old value is neither
    // before or after (concurrent) with the newValue. It will be preserved
    private List<VersionedValue> merge(VersionedValue newValue,
                                       List<VersionedValue> existingValues) {

        var retainedValues = removeOlderVersions(newValue, existingValues);
        retainedValues.add(newValue);
        return retainedValues;
    }

    private List<VersionedValue> removeOlderVersions(VersionedValue newValue,
                                       List<VersionedValue> existingValues) {

        //keep versions which are not directly dominated by newValue.
        return existingValues
                .stream()
                .filter(v -> !newValue.descendsVersion(v))
                .collect(Collectors.toList());
    }
```

If concurrent values are detected while reading from multiple nodes, an error is thrown, allowing the client to do possible conflict resolution.

Resolving Conflicts

If multiple versions are returned from different replicas, version vector comparison allows the latest value to be detected.

```
class ClusterClient...

    public List<VersionedValue> get(String key) {
        List<Integer> allReplicas = findReplicas(key);

        List<VersionedValue> allValues = new ArrayList<>();
        for (Integer index : allReplicas) {
            ClusterNode clusterNode = clusterNodes.get(index);
            List<VersionedValue> nodeVersions = clusterNode.get(key);

            allValues.addAll(nodeVersions);
        }
        return latestValuesAcrossReplicas(allValues);
    }

    private List<VersionedValue>
            latestValuesAcrossReplicas(List<VersionedValue> allValues) {

        var uniqueValues = removeDuplicates(allValues);
        return retainOnlyLatestValues(uniqueValues);
    }

    private List<VersionedValue>
            retainOnlyLatestValues(List<VersionedValue> versionedValues) {

        for (int i = 0; i < versionedValues.size(); i++) {
            var v1 = versionedValues.get(i);
            versionedValues.removeAll(getPredecessors(v1, versionedValues));
        }
        return versionedValues;
    }

    private List<VersionedValue> getPredecessors(VersionedValue v1,
                              List<VersionedValue> versionedValues) {

        var predecessors = new ArrayList<VersionedValue>();
        for (VersionedValue v2 : versionedValues) {
            if (!v1.sameVersion(v2) && v1.descendsVersion(v2)) {
                predecessors.add(v2);
            }
        }
        return predecessors;
    }
```

```
    private List<VersionedValue>
                removeDuplicates(List<VersionedValue> allValues) {

    return allValues
            .stream()
            .distinct()
            .collect(Collectors.toList());
    }
```

Just doing conflict resolution based on version vectors is not enough when there are concurrent updates. So it's important to allow clients to provide application-specific conflict resolvers. A conflict resolver can be provided by the client while reading a value.

```
public interface ConflictResolver {
    VersionedValue resolve(List<VersionedValue> values);
}
```

class ClusterClient...

```
    public VersionedValue getResolvedValue(String key, ConflictResolver resolver) {
        List<VersionedValue> versionedValues = get(key);
        return resolver.resolve(versionedValues);
    }
```

For example, Riak allows applications to provide conflict resolvers.[55]

Last Write Wins (LWW) Conflict Resolution

Cassandra and LWW

Apache Cassandra, while architecturally the same as Riak or Voldemort, does not use version vectors at all, and supports only the last-write-wins conflict resolution strategy. Cassandra, being a column-family database rather than a simple key-value store, stores a timestamp with each column, as opposed to a value as a whole. While this takes the burden of doing conflict resolution away from the users, you need to make sure that the NTP service is configured and working correctly across Cassandra nodes. In the worst case scenario, some latest values can get overwritten by older values because of clock drift.

---

55. https://docs.riak.com/riak/kv/latest/developing/usage/conflict-resolution/java/index.html

While version vectors allow detection of concurrent writes across a set of servers, by themselves they do not provide any help to clients in figuring out which value to choose in case of conflicts. The burden is on the client to do the resolution. Sometimes, clients want the key-value store to do conflict resolution based on timestamps. While there are known issues with timestamps across servers, the simplicity of this approach makes it a good choice for clients, even with the risk of losing some updates because of clock drift. This relies on time services like NTP to be configured and working across the cluster. Databases like Riak and Voldemort allow users to select the last-write-wins conflict resolution strategy.

To support LWW conflict resolution, a timestamp is stored with each value while its written.

```
class TimestampedVersionedValue...

  class TimestampedVersionedValue {
      String value;
      VersionVector versionVector;
      long timestamp;

      public TimestampedVersionedValue(String value, VersionVector versionVector,
                                    long timestamp) {
          this.value = value;
          this.versionVector = versionVector;
          this.timestamp = timestamp;
      }
```

When reading the value, the client can use the timestamp to pick up the latest value. The version vector is completely ignored in this case.

```
class ClusterClient...

  public Optional<TimestampedVersionedValue>
              getWithLWW(List<TimestampedVersionedValue> values) {

      return values.stream().max(Comparator.comparingLong(v -> v.timestamp));
  }
```

Read Repair

Allowing any cluster node to accept write requests improves availability. However, it's important that eventually all of the replicas have the same data. One of the common methods to repair replicas is applied when the client reads the data.

When conflicts are resolved, it's also possible to detect which nodes have older versions. The nodes with older versions can be sent the latest versions as part of the read request handling from the client. This is called read repair.

Consider a scenario shown in Figure 18.3. Two nodes, blue and green, have values for a key "name". The green node has the latest version with version vector [blue: 1, green: 1]. When the values are read from both replicas, blue and green, they are compared to find out which node is missing the latest version, and a put request with the latest version is sent to that cluster node.

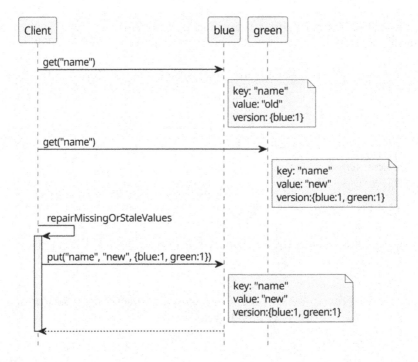

Figure 18.3   *Read repair*

Allowing Concurrent Updates on the Same Cluster Node

There is a possibility of two clients writing concurrently to the same node. In the default implementation shown above, the second write will be rejected. The basic implementation with the version number per cluster node is not enough in this case.

Consider the following scenario. With two clients trying to update the same key, the second client will get an exception, as the version it passes in its put request is stale (Figure 18.4).

A database like Riak gives flexibility to clients who can allow this kind of concurrent writes without getting error responses.

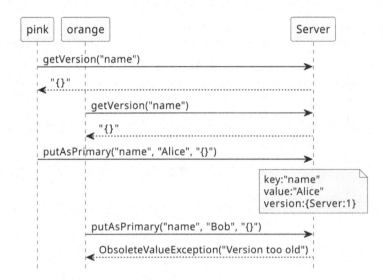

Figure 18.4 *Two clients concurrently updating the same key with server ID*

Using Client IDs Instead of Server IDs

If each cluster client can have a unique ID, client ID can be used. A version number is stored per client ID. Every time a client writes a value, it first reads the existing version, increments the number associated with the client ID, and writes it to the server.

class ClusterClient...

```
private VersionedValue putWithClientId(String clientId,
                                       int nodeIndex,
                                       String key,
                                       String value,
                                       VersionVector version) {
    var node = clusterNodes.get(nodeIndex);
    var newVersion = version.increment(clientId);
    var versionedValue = new VersionedValue(value, newVersion);
    node.put(key, versionedValue);
    return versionedValue;
}
```

Since each client increments its own counter, concurrent writes create sibling values on the servers, but concurrent writes never fail.

The scenario discussed in the previous section, which gives error to the second client, works as shown in Figure 18.5.

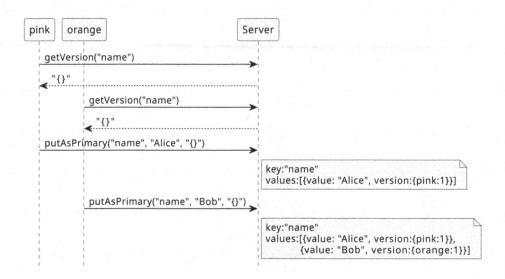

Figure 18.5 *Two clients concurrently updating the same key with client ID*

Dotted Version Vectors

One of the major problems with client-ID-based version vectors is that the size of the version vector directly depends on the number of clients. This causes cluster nodes to accumulate too many concurrent values for a given key over time. The problem is called sibling explosion.[56] To solve this issue and still allow cluster-node-based version vectors, Riak uses a variant of version vector called dotted version vector.[57]

Examples

- Voldemort uses version vector as described here. It allows timestamp-based last-write-wins conflict resolution.

- Riak started by using client-ID-based version vectors, but moved to cluster-node-based version vectors and eventually to dotted version vectors. Riak also supports last-write-wins conflict resolution based on the system timestamp.

- Apache Cassandra does not use version vectors. It supports only last-write-wins conflict resolution based on system timestamp.

---

56. https://docs.riak.com/riak/kv/2.2.3/learn/concepts/causal-context/index.html#sibling-explosion
57. https://riak.com/posts/technical/vector-clocks-revisited-part-2-dotted-version-vectors/index.html

Part III

Patterns of Data Partitioning

Partitioning data across servers is crucial for scaling distributed systems. However, it comes with challenges. We need to ensure that clients can quickly find the right server for their data and that adding or removing servers doesn't require moving a lot of data. Also, when data needs to be added to multiple partitions hosted on different servers, we face the question of how to do that atomically.

In the following chapters, we will explore commonly used patterns for partitioning data.

While these patterns primarily focus on partitioning schemes, it's important to remember that each partition is typically replicated using *Patterns of Data Replication* to achieve fault tolerance.

Chapter 19

Fixed Partitions

Keep the number of partitions fixed so that the mapping of data to partition stays the same when the size of a cluster changes.

Problem

To split data across a set of cluster nodes, each data item needs to be mapped to them. There are two requirements for mapping data to the cluster nodes.

- The distribution should be uniform.

- It should be possible to know which cluster node stores a particular data item without making a request to all the nodes.

Consider a key-value store, which is a good proxy for many storage systems. Both requirements can be fulfilled by taking a hash of the key and using the modulo operation to map it to a cluster node. So if we have a three-node cluster, we can map keys Alice, Bob, Mary, and Philip, as Table 19.1 demonstrates.

Table 19.1 *Key Mapping in a Three-Node Cluster*

Keys	Hash	Node Index = Hash % 3
Alice	133299819613694460644197938031451912208	0
Bob	63479738429015246738359000453022047291	1
Mary	37724856304035789372490171084843241126	2
Philip	83980963731216160506671196398339418866	2

However, this method creates a problem when the cluster size changes. If two more nodes are added to the cluster, we will have five nodes. The mapping will then look as shown in Table 19.2.

Table 19.2 *Key Mapping in a Five-Node Cluster*

Keys	Hash	Node Index = Hash % 5
Alice	133299819613694446064419793803145191 2208	3
Bob	6347973842901524673835900045302204 7291	1
Mary	37724856304035789372490171084843241126	1
Philip	83980963731216160506671196398339418866	1

This way, mapping for almost all the keys changes. Even after adding only a few new cluster nodes, all the data needs to be moved. When the data size is large, this is undesirable.

Solution

A message broker such as Apache Kafka needs an ordering guarantee for the data per partition. With fixed partitions, the data per partition doesn't change even when partitions are moved around the cluster nodes after new nodes are added. This maintains the ordering of data per partition.

One of the most commonly used solution is to map data to logical partitions. Logical partitions are mapped to the cluster nodes. Even if cluster nodes are added or removed, the mapping of data to partitions doesn't change. The cluster is launched with a preconfigured number of partitions—for the sake of this example, 1024. This number does not change when new nodes are added to the cluster. So the way data is mapped to partitions using a hash of the key remains the same.

It's important that partitions are evenly distributed across cluster nodes. When partitions are moved to new nodes, it should be relatively quick with only a smaller portion of the data being moved.

Once configured, the partition number won't change. This means it should have enough room for future growth of data volumes—it should be significantly higher than the number of cluster nodes. For example, Akka suggests you should have the number of shards ten times the number of nodes. Partitioning in Apache Ignite[58] has its default value at 1024. Hazelcast has a default value of 271 for cluster size smaller than 100.

Data storage or retrieval is then a two-step process.

1. First, you find the partition for the given data item.

2. Then you find the cluster node where the partition is stored.

To balance data across the cluster nodes when new ones are added, some of the partitions can be moved to the new nodes.

Choosing the Hash Function

It's critical to choose the hashing method that gives the same hash values independent of the platform and runtime. For example, programming languages like Java provide a hash for every object. However, that hash value is dependent on the JVM runtime, so two different JVMs could give a different hash for the same key. To tackle this, use hashing algorithms such as MD5 hash or Murmur hash.

```
class HashingUtil...

    public static BigInteger hash(String key)
    {
        try {
            var messageDigest = MessageDigest.getInstance("MD5");
            return new BigInteger(messageDigest.digest(key.getBytes()));
        } catch (NoSuchAlgorithmException e) {
            throw new RuntimeException(e);
        }
    }
```

The keys are mapped to partitions, not to nodes. If there are nine partitions, the result might look like Table 19.3.

Table 19.3 *Key Mapping with Fixed Logical Partitions*

Keys	Hash	Partition = Hash % 9	Node
Alice	133299819613694460644197938031451912208	0	0
Bob	63479738429015246738359000453022047291	1	1
Mary	37724856304035789372490171084843241126	5	1
Philip	83980963731216160506671196398339418866	2	2

---

58. https://ignite.apache.org/docs/latest/data-modeling/data-partitioning

When new nodes are added to the cluster, the mapping of a key to partition does not change.

Mapping Partitions to Cluster Nodes

Partitions need to be mapped to cluster nodes. This mapping also needs to be stored and made accessible to the clients. It's common to use a dedicated *Consistent Core* that handles both. The dedicated Consistent Core acts as a coordinator that keeps track of all nodes in the cluster and maps partitions to nodes. It also stores the mapping in a fault-tolerant way by using a *Replicated Log*. The master cluster in YugabyteDB and the controller implementation in Kafka [McCabe2021] are both good examples of this.

Peer-to-peer systems such as Akka or Hazelcast also need a particular cluster node to act as a coordinator. They use *Emergent Leader* as the coordinator.

Systems like Kubernetes use a generic Consistent Core, such as etcd. They need to elect one of the cluster nodes to play the role of coordinator as discussed in the section "Leader Election Using a Consistent Core" of the *Leader and Followers* pattern.

Tracking Cluster Membership

Each cluster node will register itself with the consistent core (Figure 19.1). It also periodically sends a *HeartBeat* to allow the consistent core detect node failures.

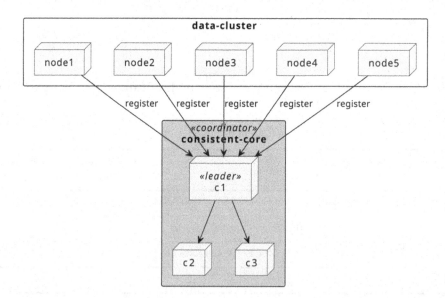

Figure 19.1 *Consistent Core tracking cluster membership*

```
class KVStore...

  public void start() {
      socketListener.start();
      requestHandler.start();
      network.sendAndReceive(coordLeader,
              new RegisterClusterNodeRequest(generateMessageId(),
                      listenAddress));
      scheduler.scheduleAtFixedRate(() -> {
          network
                  .send(coordLeader,
                      new HeartbeatMessage(generateMessageId(),
                              listenAddress));
      }, 200, 200, TimeUnit.MILLISECONDS);
  }
```

The coordinator handles the registration and then stores member information.

```
class ClusterCoordinator...

  ReplicatedLog replicatedLog;
  Membership membership = new Membership();
  TimeoutBasedFailureDetector failureDetector
          = new TimeoutBasedFailureDetector(Duration.ofMillis(TIMEOUT_MILLIS));

  private void handleRegisterClusterNodeRequest(Message message) {
      logger.info("Registering node " + message.from);
      var completableFuture = registerClusterNode(message.from);
      completableFuture.whenComplete((response, error) -> {
          logger.info("Sending register response to node " + message.from);
          network.send(message.from,
                  new RegisterClusterNodeResponse(message.messageId,
                          listenAddress));
      });
  }

  public CompletableFuture registerClusterNode(InetAddressAndPort address) {
      return replicatedLog.propose(new RegisterClusterNodeCommand(address));
  }
```

When a registration is committed in the *Replicated Log,* the membership will be updated.

```
class ClusterCoordinator...

  private void applyRegisterClusterNodeEntry(
          RegisterClusterNodeCommand command) {

      updateMembership(command.memberAddress);
  }
```

class ClusterCoordinator...

```
private void updateMembership(InetAddressAndPort address) {
    membership = membership.addNewMember(address);
    failureDetector.heartBeatReceived(address);
}
```

The coordinator maintains a list of all nodes that are part of the cluster:

class Membership...

```
List<Member> liveMembers = new ArrayList<>();
List<Member> failedMembers = new ArrayList<>();

public boolean isFailed(InetAddressAndPort address) {
    return failedMembers.stream().anyMatch(m -> m.address.equals(address));
}
```

class Member...

```
public class Member implements Comparable<Member> {
    InetAddressAndPort address;
    MemberStatus status;
```

The coordinator will detect cluster node failures using a mechanism similar to *Lease*. If a cluster node stops sending the heartbeat, the node will be marked as failed.

class ClusterCoordinator...

```
@Override
public void onBecomingLeader() {
    scheduledTask = executor.scheduleWithFixedDelay(this::checkMembership,
            1000,
            1000,
            TimeUnit.MILLISECONDS);
    failureDetector.start();
}

private void checkMembership() {
    var failedMembers = getFailedMembers();
    if (!failedMembers.isEmpty()) {
        replicatedLog.propose(new MemberFailedCommand(failedMembers));
    }
}

private List<Member> getFailedMembers() {
    var liveMembers = membership.getLiveMembers();
    return liveMembers.stream()
            .filter(m ->
                    failureDetector.isMonitoring(m.getAddress())
                        && !failureDetector.isAlive(m.getAddress()))
            .collect(Collectors.toList());
}
```

The coordinator updates membership once the `MemberFailedCommand` is committed.

```
class ClusterCoordinator...

  private void applyMemberFailedCommand(MemberFailedCommand command) {
      membership = membership.failed(command.getFailedMember());
  }
```

```
class Membership...

  public Membership failed(List<Member> failedMembers) {
      List<Member> liveMembers = new ArrayList<>(this.liveMembers);
      liveMembers.removeAll(failedMembers);

      for (Member m : failedMembers) {
          m.markDown();
      }
      return new Membership(version + 1, liveMembers, failedMembers);
  }
```

Assigning Partitions to Cluster Nodes

For data stores like Apache Kafka or Hazelcast that have logical storage structures such as topics, caches, or tables, the partitions are created at the same time as these logical structures. The expectation is that the storage structures will be created after all nodes in the cluster are launched and have registered with the consistent core.

The coordinator assigns partitions to cluster nodes that are known at that point in time. If it's triggered every time a new cluster node is added, it might map partitions too early before the cluster reaches a stable state. This is why the coordinator should be configured to wait until the cluster reaches a minimum size.

The first time the partitions are assigned, it can be done simply in a round robin fashion. Apache Ignite uses a more sophisticated mapping using rendezvous hashing.[59]

```
class ClusterCoordinator...

  CompletableFuture assignPartitionsToClusterNodes() {
      if (!minimumClusterSizeReached()) {
          var e = new NotEnoughClusterNodesException(MINIMUM_CLUSTER_SIZE);
          return CompletableFuture.failedFuture(e);
      }
      return initializePartitionAssignment();
  }
```

---

59. https://www.gridgain.com/resources/blog/data-distribution-in-apache-ignite

```
private boolean minimumClusterSizeReached() {
    return membership.getLiveMembers().size() >= MINIMUM_CLUSTER_SIZE;
}

private CompletableFuture initializePartitionAssignment() {
    partitionAssignmentStatus = PartitionAssignmentStatus.IN_PROGRESS;
    var partitionTable = arrangePartitions();
    return replicatedLog.propose(new PartitiontableCommand(partitionTable));
}

public PartitionTable arrangePartitions() {
    var partitionTable = new PartitionTable();
    var liveMembers = membership.getLiveMembers();

    for (int partitionId = 1; partitionId <= noOfPartitions;
         partitionId++) {

        var index = partitionId % liveMembers.size();
        var member = liveMembers.get(index);
        partitionTable.addPartition(partitionId,
                new PartitionInfo(partitionId,
                                  member.getAddress(),
                                  PartitionStatus.ASSIGNED));
    }
    return partitionTable;
}
```

The *Replicated Log* makes the partition table persistent.

```
class ClusterCoordinator...

PartitionTable partitionTable;
PartitionAssignmentStatus partitionAssignmentStatus
        = PartitionAssignmentStatus.UNASSIGNED;

private void applyPartitionTableCommand(PartitiontableCommand command) {
    this.partitionTable = command.partitionTable;
    partitionAssignmentStatus = PartitionAssignmentStatus.ASSIGNED;
    if (isLeader()) {
        sendMessagesToMembers(partitionTable);
    }
}
```

Once the partition assignment is persisted, the coordinator sends messages to all cluster nodes to tell each node which partitions it now owns.

```
class ClusterCoordinator...

List<Integer> pendingPartitionAssignments = new ArrayList<>();

private void sendMessagesToMembers(PartitionTable partitionTable) {
    var partitionsTobeHosted = partitionTable.getPartitionsTobeHosted();
    partitionsTobeHosted.forEach((partitionId, partitionInfo) -> {
```

```
            pendingPartitionAssignments.add(partitionId);
            var message = new HostPartitionMessage(requestNumber++,
                    this.listenAddress, partitionId);
            scheduler.execute(new RetryableTask(partitionInfo.hostedOn,
                    network, this, partitionId, message));
        });
    }
```

The controller will keep trying to reach nodes continuously until its message is successful.

class RetryableTask...

```
    static class RetryableTask implements Runnable {
        Logger logger = LogManager.getLogger(RetryableTask.class);
        InetAddressAndPort address;
        Network network;
        ClusterCoordinator coordinator;
        Integer partitionId;
        int attempt;
        private Message message;

        public RetryableTask(InetAddressAndPort address,
                             Network network,
                             ClusterCoordinator coordinator,
                             Integer partitionId,
                             Message message) {
            this.address = address;
            this.network = network;
            this.coordinator = coordinator;
            this.partitionId = partitionId;
            this.message = message;
        }

        @Override
        public void run() {
            attempt++;
            try {
                //stop trying if the node has failed.
                if (coordinator.isSuspected(address)) {
                    return;
                }
                network.send(address, message);
            } catch (Exception e) {
                scheduleWithBackOff();
            }
        }

        private void scheduleWithBackOff() {
            scheduler.schedule(this, getBackOffDelay(attempt),
                    TimeUnit.MILLISECONDS);
        }
```

```
        private long getBackOffDelay(int attempt) {
            long baseDelay = (long) Math.pow(2, attempt);
            long jitter = randomJitter();
            return baseDelay + jitter;
        }

        private long randomJitter() {
            int i = new Random(1).nextInt();
            i = i < 0 ? i * -1 : i;
            long jitter = i % 50;
            return jitter;
        }
    }
```

When a cluster node receives the request to create a partition, it creates one with the given partition ID. If we imagine this happening within a simple key-value store, its implementation could look something like this:

class KVStore...

```
    Map<Integer, Partition> allPartitions = new ConcurrentHashMap<>();
    private void handleHostPartitionMessage(Message message) {
        var partitionId = ((HostPartitionMessage) message).getPartitionId();
        addPartitions(partitionId);

        logger.info("Adding partition " + partitionId + " to " + listenAddress);

        network.send(message.from,
                new HostPartitionAcks(message.messageId,
                        this.listenAddress, partitionId));
    }

    public void addPartitions(Integer partitionId) {
        allPartitions.put(partitionId, new Partition(partitionId));
    }
```

class Partition...

```
    SortedMap<String, String> kv = new TreeMap<>();
    private Integer partitionId;
```

Once the coordinator receives the message that the partition has been successfully created, it persists it in the replicated log and updates the partition status to be online:

class ClusterCoordinator...

```
    private void handleHostPartitionAck(Message message) {
        var partitionId = ((HostPartitionAcks) message).getPartitionId();

        pendingPartitionAssignments.remove(Integer.valueOf(partitionId));

        var future =
```

```
            replicatedLog.propose(
                  new UpdatePartitionStatusCommand(partitionId,
                        PartitionStatus.ONLINE));
      future.join();
   }
```

Once the *High-Water Mark* is reached and the record is applied, the partition's status will be updated.

class ClusterCoordinator...

```
   private void updateParitionStatus(UpdatePartitionStatusCommand command) {
      removePendingRequest(command.partitionId);
      partitionTable.updateStatus(command.partitionId, command.status);
   }
```

Client Interface

Again, consider the example of a simple key-value store. If a client needs to store or get a value for a particular key, it can do so by following these steps:

1. The client applies the hash function to the key and finds the relevant partition based on the total number of partitions.

2. The client gets the partition table from the coordinator and finds the cluster node that is hosting the partition. The client also periodically refreshes the partition table.

> Apache Kafka encountered an issue[60] when all the producers and consumers simultaneously fetched partition metadata. This placed a heavy load on Kafka brokers as they retrieved all the metadata from ZooKeeper. As a solution, the decision was made to cache metadata across all the brokers.
> A similar issue[61] was also observed in YugabyteDB.

Clients fetching a partition table from the coordinator can quickly lead to bottlenecks, especially if all requests are being served by a single coordinator leader. That is why it is common practice to keep metadata available on all cluster nodes. The coordinator can either push metadata to cluster nodes, or cluster nodes can pull it from the coordinator. Clients can then connect with any cluster node to refresh the metadata.

This can be implemented inside the client library provided by the key-value store or inside client request handling which happens on the cluster nodes.

---

60. https://issues.apache.org/jira/browse/KAFKA-901
61. https://gist.github.com/jrudolph/be4e04a776414ce07de6019ccb0d3e42

class Client...

```
public void put(String key, String value) throws IOException {
    var partitionId = findPartition(key, noOfPartitions);
    var nodeAddress = getNodeAddressFor(partitionId);
    sendPutMessage(partitionId, nodeAddress, key, value);
}

private InetAddressAndPort getNodeAddressFor(Integer partitionId) {
    var partitionInfo = partitionTable.getPartition(partitionId);
    var nodeAddress = partitionInfo.getAddress();
    return nodeAddress;
}

private void sendPutMessage(Integer partitionId,
                            InetAddressAndPort address,
                            String key, String value) throws IOException {
    var partitionPutMessage = new PartitionPutMessage(partitionId, key, value);
    var socketClient = new SocketClient(address);
    socketClient
            .blockingSend(new RequestOrResponse(partitionPutMessage));
}

public String get(String key) throws IOException {
    var partitionId = findPartition(key, noOfPartitions);
    var nodeAddress = getNodeAddressFor(partitionId);
    return sendGetMessage(partitionId, key, nodeAddress);
}

private String sendGetMessage(Integer partitionId,
                              String key,
                              InetAddressAndPort address) throws IOException {
    var partitionGetMessage = new PartitionGetMessage(partitionId, key);
    var socketClient = new SocketClient(address);
    var response =
            socketClient
                    .blockingSend(new RequestOrResponse(partitionGetMessage));
    var partitionGetResponseMessage =
                    deserialize(response.getMessageBody(),
                    PartitionGetResponseMessage.class);
    return partitionGetResponseMessage.getValue();
}
```

Moving Partitions to Newly Added Members

When new nodes are added to a cluster, some partitions can be moved to other nodes. This can be done automatically once a new cluster node is added. But it can involve a lot of data being moved across the cluster, which is why an administrator will typically trigger the repartitioning. One simple method to do this is to calculate the average number of partitions each node should host and then move this many partitions to the new node. For example, if the number of partitions is 30 and there are three existing nodes in the cluster, each node should host 10 partitions. If a new node is added, the average per node is about 7. The coordinator will therefore try to move 3 partitions from each cluster node to the new node.

class ClusterCoordinator...

```
List<Migration> pendingMigrations = new ArrayList<>();

boolean reassignPartitions() {
    if (partitionAssignmentInProgress()) {
        logger.info("Partition assignment in progress");
        return false;
    }
    var migrations = repartition(this.partitionTable);
    var proposalFuture =
            replicatedLog.propose(new MigratePartitionsCommand(migrations));
    proposalFuture.join();
    return true;
}

public List<Migration> repartition(PartitionTable partitionTable) {
    int averagePartitionsPerNode = getAveragePartitionsPerNode();
    List<Member> liveMembers = membership.getLiveMembers();
    var overloadedNodes = partitionTable
            .getOverloadedNodes(averagePartitionsPerNode, liveMembers);
    var underloadedNodes = partitionTable
            .getUnderloadedNodes(averagePartitionsPerNode, liveMembers);

    return tryMovingPartitionsToUnderLoadedMembers(averagePartitionsPerNode,
            overloadedNodes, underloadedNodes);
}

private List<Migration>
    tryMovingPartitionsToUnderLoadedMembers(int averagePartitionsPerNode,
            Map<InetAddressAndPort, PartitionList> overloadedNodes,
            Map<InetAddressAndPort, PartitionList> underloadedNodes) {

    List<Migration> migrations = new ArrayList<>();
    for (InetAddressAndPort member : overloadedNodes.keySet()) {
        var partitions = overloadedNodes.get(member);
        var toMove = partitions
                .subList(averagePartitionsPerNode, partitions.getSize());
        overloadedNodes.put(member,
                partitions.subList(0, averagePartitionsPerNode));
        var moveQ = new ArrayDeque<Integer>(toMove.partitionList());
        while (!moveQ.isEmpty() && nodeWithLeastPartitions(underloadedNodes,
                averagePartitionsPerNode).isPresent()) {
            assignToNodesWithLeastPartitions(migrations,
                    member, moveQ,
                    underloadedNodes, averagePartitionsPerNode);
        }
    }
```

```
            if (!moveQ.isEmpty()) {
                overloadedNodes.get(member).addAll(moveQ);
            }
        }
        return migrations;
    }

    int getAveragePartitionsPerNode() {
        return noOfPartitions / membership.getLiveMembers().size();
    }
```

The coordinator will persist the computed migrations in the replicated log and then send requests to move partitions across the cluster nodes.

```
    private void applyMigratePartitionCommand(
            MigratePartitionsCommand command) {

        logger.info("Handling partition migrations " + command.migrations);
        for (Migration migration : command.migrations) {
            var message = new RequestPartitionMigrationMessage(requestNumber++,
                    this.listenAddress, migration);
            pendingMigrations.add(migration);
            if (isLeader()) {
                scheduler.execute(new RetryableTask(migration.fromMember,
                        network, this, migration.getPartitionId(), message));
            }
        }
    }
```

When a cluster node receives a request to migrate, it will mark the partition as migrating. This stops any further modifications to the partition. It will then send the entire partition data to the target node.

```
class KVStore...

    private void handleRequestPartitionMigrationMessage(
            RequestPartitionMigrationMessage message) {

        Migration migration = message.getMigration();
        Integer partitionId = migration.getPartitionId();
        InetAddressAndPort toServer = migration.getToMember();
        if (!allPartitions.containsKey(partitionId)) {
            return;// The partition is not available with this node.
        }
        Partition partition = allPartitions.get(partitionId);
        partition.setMigrating();
        network.send(toServer,
                new MovePartitionMessage(requestNumber++, this.listenAddress,
                        toServer, partition));
    }
```

The cluster node that receives the request will add the new partition to itself and return an acknowledgment.

class KVStore...

```
private void handleMovePartition(Message message) {
    var movePartitionMessage = (MovePartitionMessage) message;
    var partition = movePartitionMessage.getPartition();
    allPartitions.put(partition.getId(), partition);
    network.send(message.from,
            new PartitionMovementComplete(message.messageId, listenAddress,
            new Migration(movePartitionMessage.getMigrateFrom(),
                movePartitionMessage.getMigrateTo(),
                partition.getId()))));
}
```

The cluster node that previously owned the partition will then send the "migration complete" message to the cluster coordinator.

class KVStore...

```
private void handlePartitionMovementCompleteMessage(
        PartitionMovementComplete message) {

    allPartitions.remove(message.getMigration().getPartitionId());
    network.send(coordLeader,
            new MigrationCompleteMessage(requestNumber++, listenAddress,
            message.getMigration()));
}
```

The cluster coordinator will then mark the migration as complete. The change will be stored in the replicated log.

class ClusterCoordinator...

```
private void
        handleMigrationCompleteMessage(MigrationCompleteMessage message) {

    var command = new MigrationCompletedCommand(message.getMigration());
    var propose = replicatedLog.propose(command);
    propose.join();
}
```

class ClusterCoordinator...

```
private void applyMigrationCompleted(MigrationCompletedCommand command) {
    pendingMigrations.remove(command.getMigration());
    logger.info("Completed migration " + command.getMigration());
    logger.info("pendingMigrations = " + pendingMigrations);
    partitionTable.migrationCompleted(command.getMigration());
}
```

```
class PartitionTable...

  public void migrationCompleted(Migration migration) {
      this
              .addPartition(migration.partitionId,
                  new PartitionInfo(migration.partitionId,
                      migration.toMember,
                      ClusterCoordinator.PartitionStatus.ONLINE));
  }
```

An Example Scenario

Once again, we have three data servers Athens, Byzantium, and Cyrene. If there are nine partitions, the flow might look as shown in Figure 19.2. Note that, replication messages from leader to followers of the *Consistent Core* are not shown in the diagram.

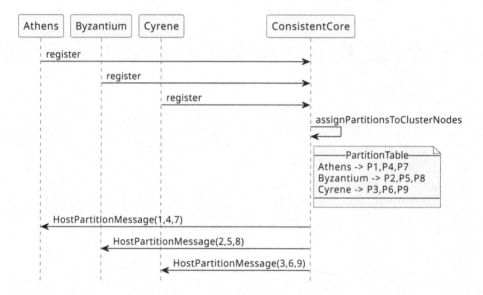

Figure 19.2 *Partition assignment by a Consistent Core*

The client can then use the partition table to map a given key to a particular cluster node (Figure 19.3).

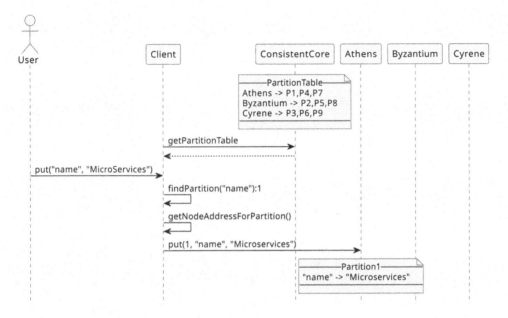

Figure 19.3 *Client writing to a partition*

Now a new node, Ephesus, is added to the cluster. The admin triggers a reassignment and the coordinator verifies which nodes are underloaded by checking the partition table. It figures out that Ephesus is a node which is underloaded, and decides to allocate partition 7 to it, moving it from Athens. The coordinator stores the migrations and then sends the request to Athens to move partition 7 to Ephesus. Once the migration is complete, Athens lets the coordinator know. The coordinator then updates the partition table (Figure 19.4).

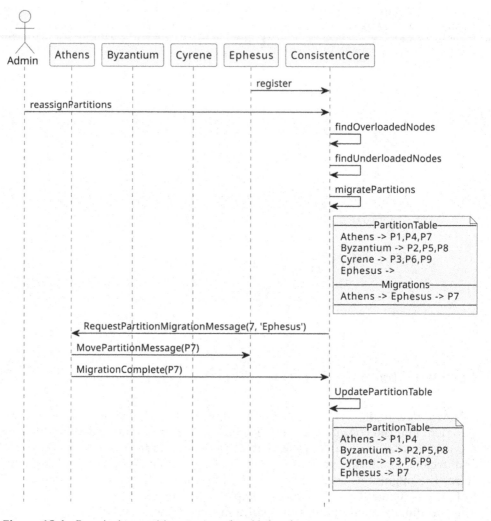

Figure 19.4 *Reassigning partitions to a newly added node*

Alternative Solution: Partitions Proportional to Number of Nodes

An alternative to fixed partitions, popularized by Apache Cassandra, is to have the number of partitions proportional to the number of nodes in the cluster. The number of partitions increases when new nodes are added to the cluster. This technique is also sometimes called consistent hashing. It requires storing a randomly generated hash per partition, and needs to search through the sorted list of hashes. This takes more time compared to O(1) computation of hash % number of partitions. This technique is also shown to create some imbalance in data assigned to partitions, so most data systems use fixed-partitions technique.

The basic mechanism works as follows. Each node is assigned a random integer token. This value is typically generated as hash of a random GUID.

The client maps the key to the cluster nodes as follows:

- It computes the hash of the key.

- It gets the sorted list of all the available tokens. It then searches for the smallest token value that is higher than the hash of the key. The cluster node owning that token is the node storing the given key.

- The list is considered circular, so any hash value of a key which is greater than the last token in the list maps to the first token.

Here's what the code looks like:

class TokenMetadata...

```
Map<BigInteger, Node> tokenToNodeMap;

public Node getNodeFor(BigInteger keyHash) {
    List<BigInteger> tokens = sortedTokens();
    BigInteger token = searchToken(tokens, keyHash);
    return tokenToNodeMap.get(token);
}

private static BigInteger searchToken(List<BigInteger> tokens,
                                      BigInteger keyHash) {

    int index = Collections.binarySearch(tokens, keyHash);
    if (index < 0) {
        index = (index + 1) * (-1);
        if (index >= tokens.size())
            index = 0;
    }
    BigInteger token = tokens.get(index);
    return token;
}

List<BigInteger> sortedTokens() {
    List<BigInteger> tokens = new ArrayList<>(tokenToNodeMap.keySet());
    Collections.sort(tokens);
    return tokens;
}
```

To see how this works, we take some example values for tokens. Consider a three-node cluster, with Athens, Byzantium, and Cyrene having the token values of 10, 20, and 30, respectively (Figure 19.5).

For this example, imagine this metadata stored with the *Consistent Core*. The client library gets the token metadata and uses it to map a given key to the cluster node (Figure 19.6).

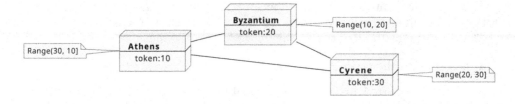

Figure 19.5 *Cluster nodes forming a token ring*

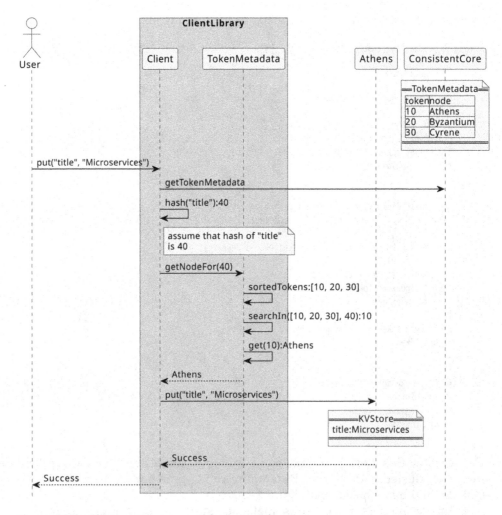

Figure 19.6 *Client writing to a partition using token ring*

Adding New Node to the Cluster

The main advantage of this scheme is that we have more partitions when new nodes are added to the cluster (Figure 19.7).

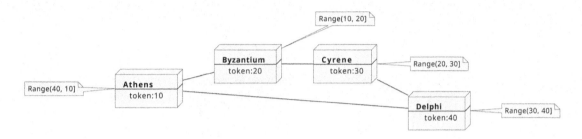

Figure 19.7 *New node owns a part of existing token range.*

Consider a new node, Delphi, is added to the cluster, with a random token of 40 assigned to it. We can see that Athens, which was hosting all the keys with hashes above 30, now needs to move the keys with hashes between 30 and 40 to the new node. This does not involve moving all the keys—only a small portion needs to be moved to the new node.

As before, let's consider a *Consistent Core* tracking the cluster membership and mapping partitions to the cluster nodes. When Delphi registers with the consistent core, it first figures out which existing nodes are affected because of this new addition. In our example, Athens needs to move part of the data to the new node. The Consistent Core tells Athens to move all the keys with hashes between 30 and 40 to Delphi. After the move is complete, Delphi's token is added to token metadata (Figure 19.8).

This basic technique of assigning a single token to each node has shown to create data imbalance. When a new node is added, it also puts all the burden of moving data on one of the existing nodes. For this reason, Apache Cassandra changed its design to have multiple random tokens[62] assigned to each node. This allows a more even distribution of data. When a new node is added to the cluster, a small amount of data is moved from multiple existing nodes, without overloading a single node.

In our example, instead of a single token, each of Athens, Byzantium, and Cyrene can have three tokens each. (Three is taken to simplify the example; the default value for Apache Cassandra was 256.) The tokens are randomly allocated to nodes. It is important to note that tokens assigned to nodes are randomly generated GUID hashes, so they are not contiguous. If contiguous numbers like

---

62. https://www.datastax.com/blog/virtual-nodes-cassandra-12

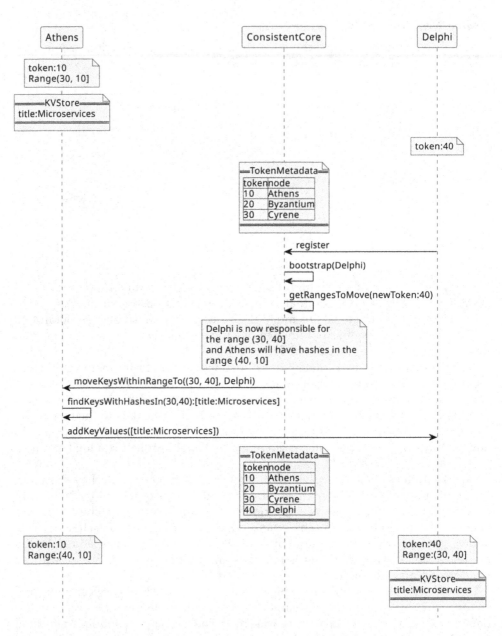

Figure 19.8 *Moving a part of the token range to a newly added node*

10, 20, 30 are assigned to each node, that will have the same problem as a single token per node when a new node is added (Figure 19.9).

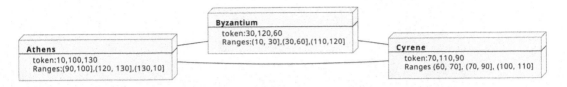

Figure 19.9 *Nodes owning multiple token ranges*

When a new node, Delphi, is added, with tokens of 40, 50, and 200, the key ranges of Athens and Byzantium are responsible for changes. The range (130, 10] on Athens is split with Delphi which now owns the keys with hashes within (130, 200]. The range (30, 60] on Byzantium is split, passing to Delphi the keys with hashes within (40, 50]. All keys in the range (130, 200] from Athens and (40, 50] from Byzantium are moved to Delphi (Figure 19.10).

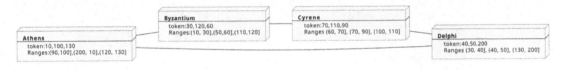

Figure 19.10 *Data ranges moved from multiple nodes*

Examples

- In Apache Kafka, each topic is created with a fixed number of partitions.

- Shard allocation in Akka[63] has a fixed number of shards configured. The guideline is to have the number of shards 10 times the size of the cluster.

- In-memory data grid products like partitioning in Apache Ignite[64] and partitioning in Hazelcast[65] have a fixed number of partitions that are configured for their caches.

---

63. https://doc.akka.io/docs/akka/current/typed/cluster-sharding.html#shard-allocation
64. https://ignite.apache.org/docs/latest/data-modeling/data-partitioning
65. https://docs.hazelcast.com/imdg/4.2/overview/data-partitioning

Chapter 20

Key-Range Partitions

Partition data in sorted key ranges to efficiently handle range queries.

Problem

To split data across a set of cluster nodes, each data item needs to be mapped to a node. If users want to query a range of keys, specifying only the start and end key, all partitions will need to be queried for the values to be acquired. Querying every partition for a single request is far from optimal.

Take a key-value store as an example. We can store the author names using hash-based mapping, as in *Fixed Partitions* (Table 20.1).

Table 20.1 *Key Mapping to Cluster Nodes Using Hash of a Key*

Keys	Hash	Partition = Hash % Number of partitions (9)	Node
alice	133299819613694460644197938031451912208	0	0
bob	63479738429015246738359000453022047291	1	1
mary	37724856304035789372490171084843241126	5	1
philip	83980963731216160506671196398339418866	2	2

243

If a user wants to get values for a range of names—say, beginning with letter "a" to "f"—there's no way to know which partitions we should fetch data from if the hash of the key is being used to map keys to partitions. All partitions need to be queried to get the values required.

Solution

Create logical partitions for keys ranged in a sorted order. The partitions can then be mapped to cluster nodes. To query a range of data, the client can get all partitions that contain keys from a given range and query only those specific partitions to get the values required.

Predefining Key Ranges

If we already know the whole key space and the distribution of keys, the ranges for partitions can be specified upfront.

Let's return to our simple key-value store with string keys and values. In this example, we are storing author names and their books. If we know the author name distribution upfront, we can then define partition splits at specific letters—let's say, in this instance, "b" and "d".

The start and end of the entire key range need to be specifically marked. We can use an empty string to mark the lowest and the highest key. The ranges will be created as shown in Table 20.2.

Table 20.2 *Example Key-Ranges Partitions*

Key Range	Description
["", "b")	Covers all the names starting from "a" to "b", excluding "b"
["b", "d")	Covers all the names starting from "b" to "d", excluding "d"
["d", "")	Covers everything else

The range will be represented by a start and an end key:

class Range...

```
private String startKey;
private String endKey;
```

The cluster coordinator creates ranges from the specified split points. The partitions will then be assigned to cluster nodes.

```
class ClusterCoordinator...

  PartitionTable createPartitionTableFor(List<String> splits) {
      var ranges = createRangesFromSplitPoints(splits);
      return arrangePartitions(ranges, membership.getLiveMembers());
  }

  List<Range> createRangesFromSplitPoints(List<String> splits) {
      var ranges = new ArrayList<Range>();
      String startKey = Range.MIN_KEY;
      for (String split : splits) {
          String endKey = split;
          ranges.add(new Range(startKey, endKey));
          startKey = split;
      }
      ranges.add(new Range(startKey, Range.MAX_KEY));
      return ranges;
  }

  PartitionTable arrangePartitions(List<Range> ranges,
                                   List<Member> liveMembers) {
      var partitionTable = new PartitionTable();
      for (int i = 0; i < ranges.size(); i++) {
          //simple round-robin assignment.
          var member = liveMembers.get(i % liveMembers.size());
          var partitionId = newPartitionId();
          var range = ranges.get(i);
          var partitionInfo = new PartitionInfo(partitionId,
                  member.getAddress(), PartitionStatus.ASSIGNED, range);
          partitionTable.addPartition(partitionId, partitionInfo);
      }
      return partitionTable;
  }
```

The consistent core, acting as a cluster coordinator, stores the mapping in a fault-tolerant way by using a *Replicated Log*. The implementation is similar to the one explained in the section "Mapping Partitions to Cluster Nodes" of the *Fixed Partitions* pattern.

Client Interface

If a client needs to store or get a value for a particular key in a key-value store, it needs to follow these steps:

```
class Client...

  public List<String> getValuesInRange(Range range) throws IOException {
      var partitionTable = getPartitionTable();
```

```
    var partitionsInRange = partitionTable.getPartitionsInRange(range);
    var values = new ArrayList<String>();

    for (PartitionInfo partitionInfo : partitionsInRange) {
        var partitionValues =
                sendGetRangeMessage(partitionInfo.getPartitionId(),
                        range, partitionInfo.getAddress());
        values.addAll(partitionValues);
    }
    return values;
}
```

class PartitionTable...

```
public List<PartitionInfo> getPartitionsInRange(Range range) {
    var allPartitions = getAllPartitions();
    var partitionsInRange =
            allPartitions
                    .stream()
                    .filter(p -> p.getRange().isOverlapping(range))
                    .collect(Collectors.toList());
    return partitionsInRange;
}
```

class Range...

```
public boolean isOverlapping(Range range) {
    return this.contains(range.startKey)
            || range.contains(this.startKey)
            || contains(range.endKey);
}

public boolean contains(String key) {
    return key.compareTo(startKey) >= 0 &&
            (endKey.equals(Range.MAX_KEY) || endKey.compareTo(key) > 0);

}
```

class Partition...

```
public List<String> getAllInRange(Range range) {
    return kv.subMap(range.getStartKey(), range.getEndKey())
            .values().stream().toList();
}
```

Storing a Value

To store a value, the client needs to find the right partition for the given key.
Once a partition is found, the request is sent to the cluster node that is hosting
that partition.

```
class Client...

    public void put(String key, String value) throws IOException {
        var partition = findPartition(key);
        sendPutMessage(partition.getPartitionId(),
                partition.getAddress(), key, value);
    }

    private PartitionInfo findPartition(String key) {
        return partitionTable.getPartitionFor(key);
    }

class PartitionTable...

    public PartitionInfo getPartitionFor(String key) {
        List<PartitionInfo> allPartitions = getAllPartitions();
        Optional<PartitionInfo> partition = allPartitions.stream()
                .filter(p -> !p.isMarkedForSplit() && p.containsKey(key))
                .findFirst();
        return partition
                .orElseThrow(()->
                new RuntimeException("No partition available for key " + key));
    }
```

An Example Scenario

Let's explore this with another example. Consider three data servers: Athens, Byzantium, and Cyrene. The partition splits are defined at "b" and "d". The three ranges will be created as in Table 20.3.

Table 20.3 *Key-Ranges Partitions with Splits at "b" and "d"*

Key Range	Description
["", "b")	Covers all the names starting from "a" to "b", excluding "b"
["b", "d")	Covers all the names starting from "b" to "d", excluding "d"
["d", "")	Covers everything else

The coordinator then creates three partitions for these ranges and maps them to the cluster nodes (Figure 20.1).

Now, if a client wants to get all the values for names starting with "a" and "c", it gets all the partitions which have key ranges containing keys starting with "a" and "c". It then sends requests to only those partitions to get the values (Figure 20.2).

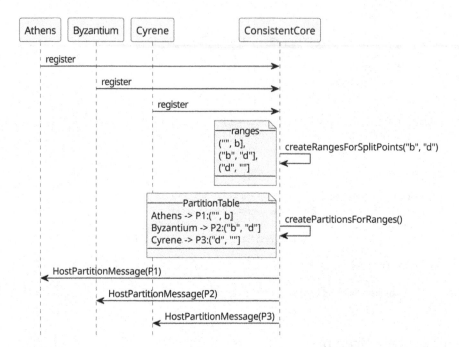

Figure 20.1 *Partition assignment by a Consistent Core*

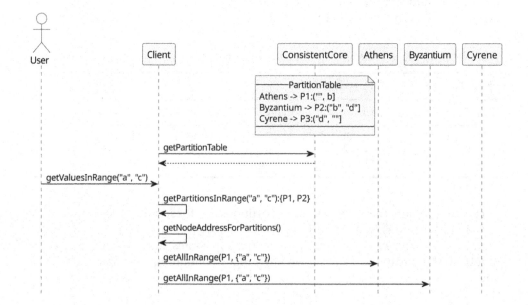

Figure 20.2 *Client reading a range*

Auto-Splitting Ranges

Often, it can be difficult to know what the suitable split points are upfront. In this case, we can implement auto-splitting.

Here, the coordinator will create only one partition with a key range that includes all the key space:

```
class ClusterCoordinator...

    private CompletableFuture initializeRangePartitionAssignment(
            List<String> splits) {

        partitionAssignmentStatus = PartitionAssignmentStatus.IN_PROGRESS;
        var partitionTable = splits.isEmpty() ?
                createPartitionTableWithOneRange()
                :createPartitionTableFor(splits);

        return replicatedLog.propose(new PartitiontableCommand(partitionTable));
    }

    public PartitionTable createPartitionTableWithOneRange() {
        var partitionTable = new PartitionTable();
        var liveMembers = membership.getLiveMembers();
        var member = liveMembers.get(0);
        var firstRange = new Range(Range.MIN_KEY, Range.MAX_KEY);
        int partitionId = newPartitionId();
        partitionTable
                .addPartition(partitionId,
                        new PartitionInfo(partitionId,
                                member.getAddress(),
                                PartitionStatus.ASSIGNED, firstRange));
        return partitionTable;
    }
```

Each partition can be configured with a fixed maximum size. A background task then runs on each cluster node to track the size of the partitions. When a partition reaches its maximum size, it's split into two partitions, each one being approximately half the size of the original.

```
class KVStore...

    public void scheduleSplitCheck() {
        scheduler.scheduleAtFixedRate(() -> {
            splitCheck();
        }, 1000, 1000, TimeUnit.MILLISECONDS);
    }

    public void splitCheck() {
        for (Integer partitionId : allPartitions.keySet()) {
            splitCheck(allPartitions.get(partitionId));
        }
    }
```

```
int MAX_PARTITION_SIZE = 1000;
public void splitCheck(Partition partition) {
    var middleKey = partition.getMiddleKeyIfSizeCrossed(MAX_PARTITION_SIZE);

    if (!middleKey.isEmpty()) {
        logger.info("Partition " + partition.getId()
                + " reached size " + partition.size() + ". Triggering " +
                "split");
        network.send(coordLeader,
                new SplitTriggerMessage(partition.getId(),
                        middleKey, requestNumber++, listenAddress));
    }
}
```

Calculating Partition Size and Finding the Middle Key

Scanning the complete partition to find the split key is resource-intensive. This is why databases such as TiKV[66] store the size of the partition and corresponding key in the data store. The middle key can then be found without scanning the full partition.

Databases such as YugabyteDB[67] or HBase[68] which use a store per partition find an approximate middle key by scanning through the metadata of the store files.

Getting the size of the partition and finding the middle key depends on what storage engines are being used. A simple way of doing this is by scanning through the entire partition to calculate its size. TiKV initially used this approach. To be able to split the tablet, the key situated at the midpoint needs to be found as well. To avoid scanning through the partition twice, a simple implementation can get the middle key if the size is more than the configured maximum.

class Partition...

```
public String getMiddleKeyIfSizeCrossed(int partitionMaxSize) {
    int kvSize = 0;
    for (String key : kv.keySet()) {
        kvSize += key.length() + kv.get(key).length();
        if (kvSize >= partitionMaxSize / 2) {
            return key;
        }
    }
    return "";
}
```

---

66. https://tikv.org
67. https://github.com/yugabyte/yugabyte-db/issues/1463
68. https://hbase.apache.org

The coordinator, handling the split trigger message, updates the key range metadata for the original partition and creates a new partition metadata for the split range.

```
class ClusterCoordinator...

    private void handleSplitTriggerMessage(SplitTriggerMessage message) {
        logger.info("Handling SplitTriggerMessage "
                + message.getPartitionId()
                + " split key " + message.getSplitKey());
        splitPartition(message.getPartitionId(), message.getSplitKey());
    }

    public CompletableFuture splitPartition(int partitionId, String splitKey) {
        logger.info("Splitting partition " + partitionId + " at key " +
                splitKey);

        var parentPartition = partitionTable.getPartition(partitionId);
        var originalRange = parentPartition.getRange();
        var splits = originalRange.split(splitKey);
        var shrunkOriginalRange = splits.get(0);
        var newRange = splits.get(1);
        return replicatedLog
                .propose(new SplitPartitionCommand(partitionId,
                        splitKey, shrunkOriginalRange, newRange));
    }
```

After the partitions metadata is stored successfully, it sends a message to the cluster node that is hosting the parent partition to split the parent partition's data.

```
class ClusterCoordinator...

    private void applySplitPartitionCommand(SplitPartitionCommand command) {
        var originalPartition =
                partitionTable.getPartition(command.getOriginalPartitionId());
        var originalRange = originalPartition.getRange();
        if (!originalRange
                .coveredBy(command.getUpdatedRange().getStartKey(),
                        command.getNewRange().getEndKey())) {
            logger.error("The original range start and end keys "
                    + originalRange + " do not match split ranges");
            return;
        }

        originalPartition.setRange(command.getUpdatedRange());
        var newPartitionInfo = new PartitionInfo(newPartitionId(),
                originalPartition.getAddress(),
                PartitionStatus.ASSIGNED, command.getNewRange());
        partitionTable.addPartition(newPartitionInfo.getPartitionId(),
                newPartitionInfo);

        //send requests to cluster nodes if this is the leader node.
```

```
            if (isLeader()) {
                var message
                        = new SplitPartitionMessage(
                                command.getOriginalPartitionId(),
                                command.getSplitKey(), newPartitionInfo,
                                requestNumber++, listenAddress);

                scheduler.execute(new RetryableTask(originalPartition.getAddress(),
                        network, this, originalPartition.getPartitionId(),
                        message));
            }
        }
```

class Range...

```
    public boolean coveredBy(String startKey, String endKey) {
        return getStartKey().equals(startKey)
                && getEndKey().equals(endKey);
    }
```

The cluster node splits the original partition and creates a new partition. The data from the original partition is then copied to the new partition. It then responds to the coordinator telling it that the split is complete.

class KVStore...

```
    private void handleSplitPartitionMessage(
            SplitPartitionMessage splitPartitionMessage) {

        splitPartition(splitPartitionMessage.getPartitionId(),
                            splitPartitionMessage.getSplitKey(),
                            splitPartitionMessage.getSplitPartitionId());
        network.send(coordLeader,
                new SplitPartitionResponseMessage(
                        splitPartitionMessage.getPartitionId(),
                        splitPartitionMessage.getPartitionId(),
                        splitPartitionMessage.getSplitPartitionId(),
                        splitPartitionMessage.messageId, listenAddress));
    }

    private void splitPartition(int parentPartitionId, String splitKey,
                            int newPartitionId) {

        var partition = allPartitions.get(parentPartitionId);
        var splitPartition = partition.splitAt(splitKey, newPartitionId);
        logger.info("Adding new partition "
                + splitPartition.getId()
                + " for range " + splitPartition.getRange());
        allPartitions.put(splitPartition.getId(), splitPartition);
    }
```

class Partition...

```
public Partition splitAt(String splitKey, int newPartitionId) {
    var splits = this.range.split(splitKey);
    var shrunkOriginalRange = splits.get(0);
    var splitRange = splits.get(1);

    var partition1Kv =
            (range.getStartKey().equals(Range.MIN_KEY))
                    ? kv.headMap(splitKey)
                    : kv.subMap(range.getStartKey(), splitKey);

    var partition2Kv =
            (range.getEndKey().equals(Range.MAX_KEY))
                    ? kv.tailMap(splitKey)
                    : kv.subMap(splitKey, range.getEndKey());

    this.kv = partition1Kv;
    this.range = shrunkOriginalRange;

    return new Partition(newPartitionId, partition2Kv, splitRange);
}
```

class Range...

```
public List<Range> split(String splitKey) {
    return Arrays.asList(new Range(startKey, splitKey),
            new Range(splitKey, endKey));
}
```

Once the coordinator receives the message, it marks the partitions online

class ClusterCoordinator...

```
private void handleSplitPartitionResponse(
        SplitPartitionResponseMessage message) {

    replicatedLog
        .propose(new UpdatePartitionStatusCommand(message.getPartitionId(),
            PartitionStatus.ONLINE));
}
```

One of the issues that can arise when trying to modify an existing partition is that the client cannot cache and always needs to get the latest partition metadata before it can send any requests to the cluster node. Data stores use *Generation Clock* for partitions, updating it every time a partition is split. Any client requests with an older generation number will be rejected. Clients can then reload the partition table from the coordinator and retry the request. This ensures that clients that possess older metadata don't get the wrong results. YugabyteDB chooses to create two separate new partitions and marks the original partition as split. The split partition stops accepting any read-write requests from clients as explained in their automatic table splitting design document.[69]

Example Scenario

Consider an example where the cluster node Athens holds partition P1 covering the entire key range (Figure 20.3). The maximum partition size is configured to be 10 bytes. The SplitCheck detects the size has grown beyond 10, and finds the approximate middle key to be Bob. It then sends a message to the cluster coordinator, asking it to create metadata for the split partition. Once this metadata

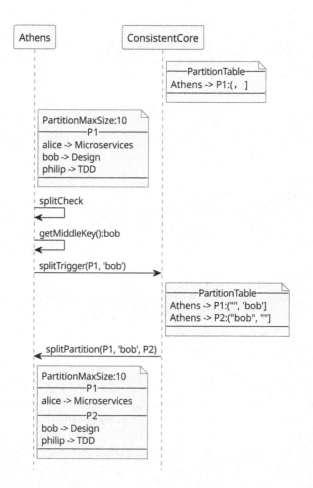

Figure 20.3 *Auto-splitting a range partition*

69. https://github.com/yugabyte/yugabyte-db/blob/master/architecture/design/docdb-automatic-tablet-splitting.md

has been successfully created by the coordinator, the coordinator then asks Athens to split partition P1 and passes it the `partitionId` from the metadata. Athens can then shrink P1 and create a new partition, copying the data from P1 to the new partition. After the partition has been successfully created, it sends confirmation to the coordinator. The coordinator then marks the new partition as online.

Load-Based Splitting

With auto-splitting, we only ever begin with one range. This means all client requests go to a single server even if there are other nodes in the cluster. All requests will continue to go to that single server hosting the single range until the range is split and moved to other servers. This is why partition splitting on parameters, such as the total number of requests, CPU usage, or memory usage, is also used. Modern databases such as CockroachDB[70] and YugabyteDB support load-based splitting. More details can be found in their documentation.

Examples

- Databases including HBase, CockroachDB, YugabyteDB, and TiKV support range partitioning.

---

70. https://www.cockroachlabs.com/docs/stable/load-based-splitting.html

Chapter 21

Two-Phase Commit

Update resources on multiple nodes in one atomic operation.

Problem

When data needs to be atomically stored on multiple cluster nodes, nodes cannot make the data accessible to clients until the decision of other cluster nodes is known. Each node needs to know if other nodes successfully stored the data or if they failed.

Solution

> **Comparison with Paxos and Replicated Log**
>
> *Paxos* and *Replicated Log* implementations also have two phases of execution. But the key difference is that those consensus algorithms are used when all the cluster nodes involved store the same values.
>
> Two-phase commit works across cluster nodes storing different values—for example, across different partitions of a database. Each partition can be using Replicated Log to replicate the state involved in a two-phase commit.

The essence of two-phase commit, unsurprisingly, is that it carries out an update in two phases:

1. The prepare phase asks each node if it can promise to carry out the update.

2. The commit phase actually carries it out.

As part of the prepare phase, each node participating in the transaction acquires whatever it needs to assure that it will be able to do the commit in the second phase—for example, any locks that are required. Once each node is able to ensure it can commit in the second phase, it lets the coordinator know, promising the coordinator that it can and will commit in the second phase. If any node is unable to make that promise, then the coordinator tells all nodes to roll back, releasing any locks they have, and the transaction is aborted. Only if all the participants agree to go ahead does the second phase commence—at which point it's expected they will all successfully update. It is crucial for each participant to ensure the durability of their decisions using a pattern like *Write-Ahead Log*. This means that even if a node crashes and subsequently restarts, it should be capable of completing the protocol without any issues.

In a simple distributed key-value store implementation, the two-phase commit protocol works as follows.

The transactional client creates a unique identifier called a transaction identifier. The client also keeps track of other details like the transaction start time. This is used, as described later, by the locking mechanism to prevent deadlocks. The unique ID, along with the additional details such as the start timestamp, is used to track the transaction across the cluster nodes. The client maintains a transaction reference, which is passed along with every request from the client to other cluster nodes:

```
class TransactionRef...

  private UUID txnId;
  private long startTimestamp;


  public TransactionRef(long startTimestamp) {
      this.txnId = UUID.randomUUID();
      this.startTimestamp = startTimestamp;
  }

class TransactionClient...

  TransactionRef transactionRef;

  public TransactionClient(ReplicaMapper replicaMapper, SystemClock systemClock) {
      this.clock = systemClock;
      this.transactionRef = new TransactionRef(clock.now());
      this.replicaMapper = replicaMapper;
  }
```

One of the cluster nodes acts as a coordinator which tracks the status of the transaction on behalf of the client. In a key-value store, it is generally the cluster node holding data for one of the keys. It is generally picked up as the cluster node storing data for the first key used by the client.

Before storing any value, the client communicates with the coordinator to notify it about the start of the transaction. Since the coordinator is one of the cluster nodes storing values, it is picked dynamically when the client initiates a get or put operation with a specific key.

class TransactionClient...

```
private TransactionalKVStore coordinator;
private void maybeBeginTransaction(String key) {
    if (coordinator == null) {
        coordinator = replicaMapper.serverFor(key);
        coordinator.begin(transactionRef);
    }
}
```

The transaction coordinator keeps track of the status of the transaction. It records every change in a Write-Ahead Log to make sure that the details are available in case of a crash.

class TransactionCoordinator...

```
Map<TransactionRef, TransactionMetadata> transactions
        = new ConcurrentHashMap<>();
WriteAheadLog transactionLog;

public void begin(TransactionRef transactionRef) {
    var txnMetadata = new TransactionMetadata(transactionRef, systemClock,
            transactionTimeoutMs);
    transactionLog.writeEntry(txnMetadata.serialize());
    transactions.put(transactionRef, txnMetadata);
}
```

class TransactionMetadata...

```
private TransactionRef txn;
private List<String> participatingKeys = new ArrayList<>();
private TransactionStatus transactionStatus;
```

The example code shows that every put request goes to the respective servers. But since the values are not made visible until the transaction commits, they can very well be buffered on the client side, to optimize on the network round trips, until the client decides to commit.

The client sends each key which is part of the transaction to the coordinator. This way the coordinator tracks all the keys which are part of the transaction. The coordinator records the keys which are part of the transaction in the transaction metadata. The keys then can be used to know about all of the cluster nodes which are part of the transaction. Since each key-value is generally replicated with the Replicated Log, the leader server handling the requests for a particular key might change over the lifetime of the transaction, so the keys are tracked instead of the actual server addresses. The client then sends the put or get requests to the server holding the data for the key. The server is picked based on the partitioning strategy. The thing to note is that the client directly communicates with the server and not through the coordinator. This avoids sending data twice over the network—from client to coordinator and then from coordinator to the respective server.

class TransactionClient...

```
public CompletableFuture<String> get(String key) {
    maybeBeginTransaction(key);
    coordinator.addKeyToTransaction(transactionRef, key);
    TransactionalKVStore kvStore = replicaMapper.serverFor(key);
    return kvStore.get(transactionRef, key);
}

public void put(String key, String value) {
    maybeBeginTransaction(key);
    coordinator.addKeyToTransaction(transactionRef, key);
    replicaMapper.serverFor(key).put(transactionRef, key, value);
}
```

class TransactionCoordinator...

```
public void addKeyToTransaction(TransactionRef transactionRef,
                                        String key) {

    var metadata = transactions.get(transactionRef);
    if (!metadata.getParticipatingKeys().contains(key)) {
        metadata.addKey(key);
        transactionLog.writeEntry(metadata.serialize());
    }
}
```

The cluster node handling the request detects that the request is part of a transaction with the transaction ID. It manages the state of the transaction, where it stores the key, and the value in the request. The key values are not directly made available to the key-value store but stored separately.

class TransactionalKVStore...

```
public void put(TransactionRef transactionRef, String key, String value) {
    TransactionState state = getOrCreateTransactionState(transactionRef);
    state.addPendingUpdates(key, value);
}
```

Locks and Transaction Isolation

Problems with Non-Serializable Isolation

The serializable isolation level has an impact on overall performance—mostly because of the locks held for the duration of the transaction. That's why most data stores provide relaxed isolation levels where the locks are released earlier. This is a problem particularly when clients need to do read-modify-write operations. The operations can potentially overwrite the values from the previous transactions. So modern data stores like Google Spanner or CockroachDB provide serializable isolation.

In implementations using locks, the requests also take a lock on the keys. Particularly, the get requests take a read lock and the put requests take a write lock. The read locks are taken as the values are read.

class TransactionalKVStore...

```
public CompletableFuture<String> get(TransactionRef txn, String key) {
    CompletableFuture<TransactionRef> lockFuture
            = lockManager.acquire(txn, key, LockMode.READ);
    return lockFuture.thenApply(transactionRef -> {
        getOrCreateTransactionState(transactionRef);
        return kv.get(key);
    });
}

synchronized TransactionState getOrCreateTransactionState(
                            TransactionRef txnRef) {

    TransactionState state = this.ongoingTransactions.get(txnRef);
    if (state == null) {
        state = new TransactionState();
        this.ongoingTransactions.put(txnRef, state);
    }
    return state;
}
```

The write locks can be taken only when the transaction is about to commit and the values are to be made visible in the key-value store. Until then, the cluster node can just track the modified values as pending operations.

class TransactionalKVStore...

```
public void put(TransactionRef transactionRef, String key, String value) {
    TransactionState state = getOrCreateTransactionState(transactionRef);
    state.addPendingUpdates(key, value);
}
```

The key design decision is about which values are made visible to the concurrent transactions. Different transaction isolation levels give different levels of visibility. For example, in strictly serializable transactions, read requests are blocked till the transaction doing the write completes. To improve performance, data stores can get around two-phase locking and release locks earlier. But then consistency of the data is compromised. There are a lot of different choices[71] defined by different isolation levels that data stores provide.

It is important to note that the locks are long-lived and not released when the request completes. They are released only when the transaction commits. This technique of holding locks for the duration of the transaction and releasing them only when the transaction commits or rolls back is called two-phase locking. Two-phase locking is critical in providing the serializable isolation level. "Serializable" means that the effects of transactions are visible as if they are executed one at a time.

Deadlock Prevention

Usage of locks can cause deadlocks where two transactions wait for each other to release the locks. Deadlocks can be avoided if transactions are not allowed to wait and are aborted when a conflict is detected. There are different strategies used to decide which transactions are aborted and which are allowed to continue.

The lock manager implements these wait policies as follows:

```
class LockManager...

  WaitPolicy waitPolicy;
```

The WaitPolicy decides what to do when there are conflicting requests.

```
public enum WaitPolicy {
    WoundWait,
    WaitDie,
    Error
}
```

The lock is an object which tracks the transactions which currently own the lock and the ones which are waiting for the lock.

```
class Lock...

  Queue<LockRequest> waitQueue = new LinkedList<>();
  List<TransactionRef> owners = new ArrayList<>();
  LockMode lockMode;
```

---

71. https://jepsen.io/consistency

When a transaction requests to acquire a lock, the lock manager grants the lock immediately if there are no conflicting transactions already owning the lock.

class LockManager...

```
public synchronized CompletableFuture<TransactionRef>
                acquire(TransactionRef txn, String key,
                    LockMode lockMode) {

    return acquire(txn, key, lockMode, new CompletableFuture<>());
}

CompletableFuture<TransactionRef>
            acquire(TransactionRef txnRef,
                String key,
                LockMode askedLockMode,
                CompletableFuture<TransactionRef> lockFuture) {

    var lock = getOrCreateLock(key);

    logger.debug("acquiring lock for = " + txnRef
            + " on key = " + key + " with lock mode = " + askedLockMode);
    if (lock.isCompatible(txnRef, askedLockMode)) {
        lock.addOwner(txnRef, askedLockMode);
        lockFuture.complete(txnRef);
        logger.debug("acquired lock for = " + txnRef);
        return lockFuture;
    }
    if (lock.isLockedBy(txnRef) && lock.lockMode == askedLockMode) {
        lockFuture.complete(txnRef);
        logger.debug("Lock already acquired lock for = " + txnRef);
        return lockFuture;
    }
}
```

class Lock...

```
public boolean isCompatible(TransactionRef txnRef, LockMode lockMode) {
    if(hasOwner()) {
        return (inReadMode() && lockMode == LockMode.READ)
                || isOnlyOwner(txnRef);
    }
    return true;
}
```

If there are conflicts, the lock manager acts depending on the wait policy.

Error On Conflict

If the wait policy is to error out, it will throw an error and the calling transaction will roll back. The error is propagated to the client, who can then decide to retry after a random timeout.

```
class LockManager...

    private CompletableFuture<TransactionRef>
            handleConflict(Lock lock,
                           TransactionRef txnRef,
                           String key,
                           LockMode askedLockMode,
                           CompletableFuture<TransactionRef> lockFuture) {

        switch (waitPolicy) {
            case Error: {
                var e = new WriteConflictException(txnRef, key, lock.owners);
                lockFuture
                        .completeExceptionally(e);
                return lockFuture;
            }
            case WoundWait: {
                return lock.woundWait(txnRef, key,  askedLockMode, lockFuture,
                                this);
            }
            case WaitDie: {
                return lock.waitDie(txnRef, key,  askedLockMode, lockFuture,
                        this);
            }
        }
        throw new IllegalArgumentException("Unknown waitPolicy " + waitPolicy);
    }
```

In case of contention, when there are many user transactions trying to acquire locks and all of them need to restart, it severely limits the systems throughput. Data stores try to make sure that there are minimal transaction restarts.

A common technique is to assign a unique ID to transactions and order them. For example, Google Spanner assigns unique IDs [Malkhi2013] to transactions in such a way that they can be ordered. The technique is very similar to the one discussed in *Paxos* to order requests across cluster nodes. When transactions can be ordered, there are two techniques used to avoid deadlock but still allow transactions to continue without restarting.

The transaction reference is created in such a way that it can be compared and ordered with other transaction references. The easiest method is to assign a timestamp to each transaction and compare based on the timestamp.

```
class TransactionRef...

    boolean after(TransactionRef otherTransactionRef) {
        return this.startTimestamp > otherTransactionRef.startTimestamp;
    }
```

But in distributed systems system clocks are not monotonic, as discussed in the sidebar "Wall Clocks Are Not Monotonic" of the *Lease* pattern, so a different method can be used: assigning unique IDs to transactions in such a way that they can be ordered. Along with ordered IDs, the age of each is tracked so the transactions can be ordered. Google Spanner orders transactions by tracking the age of each transaction in the system.

To be able to order all the transactions, each cluster node is assigned a unique ID. The client picks up the coordinator at the start of the transaction and gets the transaction ID from the coordinator. The cluster node acting as a coordinator generates transaction IDs as follows:

class TransactionCoordinator...

```
private int requestId;
public MonotonicId begin() {
    return new MonotonicId(requestId++, config.getServerId());
}
```

class MonotonicId...

```
public class MonotonicId implements Comparable<MonotonicId> {
    public int requestId;
    int serverId;

    public MonotonicId(int requestId, int serverId) {
        this.serverId = serverId;
        this.requestId = requestId;
    }

    public static MonotonicId empty() {
        return new MonotonicId(-1, -1);
    }

    public boolean isAfter(MonotonicId other) {
        if (this.requestId == other.requestId) {
            return this.serverId > other.serverId;
        }
        return this.requestId > other.requestId;
    }
}
```

class TransactionClient...

```
private void beginTransaction(String key) {
    if (coordinator == null) {
        coordinator = replicaMapper.serverFor(key);
        MonotonicId transactionId = coordinator.begin();
        transactionRef = new TransactionRef(transactionId, clock.nanoTime());
    }
}
```

The client tracks the age of the transaction by recording the elapsed time since the beginning of the transaction:

```
class TransactionRef...

  public void incrementAge(SystemClock clock) {
      age = clock.nanoTime() - startTimestamp;
  }
```

The client increments the age every time a get or a put request is sent to the servers. The transactions are then ordered as per their age. The transaction ID is used to break the ties when there are same-age transactions.

```
class TransactionRef...

  public boolean isAfter(TransactionRef other) {
      return age == other.age?
                  this.id.isAfter(other.id)
                  :this.age > other.age;
  }
```

Wound-Wait

In the wound-wait method, if there is a conflict, the transaction reference asking for the lock is compared to all the transactions currently owning the lock. If the lock owners are all younger than the transaction asking for the lock, all of those transactions are aborted. But if the transaction asking the lock is younger than the ones owning the transaction, it waits for the lock:

```
class Lock...

  public CompletableFuture<TransactionRef>
                    woundWait(TransactionRef txnRef,
                          String key,
                          LockMode askedLockMode,
                          CompletableFuture<TransactionRef> lockFuture,
                          LockManager lockManager) {

      if (allOwningTransactionsStartedAfter(txnRef)
          && !anyOwnerIsPrepared(lockManager)) {

          abortAllOwners(lockManager, key, txnRef);
          return lockManager.acquire(txnRef, key, askedLockMode, lockFuture);
      }

      var lockRequest = new LockRequest(txnRef, key, askedLockMode,
              lockFuture);

      lockManager.logger.debug("Adding to wait queue = " + lockRequest);
      addToWaitQueue(lockRequest);
      return lockFuture;
  }
```

class Lock...

```
private boolean allOwningTransactionsStartedAfter(TransactionRef txn) {
    return owners.
            stream().
            filter(o -> !o.equals(txn))
            .allMatch(owner -> owner.after(txn));
}
```

One of the key things to notice is that if the transaction owning the lock is already in the prepare state of the two-phase commit, it is not aborted.

Wait-Die

The wait-die method works in the opposite way to wound-wait. If the lock owners are all younger than the transaction asking for the lock, then the transaction waits for the lock. But if the transaction asking for the lock is younger than the ones owning the transaction, the transaction is aborted.

class Lock...

```
public CompletableFuture<TransactionRef>
                    waitDie(TransactionRef txnRef,
                        String key,
                        LockMode askedLockMode,
                        CompletableFuture<TransactionRef> lockFuture,
                        LockManager lockManager) {

    if (allOwningTransactionsStartedAfter(txnRef)) {
        addToWaitQueue(new LockRequest(txnRef, key, askedLockMode, lockFuture));
        return lockFuture;
    }

    lockManager.abort(txnRef, key);
    lockFuture.completeExceptionally(
            new WriteConflictException(txnRef, key, owners));
    return lockFuture;
}
```

The wound-wait method generally has fewer restarts than the wait-die method, so data stores such as Google Spanner use the wound-wait method.

When the owner of the transaction releases a lock, the waiting transactions are granted the lock.

class LockManager...

```
private void release(TransactionRef txn, String key) {
    Optional<Lock> lock = getLock(key);
    lock.ifPresent(l -> {
        l.release(txn, this);
    });
}
```

class Lock...

```
public void release(TransactionRef txn, LockManager lockManager) {
    removeOwner(txn);
    if (hasWaiters()) {
        var lockRequest = getFirst(lockManager.waitPolicy);
        lockManager.acquire(lockRequest.txn,
                lockRequest.key, lockRequest.lockMode, lockRequest.future);
    }
}
```

Commit and Rollback

Once the client is done with its read or write operations, it initiates the commit request by sending a commit request to the coordinator.

class TransactionClient...

```
public CompletableFuture<Boolean> commit() {
    return coordinator.commit(transactionRef);
}
```

The transaction coordinator records the state of the transaction as preparing to commit. The coordinator implements the commit handling in two phases.

1. It first sends the prepare request to each of the participants.

2. Once it receives a successful response from all the participants, the coordinator marks the transaction as prepared to complete. Then it sends the commit request to all the participants.

class TransactionCoordinator...

```
public CompletableFuture<Boolean> commit(TransactionRef transactionRef)  {
    var metadata = transactions.get(transactionRef);
    metadata.markPreparingToCommit(transactionLog);
    var allPrepared = sendPrepareRequestToParticipants(transactionRef);
    var futureList = sequence(allPrepared);
    return futureList.thenApply(result -> {
        if (!result.stream().allMatch(r -> r)) {
            logger.info("Rolling back = " + transactionRef);
            rollback(transactionRef);
            return false;
        }
        metadata.markPrepared(transactionLog);
        sendCommitMessageToParticipants(transactionRef);
        metadata.markCommitComplete(transactionLog);
        return true;
    });
}
```

The cluster node receiving the prepare request does two things:

1. It tries to grab the write locks for all of the keys.

2. Once successful, it writes all of the changes to the write-ahead log.

If it can successfully do these, it can guarantee that there are no conflicting transactions, and even in case of a crash the cluster node can recover all the required state to complete the transaction.

```
class TransactionalKVStore...

  public CompletableFuture<Boolean>
                  handlePrepare(TransactionRef txn) {

    try {
      TransactionState state = getTransactionState(txn);
      if (state.isPrepared()) {
        //already prepared.
        return CompletableFuture.completedFuture(true);
      }

      if (state.isAborted()) {
        //aborted by another transaction.
        return CompletableFuture.completedFuture(false);
      }

      var pendingUpdates = state.getPendingUpdates();
      var prepareFuture = prepareUpdates(txn, pendingUpdates);
      return prepareFuture.thenApply(ignored -> {
        var locksHeldByTxn = lockManager.getAllLocksFor(txn);
        state.markPrepared();
        writeToWAL(new TransactionMarker(txn, locksHeldByTxn,
              TransactionStatus.PREPARED));
        return true;
      });

    } catch (TransactionException| WriteConflictException e) {
      logger.error(e);
    }
    return CompletableFuture.completedFuture(false);
  }

  private CompletableFuture<Boolean> prepareUpdates(TransactionRef txn,
                  Optional<Map<String, String>> pendingUpdates)  {

    if (pendingUpdates.isPresent()) {
      var pendingKVs = pendingUpdates.get();
      var lockFuture = acquireLocks(txn, pendingKVs.keySet());
      return lockFuture.thenApply(ignored -> {
        writeToWAL(txn, pendingKVs);
        return true;
      });
    }
```

```
        return CompletableFuture.completedFuture(true);
    }

    TransactionState getTransactionState(TransactionRef txnRef) {
        return ongoingTransactions.get(txnRef);
    }

    private void writeToWAL(TransactionRef txn,
                           Map<String, String> pendingUpdates) {

        for (String key : pendingUpdates.keySet()) {
            var value = pendingUpdates.get(key);
            wal.writeEntry(new SetValueCommand(txn, key, value).serialize());
        }
    }

    private CompletableFuture<List<TransactionRef>>
                            acquireLocks(TransactionRef txn,
                                         Set<String> keys) {

        var lockFutures = new ArrayList<CompletableFuture<TransactionRef>>();
        for (String key : keys) {
            var lockFuture = lockManager.acquire(txn, key, LockMode.READWRITE);
            lockFutures.add(lockFuture);
        }
        return sequence(lockFutures);
    }
```

When the cluster node receives the commit message from the coordinator, it is safe to make the key-value changes visible. The cluster node does three things while committing the changes:

1. It marks the transaction as committed. Should the cluster node fail at this point, it knows the outcome of the transaction, and can repeat the following steps.

2. It applies all the changes to the key-value storage.

3. It releases all the acquired locks.

class TransactionalKVStore...

```
    public void handleCommit(TransactionRef transactionRef,
                             List<String> keys) {
        if (!ongoingTransactions.containsKey(transactionRef)) {
            return; //this is a no-op. Already committed.
        }

        if (!lockManager.hasLocksFor(transactionRef, keys)) {
            throw new IllegalStateException("Transaction " + transactionRef
                    + " should hold all the required locks for keys " + keys);
        }
```

```
    writeToWAL(new TransactionMarker(transactionRef,
            TransactionStatus.COMMITTED, keys));

    applyPendingUpdates(transactionRef);

    releaseLocks(transactionRef, keys);
}

private void removeTransactionState(TransactionRef txnRef) {
    ongoingTransactions.remove(txnRef);
}

private void applyPendingUpdates(TransactionRef txnRef) {
    var state = getTransactionState(txnRef);
    var pendingUpdates = state.getPendingUpdates();
    apply(txnRef, pendingUpdates);
}

private void apply(TransactionRef txnRef,
                   Optional<Map<String, String>> pendingUpdates) {
    if (pendingUpdates.isPresent()) {
        var pendingKv = pendingUpdates.get();
        apply(pendingKv);
    }
    removeTransactionState(txnRef);
}

private void apply(Map<String, String> pendingKv) {
    for (String key : pendingKv.keySet()) {
        String value = pendingKv.get(key);
        kv.put(key, value);
    }
}
private void releaseLocks(TransactionRef txn, List<String> keys) {
        lockManager.release(txn, keys);
}

private Long writeToWAL(TransactionMarker transactionMarker) {
    return wal.writeEntry(transactionMarker.serialize());
}
```

The rollback is implemented in a similar way. If there is any failure, the client communicates with the coordinator to roll back the transaction.

```
class TransactionClient...

public void rollback() {
    coordinator.rollback(transactionRef);
}
```

The transaction coordinator records the state of the transaction as preparing to roll back. Then it forwards the rollback request to all of the servers that stored the values for the given transaction. Once all of the requests are successful, the coordinator marks the transaction rollback as complete. In case the coordinator crashes and restarts after the transaction is marked as "prepared to roll back," it can keep on sending the rollback messages to all the participating cluster nodes.

```
class TransactionCoordinator...

  public void rollback(TransactionRef transactionRef) {
      var transactionMetadata = transactions.get(transactionRef);

      transactionMetadata.markPrepareToRollback(this.transactionLog);

      sendRollbackMessageToParticipants(transactionRef);

      transactionMetadata.markRollbackComplete(this.transactionLog);
  }

  private void sendRollbackMessageToParticipants(TransactionRef transactionRef) {

      var transactionMetadata = transactions.get(transactionRef);
      var participants
              = getParticipants(transactionMetadata.getParticipatingKeys());
      for (var kvStore : participants.keySet()) {
          var keys = participants.get(kvStore);
          kvStore.sendRollback(transactionMetadata.getTxn(), keys);
      }
  }
```

A cluster node receiving the rollback request does three things:

1. It records the state of the transaction as rolled back in the write-ahead log.
2. It discards the transaction state.
3. It releases all of the locks.

```
class TransactionalKVStore...

  public void handleRollback(TransactionRef transactionRef,
                                       List<String> keys) {

      if (!ongoingTransactions.containsKey(transactionRef)) {
          return; //no-op. Already rolled back.
      }
      writeToWAL(new TransactionMarker(transactionRef,
              TransactionStatus.ROLLED_BACK, keys));
      this.ongoingTransactions.remove(transactionRef);
      this.lockManager.release(transactionRef, keys);
  }
```

Idempotent Operations

In case of network failures, the coordinator can retry calls to prepare, commit, or abort. So these operations need to be idempotent, as discussed in the sidebar "Idempotent and Non-Idempotent Requests" of the *Idempotent Receiver* pattern.

An Example Scenario

Atomic Writes

Consider the following scenario. Paula Blue has a truck and Steven Green has a backhoe. The availability and the booking status of the truck and the backhoe are stored on a distributed key-value store. Depending on how the keys are mapped to servers, Blue's truck and Green's backhoe bookings are stored on separate cluster nodes. Alice is trying to book a truck and backhoe for the construction work she is planning to start on Monday. She needs both the truck and the backhoe to be available.

The booking scenario goes as follows.

Alice checks the availability of Blue's truck and Green's backhoe by reading the keys truck_booking_on_monday (Figure 21.1) and backhoe_booking_on_monday (Figure 21.2).

If the values are empty, the booking is free. She reserves the truck and the backhoe. It is important that both values are set atomically. If there is any failure, then none of the values is set.

The commit happens in two phases. The first server Alice contacts acts as the coordinator and executes the two phases (Figure 21.3).

> The coordinator is a separate participant in the protocol, shown that way on the sequence diagram. However, usually one of the servers (Blue or Green) acts as the coordinator, thus playing two roles in the interaction.

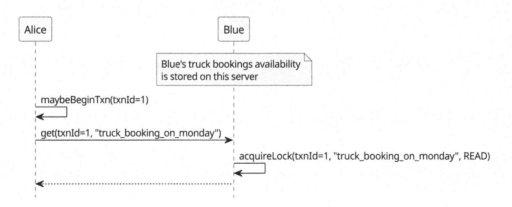

Figure 21.1 *Blue node acquires read lock.*

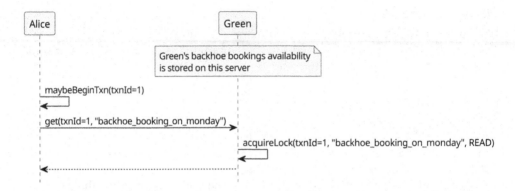

Figure 21.2 *Green node acquires read lock.*

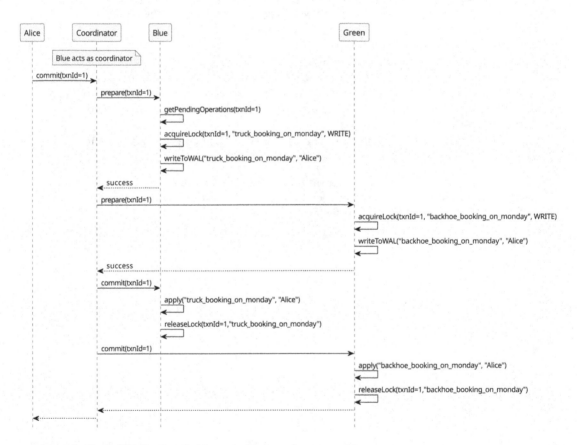

Figure 21.3 *Coordinator manages two-phase commit.*

Conflicting Transactions

Consider a scenario where another person, Bob, is also trying to book a truck and backhoe for construction work on the same Monday.

The booking scenario happens as follows:

- Both Alice and Bob read the keys `truck_booking_on_monday` and `backhoe_booking_on_monday`.

- Both see that the values are empty, meaning the booking is free.

- Both try to book the truck and the backhoe.

The expectation is that only Alice or Bob should be able to book, because the transactions are conflicting. In case of errors, the whole flow needs to be retried—and, hopefully, one will go ahead with the booking. However, in no situation should booking be done partially. Either both bookings are done or neither is done.

> The scenario gets into a deadlock because both transactions depend on the locks held by others. The way out is for transactions to back out and fail. The example implementation shown here will fail the transaction if it detects a conflicting transaction holding a lock for a given key.

To check the availability, both Alice and Bob start a transaction and contact Blue and Green's servers, respectively. Blue holds a read lock for the key `truck_booking_on_monday` (Figure 21.4) and Green holds a read lock for the key `backhoe_booking_on_monday` (Figure 21.5). Since read locks are shared, both Alice and Bob can read the values.

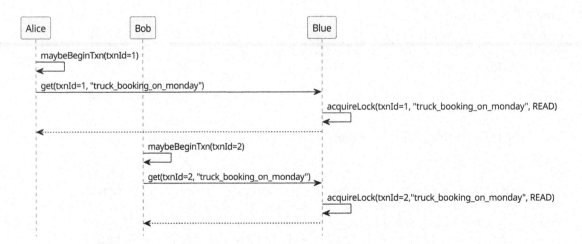

Figure 21.4 *Blue acquires read lock for both Alice and Bob.*

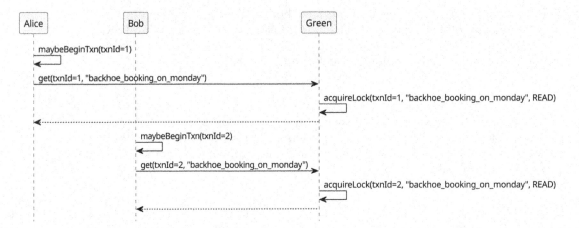

Figure 21.5 *Green acquires read lock for both Alice and Bob.*

Alice and Bob see that both bookings are available on Monday. So they reserve by sending the put requests to servers. Both servers hold the put requests in the temporary storage, as shown in Figures 21.6 and 21.7.

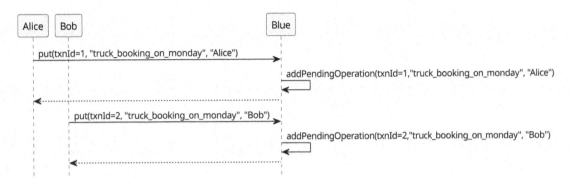

Figure 21.6 *Blue records pending operations for both Alice and Bob.*

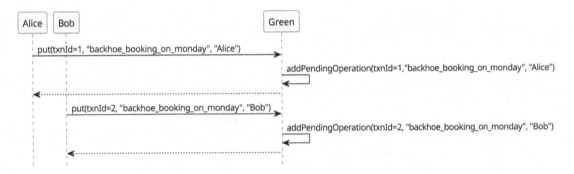

Figure 21.7 *Green records pending operations for both Alice and Bob.*

When Alice and Bob decide to commit the transactions, Blue—assuming it acts as a coordinator—triggers the two-phase commit protocol and sends the prepare requests to itself and Green.

For Alice's request, it tries to grab a write lock for the key truck_booking_on_monday, which it cannot get, because there is a conflicting read lock grabbed by another transaction. So Alice's transaction fails in the prepare phase. The same thing happens to Bob's request (Figure 21.8).

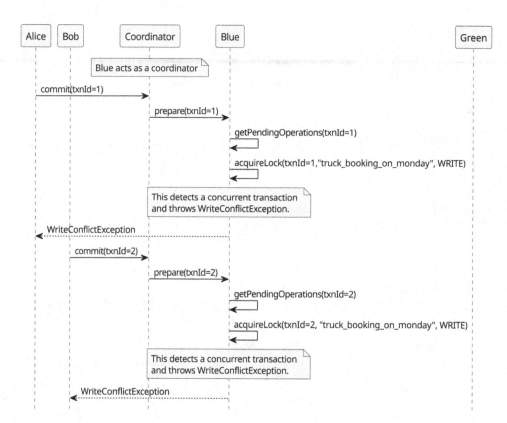

Figure 21.8 *Commit failure because of conflicts*

Transactions can be retried with a retry loop as follows:

class TransactionExecutor...

```
public boolean executeWithRetry(Function<TransactionClient, Boolean> txnMethod,
                                ReplicaMapper replicaMapper,
                                SystemClock systemClock) {
    for (int attempt = 1; attempt <= maxRetries; attempt++) {
        var client = new TransactionClient(replicaMapper, systemClock);
        try {
            txnMethod.apply(client);
            var successfullyCommitted = client.commit().get();
            return successfullyCommitted;

        } catch (WriteConflictException e) {
            logger.error("Write conflict detected while executing."
                    + client.transactionRef
                    + " Retrying attempt " + attempt);
            rollbackAndWait(client);
```

```
        } catch (ExecutionException | InterruptedException e) {
            rollbackAndWait(client);
        }

    }
    return false;
}

private void rollbackAndWait(TransactionClient client) {
    client.rollback();
    randomWait(); //wait for random interval
}
```

While it is very easy to implement, with error-on-conflict policy there will be multiple transaction restarts, reducing the overall throughput. If the wound-wait policy is used, it will have fewer transaction restarts. In the above example, only one transaction will possibly restart instead of both restarting in case of conflicts.

Using Versioned Value

It is very constraining to have conflicts for all the read and write operations, particularly so when the transactions can be read-only. It is optimal when read-only transactions can work without holding any locks and still guarantee that the values read in a transaction do not change with a concurrent read-write transaction.

Data stores generally store multiple versions of the values, as described in *Versioned Value*. The version used is the timestamp following *Lamport Clock*. A *Hybrid Clock* is used in databases such as MongoDB or CockroachDB. To use it with the two-phase commit protocol, the trick is that every server participating in the transaction sends, as its response to the prepare request, the timestamp it can write the values at. The coordinator chooses the maximum of these timestamps as the commit timestamp and sends it along with the value. The participating servers then save the value at the commit timestamp. This allows read-only requests to be executed without holding locks, because it's guaranteed that the value written at a particular timestamp is never going to change.

Consider a simple example. Philip is running a report to read all of the bookings that happened until timestamp 2. If it is a long-running operation holding a lock, then Alice, who is trying to book a truck, will be blocked until Philip's work completes. With Versioned Value, Philip's get requests, which are part of a read-only operation, can continue at timestamp 2, while Alice's booking continues at timestamp 4 (Figure 21.9).

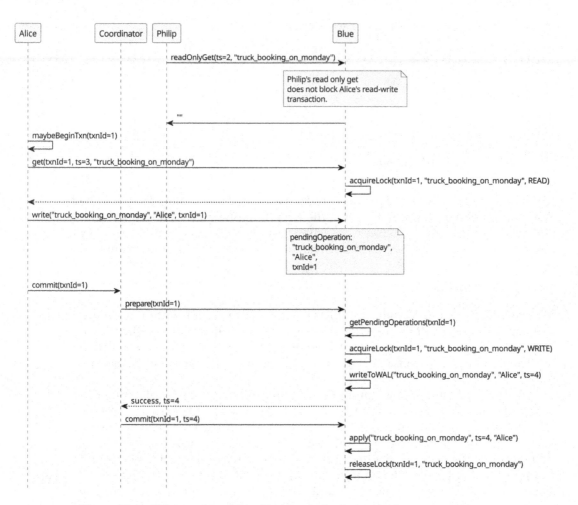

Figure 21.9 *Using versions for nonblocking read-only transactions*

Note that read requests which are part of a read-write transaction still need to hold a lock.

The example code with Lamport Clock looks as follows:

```
class MvccTransactionalKVStore...

    public String readOnlyGet(String key, int readTimestamp) {
        adjustServerTimestamp(readTimestamp);
        waitForPendingWritesBelow(readTimestamp);

        return kv.get(new VersionedKey(key, readTimestamp));
    }
```

```java
    public CompletableFuture<String> get(TransactionRef txn,
                                         String key, int requestTimestamp) {

        adjustServerTimestamp(requestTimestamp);
        var lockFuture = lockManager.acquire(txn, key, LockMode.READ);
        return lockFuture.thenApply(transactionRef -> {
            getOrCreateTransactionState(transactionRef);
            return getValue(key, this.timestamp);
            //read the latest value. no write can happen below this timestamp.
        });
    }

    private String getValue(String key, int timestamp) {
        var entry = kv.floorEntry(new VersionedKey(key, timestamp));
        return entry != null && entry.getKey().getKey().equals(key)
                ? entry.getValue() : null;
    }

    private void adjustServerTimestamp(int requestTimestamp) {
        this.timestamp = requestTimestamp > this.timestamp
                ? requestTimestamp:timestamp;
    }

    public int put(TransactionRef txnId, String key, String value,
                   int requestTimestamp) {

        adjustServerTimestamp(requestTimestamp);
        var transactionState = getOrCreateTransactionState(txnId);
        transactionState.addPendingUpdates(key, value);
        return this.timestamp;
    }

class MvccTransactionalKVStore...

    private int prepare(TransactionRef txn,
                        Optional<Map<String, String>> pendingUpdates)
            throws WriteConflictException, IOException {

        if (pendingUpdates.isPresent()) {
            var pendingKVs = pendingUpdates.get();

            acquireLocks(txn, pendingKVs);

            //increment the timestamp for write operation.
            timestamp = timestamp + 1;

            writeToWAL(txn, pendingKVs, timestamp);
        }
        return timestamp;
    }
```

```
class MvccTransactionCoordinator...

    public int commit(TransactionRef txn) {
        var commitTimestamp = prepare(txn);
        var transactionMetadata = transactions.get(txn);
        transactionMetadata.markPreparedToCommit(commitTimestamp, this.transactionLog);
        sendCommitMessageToAllTheServers(txn,
                commitTimestamp, transactionMetadata.getParticipatingKeys());
        transactionMetadata.markCommitComplete(transactionLog);
        return commitTimestamp;
    }

    public int prepare(TransactionRef txn) throws WriteConflictException {
        var transactionMetadata = transactions.get(txn);
        var keysToServers = getParticipants(transactionMetadata.getParticipatingKeys());
        var prepareTimestamps = new ArrayList<Integer>();
        for (var store : keysToServers.keySet()) {
            var keys = keysToServers.get(store);
            var prepareTimestamp = store.prepare(txn, keys);
            prepareTimestamps.add(prepareTimestamp);
        }
        return prepareTimestamps
            .stream()
            .max(Integer::compare)
            .orElse((int) txn.getStartTimestamp());
    }
```

All the participating cluster nodes then store the key-value records at the commit timestamp.

```
class MvccTransactionalKVStore...

    public void commit(TransactionRef txn, List<String> keys, int commitTimestamp) {
        if (!lockManager.hasLocksFor(txn, keys)) {
            throw new IllegalStateException(
                    "Transaction should hold all the required locks");
        }

        adjustServerTimestamp(commitTimestamp);

        applyPendingOperations(txn, commitTimestamp);

        lockManager.release(txn, keys);

        logTransactionMarker(new TransactionMarker(txn,
                TransactionStatus.COMMITTED,
                commitTimestamp,
                keys,
                Collections.EMPTY_MAP));

        removePending(commitTimestamp);
    }
```

```
private void applyPendingOperations(TransactionRef txnId,
                                    long commitTimestamp) {
    Optional<TransactionState> transactionState = getTransactionState(txnId);
    if (transactionState.isPresent()) {
        TransactionState t = transactionState.get();
        Optional<Map<String, String>> pendingUpdates = t.getPendingUpdates();
        apply(txnId, pendingUpdates, commitTimestamp);
    }
}

private void apply(TransactionRef txnId,
                   Optional<Map<String, String>> pendingUpdates,
                   long commitTimestamp) {
    if (pendingUpdates.isPresent()) {
        var pendingKv = pendingUpdates.get();
        apply(pendingKv, commitTimestamp);
    }
    ongoingTransactions.remove(txnId);
}

private void apply(Map<String, String> pendingKv, long commitTimestamp) {
    for (String key : pendingKv.keySet()) {
        var value = pendingKv.get(key);
        kv.put(new VersionedKey(key, commitTimestamp), value);
    }
}
```

Snapshot Isolation

The above implementation still uses locks for the read requests in read-write transactions. If the workload contains mostly read requests, this impacts overall throughput and latency of the system. A general observation is that, in most practical situations, even with read-write transactions, read requests are far more numerous than the write requests. So, data stores that favor better performance prefer an implementation choice which does not hold locks for read requests even in read-write transactions.

But it's a well known fact that if locks are not held for the duration of a transaction, there are various anomalies [Berenson1995] which can cause data inconsistencies.

For example, let's see what happens if read locks are not held in the above example using *Versioned Value*. Alice and Bob are trying to book a truck for Monday. They both read the key truck_booking_on_monday at timestamp 1. Both see that there is no booking (Figure 21.10).

First, Alice sends a write request to set the key truck_booking_on_monday and commits the transaction. This creates a new version at timestamp 2 for that key, as Figure 21.11 demonstrates.

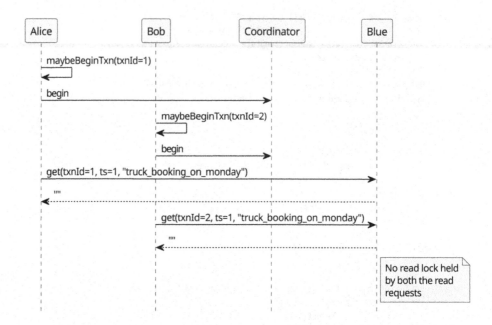

Figure 21.10 *Reads in snapshot isolation executed without read locks*

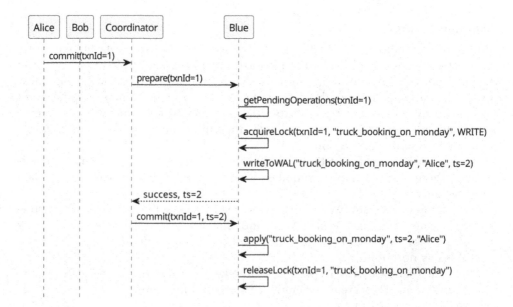

Figure 21.11 *Alice's update creates a new version.*

Now, Bob sends a write request to set the key truck_booking_on_monday. This creates a new version at timestamp 3 for the key, as shown in Figure 21.12.

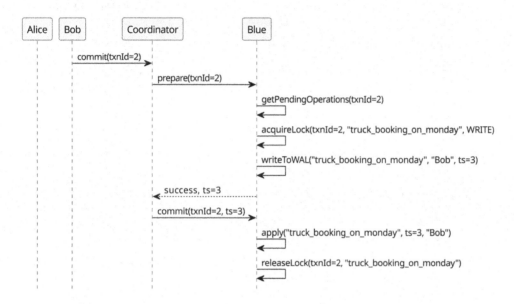

Figure 21.12   *Bob's update creates a new version.*

This is the problem of a lost update: Bob's booking overwrote Alice's booking. This happened because there was no way for Alice's transaction to know that a concurrent transaction from Bob has already read the booking value, and might have acted upon it.

> Snapshot isolation still can't avoid one particular anomaly called "write skew." So, if serializable transaction isolation is absolutely needed, a read-lock-based implementation should be used. Single-node databases, like PostgresSQL, implement a variation of snapshot isolation called serializable snapshot isolation [Cahill2009] which has no strict read locks and strikes the balance to avoid the write-skew anomaly without impacting the performance.

The snapshot isolation algorithm avoids most of anomalies, including lost updates, even when it does not hold locks while reading data. Distributed data stores Percolator [Peng2010], TiDB,[72] and Dgraph[73] implement snapshot isolation. The implementation works as follows.

- When a new transaction starts, it is assigned a new timestamp, higher than any previously committed timestamp, as its start timestamp.

- All the writes are buffered.

- All reads for that transaction happen with its start timestamp. When a key is read, the buffered value, or else a value committed before the start timestamp, is returned.

- When the client commits the transaction, it happens as a two-phase commit.

  - The prepare phase sends all the key values which are buffered to the respective servers for writing.

  - The server locks the keys which are about to be written.

  - The servers then check to see if any other transaction has updates for the same keys after the start timestamp of this transaction.

  - If the lock cannot be held, or the keys are updated after the start timestamp of the transaction, the server returns failure to the prepare request. The client can then roll back the transaction and restart.

  - If all the servers return success to the prepare request, the coordinator gets a new timestamp, called commit timestamp, which is higher than any previously assigned start or commit timestamp.

  - The request is sent to all the participant servers to write the values at the commit timestamp.

Timestamp Oracle

One of the key requirements of a snapshot isolation algorithm is that the start and the commit timestamps should be monotonic across all nodes in the cluster. Once a particular response is returned at a given timestamp, no write should happen at a lower timestamp than the one received in the read request. The system timestamp cannot be used because they are not monotonic, as discussed in the sidebar "Wall Clocks Are Not Monotonic" of the *Lease* pattern and clock values from two different servers should not be compared. A simple Lamport clock cannot be used as well because Lamport clock values are not totally ordered across a set of servers (refer to the section "Partial Order" of the *Lamport Clock* pattern). So a server initiating a transaction cannot assign a start timestamp based on its own Lamport clock value. To work around the issue with system timestamps,

---

72. https://www.pingcap.com
73. https://dgraph.io

Google Percolator and TiKV (inspired by Percolator) use a separate server, called timestamp oracle, which is guaranteed to give monotonic timestamps.

Each client communicates with the timestamp oracle service to get the start and commit transactions for the transaction. The timestamp oracle can become a single point of failure, so it is typically implemented with its own *Replicated Log*.

The above example, using the *Versioned Value*, will look as follows. The read requests won't hold lock even for the read-write transaction.

When the new transaction starts, the coordinator gets a new timestamp from the timestamp oracle (Figure 21.13).

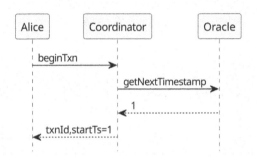

Figure 21.13   *Coordinator obtains a new timestamp using timestamp oracle.*

The read requests are sent with this timestamp. The server returns the value with the highest timestamp version below this timestamp. One subtle point to note here is that if there are pending write operations from a concurrent transaction, at a timestamp below the start timestamp, the read needs to be retried, because the pending operations might commit and should be visible to this read request (Figure 21.14).

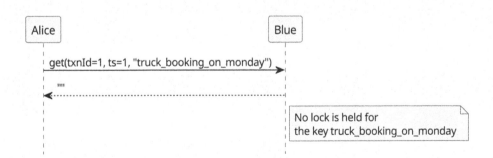

Figure 21.14   *Alice reads without acquiring a read lock.*

The write requests are buffered (Figure 21.15).

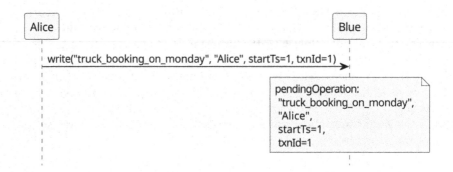

Figure 21.15 *Alice's updates are stored as pending writes.*

When client commits the transaction, it happens in two phases, just like the original example with Versioned Value. The prepare phase tries to lock the keys to be written and checks if the keys were updated after the start of this transaction (Figure 21.16).

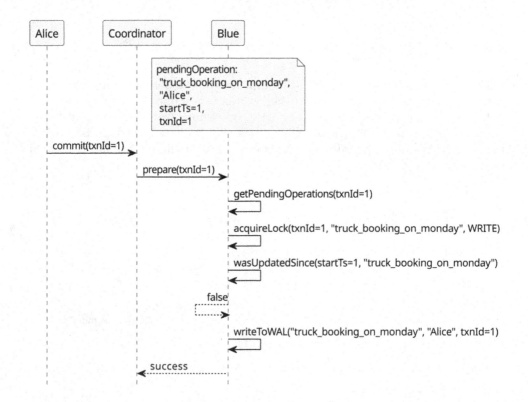

Figure 21.16 *The prepare request checks for writes since transaction start.*

Once the prepare phase returns a success, the coordinator asks for a new timestamp from the timestamp oracle. It then asks all the participants to commit the key-value records at the commit timestamp (Figure 21.17).

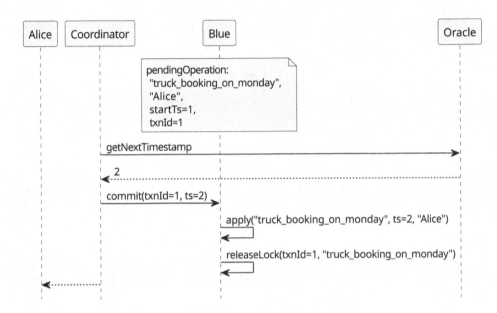

Figure 21.17 *The coordinator obtains the commit timestamp from the timestamp oracle.*

Let's look at the lost-update example with Bob's request above. Suppose Bob's transaction started after Alice's (Figure 21.18).

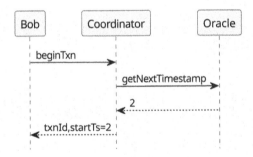

Figure 21.18 *Bob's transaction acquires a new start timestamp.*

At this point, if Alice commits the transaction, the commit timestamp will be 3.

When Bob tries to commit the transaction, the prepare phase will fail because it will detect that the key truck_booking_on_monday was updated after the start timestamp of Bob's transaction (Figure 21.19).

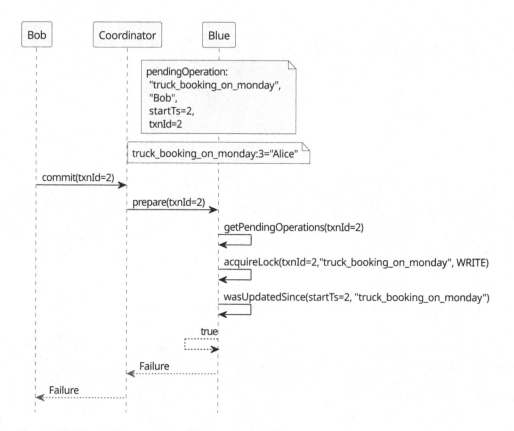

Figure 21.19   *Bob's transaction fails due to a conflict.*

Using Hybrid Clock

Databases such as MongoDB or CockroachDB use *Hybrid Clock* to guarantee monotonicity of transactions because every request will adjust the hybrid clock on each server to be the most up-to-date. The timestamp is also advanced monotonically with every write request. Finally, the commit phase picks up the maximum timestamp across the set of participating servers, making sure that the write will always follow a previous read request. *Clock-Bound Wait* is used to work around the uncertainty in timestamp ordering because of clock skew.

It is important to note that, if the client is reading at a timestamp value lower than the one at which server is writing to, it is not an issue. But if the client is reading at a timestamp while the server is about to write at that particular timestamp, then it is a problem. If a server detects that a client is reading at a timestamp for which the server might have in-flight writes (those being prepared), the server can either wait for the writes to complete or return an error, so that the client can restart the transaction. CockroachDB throws an error if a read happens at a timestamp for which there is an ongoing transaction. Google Spanner reads have a phase where the client gets the time of the last successful write on a particular partition. If a client reads at a higher timestamp, the read requests wait until the writes happen at that timestamp.

Using Replicated Log

To improve fault tolerance, cluster nodes use *Replicated Log*. The coordinator uses Replicated Log to store the transaction log entries.

For the example of Alice and Bob above, Blue and Green servers will be two groups of servers. All the booking data will be replicated across a set of servers. Each request which is part of the two-phase commit goes to the leader of the server group. The replication is implemented using Replicated Log.

The client communicates with the leader of each server group. The replication is necessary only when the client decides to commit the transaction, so it happens as part of the prepare request.

The coordinator replicates every state change to Replicated Log as well.

In a distributed data store, each cluster node handles multiple partitions. A Replicated Log is maintained per partition. When Raft is used as part of replication, it's sometimes referred to as Multi-Raft.[74]

Client communicates with the leader of each partition participating in the transaction.

Failure Handling

The two-phase commit protocol heavily relies on the coordinator node to communicate the outcome of the transaction. Until the outcome of the transaction is known, the individual cluster nodes cannot allow any other transactions to write to the keys participating in the pending transaction. The cluster nodes block until the outcome of the transaction is known. This puts some critical requirements on the coordinator.

The coordinator needs to remember the state of the transactions even in case of a process crash.

---

74. https://www.cockroachlabs.com/blog/scaling-raft

Coordinator uses *Write-Ahead Log* to record every update to the state of the transaction. This way, when the coordinator crashes and comes back up, it can continue to work on the transactions which are incomplete.

class TransactionCoordinator...

```java
public void loadTransactionsFromWAL() throws IOException {
    List<WALEntry> walEntries = this.transactionLog.readAll();
    for (WALEntry walEntry : walEntries) {
        var txnMetadata =
                (TransactionMetadata)
                        Command.deserialize(
                                new ByteArrayInputStream(
                                        walEntry.getData())));

        transactions.put(txnMetadata.getTxn(), txnMetadata);
    }
    startTransactionTimeoutScheduler();
    completePreparedTransactions();
}
private void completePreparedTransactions() throws IOException {
    var preparedTransactions
            = transactions
                .entrySet()
                .stream()
                .filter(entry -> entry.getValue().isPrepared())
            .collect(Collectors.toList());

    for (var preparedTransaction : preparedTransactions) {
        TransactionMetadata txnMetadata = preparedTransaction.getValue();
        sendCommitMessageToParticipants(txnMetadata.getTxn());
    }
}
```

The client can fail before sending the commit message to the coordinator.

The transaction coordinator tracks when each transaction state was updated. If no state update is received in a configured timeout period, it triggers a transaction rollback. To avoid getting rolled back unnecessarily, the client sends regular *HeartBeat* to the coordinator.

class TransactionCoordinator...

```java
private ScheduledThreadPoolExecutor scheduler = new ScheduledThreadPoolExecutor(1);
private ScheduledFuture<?> taskFuture;
private long transactionTimeoutMs = Long.MAX_VALUE; //for now.

public void startTransactionTimeoutScheduler() {
    taskFuture = scheduler.scheduleAtFixedRate(() -> timeoutTransactions(),
            transactionTimeoutMs,
            transactionTimeoutMs,
            TimeUnit.MILLISECONDS);
}
```

```
private void timeoutTransactions() {
    for (var txnRef : transactions.keySet()) {
        var transactionMetadata = transactions.get(txnRef);
        long now = systemClock.nanoTime();
        if (transactionMetadata.hasTimedOut(now)) {
            sendRollbackMessageToParticipants(transactionMetadata.getTxn());
            transactionMetadata.markRollbackComplete(transactionLog);
        }
    }
}
```

Transactional Intents

The key-value records that are written as part of the first phase need to be stored separately than the actual data exposed to other transactions. Data stores using existing key-value stores, such as RocksDB, instead of dealing with raw files, can use pending records themselves as locks. With some additional bookkeeping to figure out which server is acting as the coordinator, they can also be used to complete pending transactions. This is useful if the commit or rollback decision does not reach the individual servers participating in the transaction.

These provisional records are often referred to as "transactional intents." YugabyteDB, CockroachDB, and TiKV use transactional intents to implement two-phase commits.

To see how it works, consider Alice writing truck-booking-on-monday and backhoe_booking_on_monday to servers Blue and Green, respectively. Transaction begins by picking a coordinator. As discussed above, the coordinator is generally the server hosting the first key of the transaction. The coordinator records the new transaction and marks its state as pending (Figure 21.20).

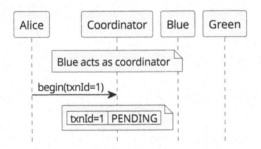

Figure 21.20 *Coordinator tracks transaction status.*

Alice then sends the write request to servers Blue and Green. The provisional records are created for both writes. The provisional records also contain the address of the server which is acting as a coordinator. Generally, the server address is not directly stored, but the first key which was used to determine the coordinator is stored. The server address can be determined from that key. In Figures 21.21 and 21.22, the server name is directly shown to simplify the explanation.

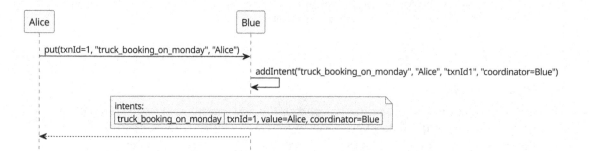

Figure 21.21   *The blue node adds pending writes as transactional intent.*

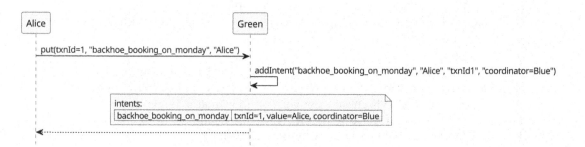

Figure 21.22   *The green node marks pending writes as transactional intent.*

When Alice decides to commit the transaction, she sends the commit request to the coordinator (Figure 21.23).

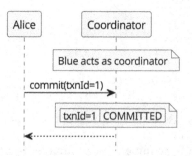

Figure 21.23   *Coordinator marks the transaction as committed.*

Once the coordinator successfully updates the status of the transaction, the client can send commit requests to Blue and Green for the keys truck_booking_on_monday and backhoe_booking_on_monday (Figure 21.24). The main advantage of having the provisional records with the details about the coordinator is that these commit requests can be sent asynchronously, without the client waiting for their results. It is fine even if the requests fail to reach the servers.

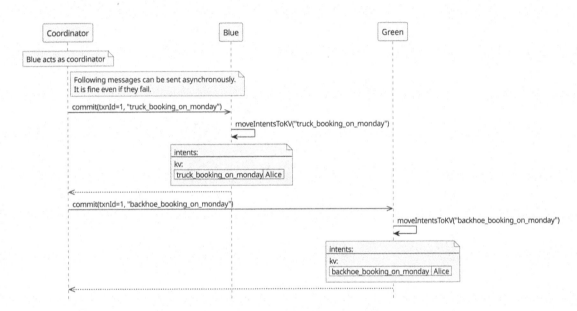

Figure 21.24 *Nodes apply transactional intents when committed.*

Let's see how intent records can be used as locks, and how they can recover pending transactions. Consider another user, Bob, reading the key backhoe_booking_on_monday from server Green while there is a pending intent record. Bob's request finds that there is a pending intent record for backhoe_booking_on_monday. It gets the transactionId and address of the server acting as the coordinator of this transaction.

It then sends a request to the coordinator to get the status of the transaction (Figure 21.25). If the transaction is committed or rolled back, the request handler commits or rolls back the transaction and removes the intent record. After this, Bob's request is resumed.

But if the transaction status is pending, then Bob is returned an error to indicate that there is a pending transaction. Bob has to retry (Figure 21.26).

This way, transaction intents act as locks and also allow resolving pending transactions even if the commit or rollback decision does not reach the servers participating in the two-phase commit execution.

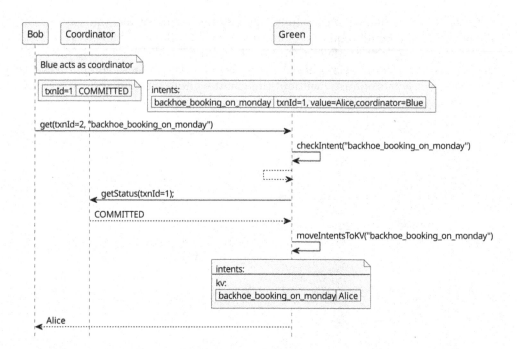

Figure 21.25   *Bob's request applies a committed transactional intent.*

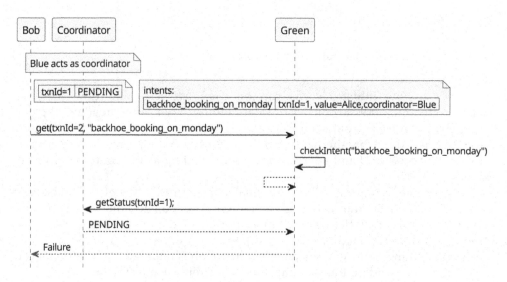

Figure 21.26   *Bob's request fails if the transaction status is pending.*

Transactions across Heterogeneous Systems

The solution outlined here demonstrates the two-phase commit implementation in a homogenous system. Homogenous means all the cluster nodes are part of the same system and store the same kind of data. Examples are a distributed data store like MongoDB or a distributed message broker like Kafka.

Historically, two-phase commit was mostly discussed in the context of heterogeneous systems. Most commonly, two-phase commits are used with XA [XA1991] transactions. In the J2EE servers, it is very common to use two-phase commits across a message broker and a database. The most common usage pattern is when a message needs to be produced on a message broker like ActiveMQ or JMS and a record needs to be inserted/updated in a database.

As we've seen in this chapter, the fault tolerance of the coordinator plays a critical role in a two-phase commit implementation. In case of XA transactions, the coordinator is an application process making the database and message broker calls. That application, in most modern scenarios, is a stateless microservice running in a containerized environment. It is not really a suitable place to put the responsibility of the coordinator. The coordinator needs to maintain state and recover quickly from failures to commit or roll back, which is difficult to implement in this case.

For this reason, while XA transactions seem attractive, they often run into issues in practice[75] and are best avoided. In the microservices world, patterns like transactional outbox[76] are preferred over XA transactions.

On the other hand, most distributed storage systems implement two-phase commits across a set of partitions, and it works well in practice.

Examples

- Distributed databases such as CockroachDB, MongoDB, and others implement two-phase commits to atomically store values across partitions.

- Apache Kafka allows producing messages across multiple partitions atomically with the implementation similar to two-phase commits.

---

75. https://docs.aws.amazon.com/amazon-mq/latest/developer-guide/recover-xa-transactions.html
76. https://microservices.io/patterns/data/transactional-outbox.html

Part IV

Patterns of Distributed Time

Servers often need to have some sense of temporal ordering to figure out which server holds the latest data and which has stale data. It might appear that we can use system timestamps to order a set of messages, but we cannot. The main reason we cannot use system clocks is that system clocks across servers are not guaranteed to be synchronized.

A time-of-the-day clock in a computer is managed by a quartz crystal and measures time based on the oscillations of the crystal. This mechanism is error-prone: Crystals can oscillate faster or slower, so different servers can have different times. The clocks across a set of servers are synchronized by a service called NTP. This service periodically checks a set of global time servers and adjusts the computer clock accordingly. Because this happens over the network, and network delays can vary, clock synchronization might be delayed because of a network issue. This can cause server clocks to drift away from each other. After the NTP sync happens, they can even move back in time. Because of these issues with computer clocks, time of day is generally not used for ordering events.

Even Google's TrueTime clock machinery built using GPS clocks has clock skew. However, that clock skew is guaranteed to be bounded by an upper bound. When the clock skew has guaranteed bounds, the system clock can be used by employing a technique called *Clock-Bound Wait*.

But when the clock skew is not bounded, which is almost always the case, distributed systems often use techniques commonly called a logical timestamp. In the following chapters, we will explore patterns for implementing logical timestamps.

Chapter 22

Lamport Clock

Use logical timestamps as a version for a value to allow ordering of values across servers.

Problem

When values are stored across multiple servers, there needs to be a way to know which values were stored before the other. The system timestamp cannot be used, because they are not monotonic, as discussed in the sidebar "Wall Clocks Are Not Monotonic" of the *Lease* pattern, and clock values from two different servers should not be compared.

The system timestamp, which represents the time of the day, is measured by clock machinery generally built with a crystal oscillator. The known problem with this mechanism is that it can drift away from the actual time of the day. To fix this, computers typically have a service such as NTP which synchronizes the computer clock with reference time sources on the Internet. Because of this, two consecutive readings of the system time on a given server can have time going backwards.

As there is no upper bound on clock drift across servers, it is impossible to compare timestamps on two different servers.

Solution

A Lamport clock maintains a single number to represent timestamps:

```
class LamportClock...

  public class LamportClock {
      int latestTime;
```

```
    public LamportClock(int timestamp) {
        latestTime = timestamp;
    }
```

Every cluster node maintains an instance of a Lamport clock.

class Server...

```
MVCCStore mvccStore;
LamportClock clock;

public Server(MVCCStore mvccStore) {
    this.clock = new LamportClock(1);
    this.mvccStore = mvccStore;
}
```

Whenever a server carries out any write operation, it should advance the Lamport clock using the tick() method:

class LamportClock...

```
public int tick(int requestTime) {
    latestTime = Integer.max(latestTime, requestTime);
    latestTime++;
    return latestTime;
}
```

This way, the server can be sure that the write is sequenced after the request and after any other action the server has carried out since the request was initiated by the client. The server returns the timestamp that was used for writing the value to the client. The requesting client then uses this timestamp to issue any further writes to the other set of servers. This way, the causal chain of requests is maintained.

Causality, Time, and Happens-Before

When an event A in a system happens before another event B, they might have a causal relationship. Causal relationship means that A might have some role in causing B. This "A happens before B" relationship is established by attaching a timestamp to each event. If A happens before B, the timestamp of A will be lower than the timestamp of B. But because we cannot rely on system time, we need some way to make sure that the happens-before relationship is maintained for the timestamp attached to the events. Leslie Lamport, in his seminal paper "Time, Clocks, and the Ordering of Events in a Distributed System" [Lamport1978], suggested a solution to use logical timestamps to track happens-before relationships. So this technique of using logical timestamps to track causality is called the Lamport timestamp.

In a database, events are about storing data. So Lamport timestamps are attached to the values stored. This also fits very well with the versioned storage mechanism discussed in *Versioned Value*.

An Example Key-Value Store

Consider an example of a simple key-value store with multiple server nodes, shown in Figure 22.1. There are two servers, Blue and Green. Each server is responsible for storing a specific set of keys. This is a typical scenario when data is partitioned across a set of servers. Values are stored as *Versioned Value* with the Lamport timestamp as a version number.

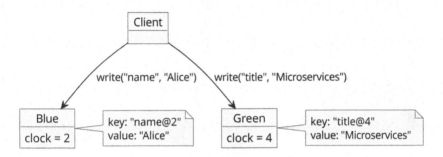

Figure 22.1 *Two servers, each responsible for specific keys*

The receiving server compares, updates its own timestamp, and uses it to write a versioned key value.

class Server...

```
public int write(String key, String value, int requestTimestamp) {
    //update own clock to reflect causality
    int writeAtTimestamp = clock.tick(requestTimestamp);
    mvccStore.put(new VersionedKey(key, writeAtTimestamp), value);
    return writeAtTimestamp;
}
```

The timestamp used for writing the value is returned to the client. The client keeps track of the maximum timestamp by updating its own timestamp. It uses this timestamp to issue any further writes.

class Client...

```
LamportClock clock = new LamportClock(1);
public void write() {
    int server1WrittenAt
            = server1.write("name",
            "Alice", clock.getLatestTime());
```

```
        clock.updateTo(server1WrittenAt);

        int server2WrittenAt
                = server2.write("title", "Microservices", clock.getLatestTime());
        clock.updateTo(server2WrittenAt);

        assertTrue(server2WrittenAt > server1WrittenAt);
    }
```

The sequence of requests is shown in Figure 22.2.

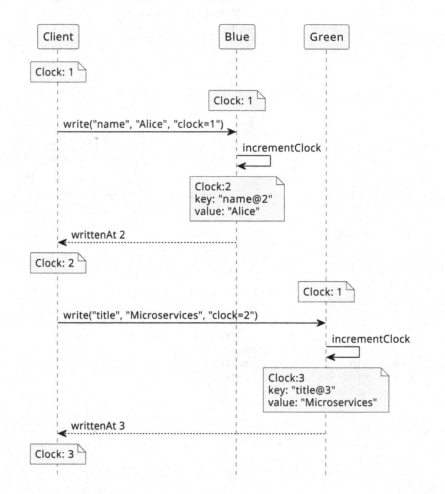

Figure 22.2   *Lamport clock tracks order of writes.*

The same technique works even when the client is communicating with leaders of *Leader and Followers* groups, with each group responsible for specific keys. The client sends requests to the leader of the group as detailed above. The Lamport clock instance is maintained by the leader of the group and is updated exactly the same way as discussed in the previous section (Figure 22.3).

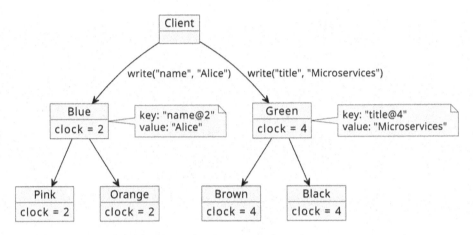

Figure 22.3 *Different leader-follower groups storing different key values*

Partial Order

The values stored by a Lamport clock are only partially ordered. If two clients store values in two separate servers, the timestamp values cannot be used to order the values across servers. In the following example, the "title" stored by Bob on server Green is at timestamp 2. But it cannot be determined if Bob stored the "title" before or after Alice stored the "name" on server Blue (Figure 22.4).

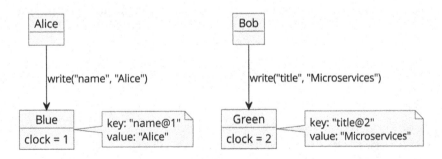

Figure 22.4 *Partial order*

A Single Leader Server Updating Values

For a single leader-follower group of servers, where a leader is always responsible for storing values, the basic implementation discussed in *Versioned Value* is enough to maintain causality (Figure 22.5).

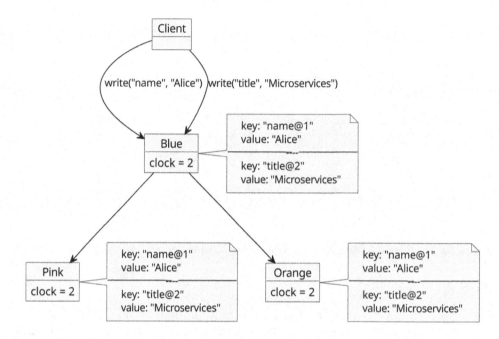

Figure 22.5 *Single leader-follower group saving key values*

In this case, the key-value store keeps an integer version counter. It increments the version counter every time the key-value write command is applied from the write-ahead log. It then constructs the new key with the incremented version counter. The leader and followers increment the version counter when applying the commands, as discussed in the *Replicated Log* pattern.

```
class ReplicatedKVStore...

    int version = 0;
    MVCCStore mvccStore = new MVCCStore();

    @Override
    public CompletableFuture<Response> put(String key, String value) {
        return replicatedLog.propose(new SetValueCommand(key, value));
    }
```

```
private Response applySetValueCommand(SetValueCommand setValueCommand) {
    version = version + 1;
    mvccStore.put(new VersionedKey(setValueCommand.getKey(), version),
            setValueCommand.getValue());
    Response response = Response.success(RequestId.SetValueResponse, version);
    return response;
}
```

Examples

- Databases such as MongoDB and CockroachDB use variants of the Lamport clock to implement MVCC storage.

- *Generation Clock* is an example of a Lamport clock.

Chapter 23

Hybrid Clock

Use a combination of system timestamp and logical timestamp to have versions as date and time, which can be ordered.

Problem

When *Lamport Clock* is used as a version in *Versioned Value*, clients do not know the actual date-time when the particular versions are stored. It's more convenient for clients to access versions using date and time like 01–01–2020 instead of an integer like 1, 2, 3.

Solution

Hybrid logical clock [Demirbas2014] provides a way to have a version which is monotonically increasing just like a simple integer, but also has relation to the actual date and time. Hybrid clocks are used in practice by databases like MongoDB[77] or CockroachDB.[78]

A hybrid logical clock is implemented as follows:

```
class HybridClock...

  public class HybridClock {
      private final SystemClock systemClock;
      private HybridTimestamp latestTime;
      public HybridClock(SystemClock systemClock) {
          this.systemClock = systemClock;
```

---

77. https://www.mongodb.com/blog/post/transactions-background-part-4-the-global-logical-clock
78. https://www.cockroachlabs.com/docs/stable/architecture/transaction-layer.html

```
                this.latestTime = new HybridTimestamp(systemClock.now(), 0);
        }
```

It maintains the latest time as an instance of the hybrid timestamp, which is constructed from the system time and an integer counter.

```
class HybridTimestamp...

  public class HybridTimestamp implements Comparable<HybridTimestamp> {
      private final long wallClockTime;
      private final int ticks;

      public HybridTimestamp(long systemTime, int ticks) {
          this.wallClockTime = systemTime;
          this.ticks = ticks;
      }

      public static HybridTimestamp fromSystemTime(long systemTime) {
          //initializing with -1 so that addTicks resets it to 0
          return new HybridTimestamp(systemTime, -1);
      }

      public HybridTimestamp max(HybridTimestamp other) {
          if (this.getWallClockTime() == other.getWallClockTime()) {
              return this.getTicks() > other.getTicks()? this:other;
          }
          return this.getWallClockTime() > other.getWallClockTime()?this:other;
      }

      public long getWallClockTime() {
          return wallClockTime;
      }

      public HybridTimestamp addTicks(int ticks) {
          return new HybridTimestamp(wallClockTime, this.ticks + ticks);
      }

      public int getTicks() {
          return ticks;
      }

      @Override
      public int compareTo(HybridTimestamp other) {
          if (this.wallClockTime == other.wallClockTime) {
              return Integer.compare(this.ticks, other.ticks);
          }
          return Long.compare(this.wallClockTime, other.wallClockTime);
      }
  }
```

Hybrid clocks can be used exactly the same way as the Lamport Clock versions. Every server holds an instance of a hybrid clock.

```
class Server...

    HybridClockMVCCStore mvccStore;
    HybridClock clock;

    public Server(HybridClockMVCCStore mvccStore) {
        this.clock = new HybridClock(new SystemClock());
        this.mvccStore = mvccStore;
    }
```

Every time a value is written, a hybrid timestamp is associated with it. The trick is to detect if the system time value is going back in time. If it does, we increment another number representing a logical part of the component to reflect clock progress.

```
class HybridClock...

    public synchronized HybridTimestamp now() {
        long currentTimeMillis = systemClock.now();
        if (latestTime.getWallClockTime() >= currentTimeMillis) {
            latestTime = latestTime.addTicks(1);
        } else {
            latestTime = new HybridTimestamp(currentTimeMillis, 0);
        }
        return latestTime;
    }
```

Every write request that a server receives from the client carries a timestamp. The receiving server compares its own timestamp to that of the request and sets its own timestamp to the higher of the two.

```
class Server...

    public HybridTimestamp write(String key, String value,
                                 HybridTimestamp requestTimestamp) {
        //update own clock to reflect causality
        var writeAtTimestamp = clock.tick(requestTimestamp);
        mvccStore.put(key, writeAtTimestamp, value);
        return writeAtTimestamp;
    }
```

```
class HybridClock...

    public synchronized HybridTimestamp tick(HybridTimestamp requestTime) {
        long nowMillis = systemClock.now();
        //set ticks to -1, so that, if this is the max,
        // the next addTicks resets it to zero.
        HybridTimestamp now = HybridTimestamp.fromSystemTime(nowMillis);
        latestTime = max(now, requestTime, latestTime);
        latestTime = latestTime.addTicks(1);
        return latestTime;
    }
```

```
private HybridTimestamp max(HybridTimestamp ...times) {
    HybridTimestamp maxTime = times[0];
    for (int i = 1; i < times.length; i++) {
        maxTime = maxTime.max(times[i]);
    }
    return maxTime;
}
```

The timestamp used for writing the value is returned to the client. The requesting client updates its own timestamp and then uses this timestamp to issue any further writes.

class Client...

```
HybridClock clock = new HybridClock(new SystemClock());
public void write() {
    HybridTimestamp server1WrittenAt = server1
            .write("name", "Alice", clock.now());
    clock.tick(server1WrittenAt);

    HybridTimestamp server2WrittenAt = server2
            .write("title", "Microservices", clock.now());

    assertTrue(server2WrittenAt
                            .compareTo(server1WrittenAt) > 0);
}
```

Multiversion Storage with Hybrid Clock

A hybrid timestamp can be used as a version when the value is stored in a key-value store. The values are stored as discussed in *Versioned Value*.

class HybridClockReplicatedKVStore...

```
private Response applySetValueCommand(
                    VersionedSetValueCommand setValueCommand) {

    mvccStore.put(setValueCommand.getKey(), setValueCommand.timestamp,
        setValueCommand.value);

    Response response =
            Response.success(RequestId.SetValueResponse,
                    setValueCommand.timestamp);
    return response;
}
```

class HybridClockMVCCStore...

```
ConcurrentSkipListMap<HybridClockKey, String> kv
        = new ConcurrentSkipListMap<>();

public void put(String key, HybridTimestamp version, String value) {
    kv.put(new HybridClockKey(key, version), value);
}
```

class HybridClockKey...

```
public class HybridClockKey implements Comparable<HybridClockKey> {
    private String key;
    private HybridTimestamp version;

    public HybridClockKey(String key, HybridTimestamp version) {
        this.key = key;
        this.version = version;
    }

    public String getKey() {
        return key;
    }

    public HybridTimestamp getVersion() {
        return version;
    }

    @Override
    public int compareTo(HybridClockKey o) {
        int keyCompare = this.key.compareTo(o.key);
        if (keyCompare == 0) {
            return this.version.compareTo(o.version);
        }
        return keyCompare;
    }
}
```

The values are read exactly as discussed in the section "Ordering of Versioned Keys" of the *Versioned Value* pattern. The versioned keys are arranged in such a way as to form a natural ordering by using hybrid timestamps as a suffix to the key. This implementation enables us to get values for a specific version using the navigable map API.

class HybridClockMVCCStore...

```
public Optional<String> get(String key, HybridTimestamp atTimestamp) {
    var versionEntry = kv.floorEntry(new HybridClockKey(key, atTimestamp));
    return Optional.ofNullable(versionEntry)
            .filter(entry -> entry.getKey().getKey().equals(key))
            .map(entry -> entry.getValue());
}
```

Using Timestamp to Read Values

Storing values with hybrid timestamp allows users to read using system timestamps in the past. For example, CockroachDB allows executing queries with "AS OF SYSTEM TIME" clause to specify date and time like "2016-10-03 12:45:00". The values can be easily read as following:

```
class HybridClockMVCCStore...

  public Optional<String> getAtSystemTime(String key,
                                String asOfSystemTimeClause) {
    long time = Utils.parseDateTime(asOfSystemTimeClause);
    HybridTimestamp atTimestamp = new HybridTimestamp(time, 0);
    return get(key, atTimestamp);
  }
```

Assigning Timestamp to Distributed Transactions

Databases like MongoDB and CockroachDB use a *Hybrid Clock* to maintain causality with distributed transactions. With distributed transactions, it's important to note that all the values stored as part of the transaction should be stored at the same timestamp across the servers when the transaction commits. The requesting server might know about a higher timestamp in later write requests. It commits the transaction with the highest known timestamp. This fits very well with the standard *Two-Phase Commit* protocol for implementing transactions.

Figure 23.1 shows an example of how the highest timestamp is determined at transaction commit. Assume that there are three servers: Blue stores names, Green stores titles, and a separate server acts as a coordinator. As can be seen, each server has a different local clock value. This can be a single integer or hybrid clock. The server acting as a coordinator starts writing to server Blue with the clock value known to it, which is 1. But Blue's clock is at 2, so it increments that and writes the value at timestamp 3. Timestamp 3 is returned to the coordinator in the response. For all subsequent requests to other servers, the coordinator uses the timestamp of 3. Green receives the timestamp value 3 in the request, but its own clock is at 4. So it picks the highest value, which is 4, increments it, and writes the value at 5 and returns timestamp 5 to the coordinator. When the transaction commits, the coordinator uses the highest timestamp it received to commit the transaction. All the values updated in the transaction will be stored at this highest timestamp.

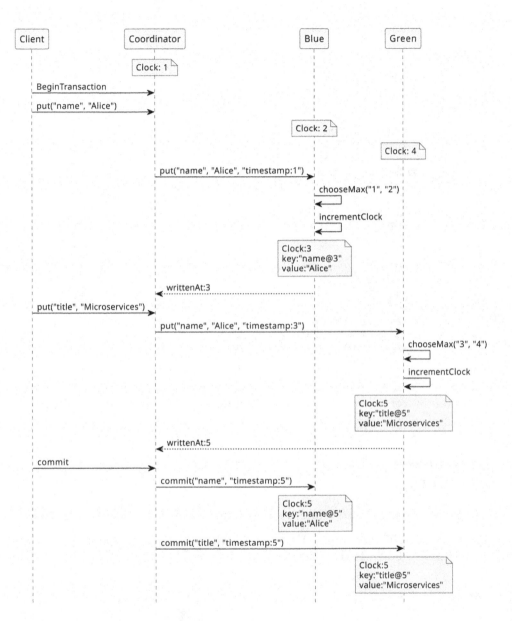

Figure 23.1 *Propagating commit timestamp across servers*

A very simplified code for timestamp handling with transactions looks like this:

```
class TransactionCoordinator...

  public Transaction beginTransaction() {
      return new Transaction(UUID.randomUUID().toString());
  }

  public void putTransactionally() {
      Transaction txn = beginTransaction();
      var coordinatorTime = new HybridTimestamp(1);
      var server1WriteTime = server1.write("name", "Alice",
                                          coordinatorTime, txn);

      var server2WriteTime
            = server2.write("title", "Microservices",
                              server1WriteTime, txn);

      var commitTimestamp = server1WriteTime.max(server2WriteTime);
      commit(txn, commitTimestamp);
  }

  private void commit(Transaction txn, HybridTimestamp commitTimestamp) {
      server1.commitTxn("name", commitTimestamp, txn);
      server2.commitTxn("title", commitTimestamp, txn);
  }
```

Transaction implementation can also use the prepare phase of the Two-Phase Commit protocol to learn about the highest timestamp used by each participating server.

Examples

- MongoDB uses hybrid timestamp to maintain versions in its MVCC storage.

- CockroachDB and YugabyteDB use hybrid timestamp to maintain causality with distributed transactions.

Chapter 24

Clock-Bound Wait

Wait to cover the uncertainty in time across cluster nodes before reading and writing values so that values can be correctly ordered across cluster nodes.

Problem

Both Alice and Bob can ask server Green for the latest version timestamp of the key they are trying to read. But that requires one extra round.

If Alice and Bob are trying to read multiple keys across a set of servers, they will need to ask the latest version for each and pick the maximum value.

Consider a key-value store where values are stored with a timestamp to designate each version. Any cluster node that handles a client request will be able to read the latest version using the current timestamp at the request processing node.

In Figure 24.1, the value "Before Dawn" is updated to value "After Dawn" at time 2 as per Green's clock. Both Alice and Bob are trying to read the latest value for "title". While Alice's request is processed by cluster node Amber, Bob's request is processed by cluster node Blue. Amber has its clock lagging at 1, which means that when Alice reads the latest value, it delivers the value "Before Dawn". Blue has its clock at 2, so when Bob reads the latest value, it returns the value as "After Dawn".

This violates what is known as external consistency. If Alice and Bob now make a phone call, Alice will be confused: Bob will tell her that the latest value is "After Dawn", while her cluster node is showing "Before Dawn".

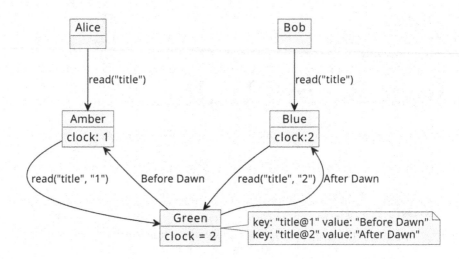

Figure 24.1 *Clock skew leads to different readings by two users.*

The same is true if Green's clock is fast and the writes happen in the future as per Amber's clock.

This is a problem if system timestamp is used as a version for storing values, because system timestamps are not monotonic, as discussed in the sidebar "Wall Clocks Are Not Monotonic" of the *Lease* pattern. Clock values from two different servers cannot and should not be compared. When *Hybrid Clock* is used as a version in *Versioned Value*, it allows values to be ordered on a single server as well as on different servers which are causally related. However, hybrid clocks (or any other kind of *Lamport Clock*) can only give partial order, as discussed in the section "Partial Order" of the Lamport Clock pattern. This means that any values which are not causally related and are stored by two different clients across different nodes cannot be ordered. This creates a problem when using a timestamp to read values across cluster nodes. If the read request originates on cluster nodes with lagging clocks, it probably won't be able to read the most up-to-date versions of given values.

Solution

While reading or writing, cluster nodes wait until the clock values on every node in the cluster are guaranteed to be above the timestamp assigned to the value.

If the difference between clocks is very small, write requests can wait without adding a great deal of overhead. As an example, assume the maximum clock offset across cluster nodes is 10 ms. (This means that, at any given point in time, the slowest clock in the cluster is lagging behind the fastest one by at most 10 ms.) To guarantee that every other cluster node has its clock past time t, the cluster node that handles any write operation will have to wait until $t + 10$ ms before storing the value.

Consider a key-value store with Versioned Value where each update is added as a new value, with a timestamp used as a version. In the Alice and Bob example described above, the write operation storing title@2 will wait until all the clocks in the cluster are at 2. This makes sure that Alice will always see the latest value of the "title" even if the clock at the cluster node of Alice is lagging behind.

Consider a slightly different scenario. Philip is updating the "title" to "After Dawn". Green's clock has its time at 2. But Green knows that there might be a server with a clock lagging behind by up to 1 unit. It will therefore have to wait in the write operation for a duration of 1 unit (Figure 24.2).

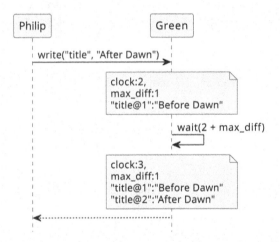

Figure 24.2 *Write request waits for clock offset.*

While Philip is updating the "title", Bob's read request is handled by server Blue. Blue's clock is at 2, so it tries to read the "title" at timestamp 2. At this point Green has not yet made the value available. This means Bob gets the value at the highest timestamp lower than 2, which is "Before Dawn" (Figure 24.3).

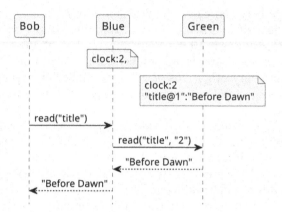

Figure 24.3 *Bob reads the initial value.*

Alice's read request is handled by server Amber. Amber's clock is at 1 so it tries to read the "title" at timestamp 1. Alice gets the value "Before Dawn" (Figure 24.4).

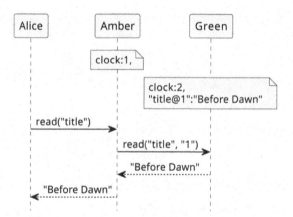

Figure 24.4 *Alice reads the initial value.*

Once Philip's write request completes (after the wait of max_diff is over), if Bob now sends a new read request, server Blue will try to read the latest value according to its clock (which has advanced to 3); this will return the value "After Dawn" (Figure 24.5).

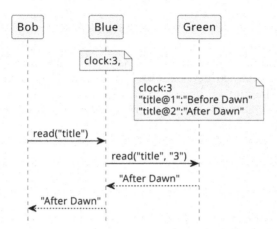

Figure 24.5 *Bob reads the new value.*

If Alice initializes a new read request, server Amber will try to read the latest value as per its clock, which is now at 2. It will therefore also return the value "After Dawn" (Figure 24.6).

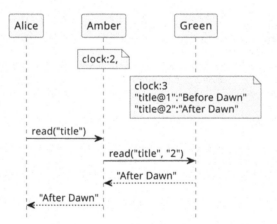

Figure 24.6 *Alice reads the new value.*

The main problem when trying to implement this solution is that getting the exact time difference across cluster nodes is simply not possible with the date/time hardware and operating system APIs that are currently available. Such is the nature of the challenge that Google has its own specialized date-time API called

TrueTime. Similarly, Amazon has AWS Time Sync Service[79] and a library called Clock Bound.[80] However, these APIs are very specific to Google and Amazon—they can't be scaled beyond the confines of those organizations.

Typically, key-value stores use Hybrid Clock to implement Versioned Value. While it is not possible to get the exact difference between clocks, a sensible default value can be chosen based on historical observations. Observed values for maximum clock drift on servers across datacenters are generally between 200 ms and 500 ms.[81]

The key-value store waits for configured max offset before storing the value:

```
class KVStore...

  int maxOffset = 200;
  NavigableMap<HybridClockKey, String> kv = new ConcurrentSkipListMap<>();
  public void put(String key, String value) {
      HybridTimestamp writeTimestamp = clock.now();
      waitTillSlowestClockCatchesUp(writeTimestamp);
      kv.put(new HybridClockKey(key, writeTimestamp), value);
  }

  private void waitTillSlowestClockCatchesUp(HybridTimestamp writeTimestamp) {
      var waitUntilTimestamp = writeTimestamp.add(maxOffset, 0);
      sleepUntil(waitUntilTimestamp);
  }

  private void sleepUntil(HybridTimestamp waitUntil) {
      HybridTimestamp now = clock.now();
      while (clock.now().before(waitUntil)) {
          var waitTime = (waitUntil.getWallClockTime() - now.getWallClockTime()) ;
          Uninterruptibles.sleepUninterruptibly(waitTime, TimeUnit.MILLISECONDS);
          now = clock.now();
      }
  }

  public String get(String key, HybridTimestamp readTimestamp) {
      return kv.get(new HybridClockKey(key, readTimestamp));
  }
```

Read Restart

To wait 200 ms for every write request may be too much of an interval. This is why databases like CockroachDB or YugabyteDB implement a check in the read requests instead.

---

79. https://aws.amazon.com/about-aws/whats-new/2021/11/amazon-time-sync-service-generate-compare-timestamps
80. https://github.com/aws/clock-bound
81. https://www.yugabyte.com/blog/evolving-clock-sync-for-distributed-databases/

While serving a read request, cluster nodes check if there is a version available in the interval between readTimestamp and readTimestamp + maximum clock drift. If the version is available, the system assumes that the reader's clock might be lagging, and asks it to restart the read request with that version:

class KVStore...

```
public void put(String key, String value) {
    HybridTimestamp writeTimestamp = clock.now();
    kv.put(new HybridClockKey(key, writeTimestamp), value);
}

public String get(String key, HybridTimestamp readTimestamp) {
    checksIfVersionInUncertaintyInterval(key, readTimestamp);
    return kv.floorEntry(new HybridClockKey(key, readTimestamp)).getValue();
}

private void checksIfVersionInUncertaintyInterval(String key,
                                     HybridTimestamp readTimestamp) {
    var uncertaintyLimit = readTimestamp.add(maxOffset, 0);
    var versionedKey = kv.floorKey(new HybridClockKey(key,
            uncertaintyLimit));
    if (versionedKey == null) {
        return;
    }
    var maxVersionBelowUncertainty = versionedKey.getVersion();
    if (maxVersionBelowUncertainty.after(readTimestamp)) {
        throw new ReadRestartException(readTimestamp,
                maxOffset,
                maxVersionBelowUncertainty);
    }
    ;
}
```

class Client...

```
String read(String key) {
    int attemptNo = 1;
    int maxAttempts = 5;
    while(attemptNo < maxAttempts) {
        try {
            HybridTimestamp now = clock.now();
            return kvStore.get(key, now);
        } catch (ReadRestartException e) {
            logger.info(" Got read restart error " + e + "Attempt No. " + attemptNo);
            Uninterruptibles
                    .sleepUninterruptibly(e.getMaxOffset(), TimeUnit.MILLISECONDS);
            attemptNo++;
        }
    }
    throw new ReadTimeoutException("Unable to read after " + attemptNo + " attempts.");
}
```

In the Alice and Bob example above, if there is a version for "title" available at timestamp 2, and Alice sends a read request with read timestamp 1, a `ReadRestartException` will be thrown asking Alice to restart the read request at timestamp 2 (Figure 24.7).

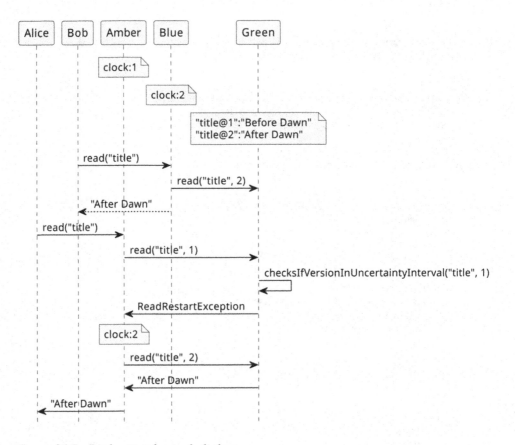

Figure 24.7 *Read restart due to clock skew*

Read restarts only happen if there is a version written in the uncertainty interval. Write requests do not need to wait.

It's important to remember that the configured value for maximum clock drift is an assumption, not a guarantee. A bad server can have a clock drift more than the assumed value. In such cases, the problem will persist.[82]

---

82. https://docs.yugabyte.com/latest/benchmark/resilience/jepsen-testing-ysql/#rare-occurrence-of-causal-reversal

Using Clock-Bound APIs

Cloud providers such as Google and Amazon implement clock machinery with atomic clocks and GPS to make sure that the clock drift across their cluster nodes is kept below a few milliseconds. As we've just discussed, Google has TrueTime; AWS has Time Sync Service and Clock Bound library.

There are two key requirements for cluster nodes to make sure these waits are implemented correctly.

- The clock drift across cluster nodes is kept to a minimum. Google's TrueTime keeps it below 1 ms in most cases, 7 ms in the worst cases.

- The possible clock drift is always available in the Date-Time API, so programmers don't need to guess the value.

The clock machinery on cluster nodes computes error bounds for date-time values. If there is a possible error in timestamps returned by the local system clock, the API makes the error explicit. It will give the lower and upper bounds on clock values. The real time value is guaranteed to be within this interval and the time span between the lower and upper bounds defines the uncertainty interval.

```
public class ClockBound {
    public final long earliest;
    public final long latest;

    public ClockBound(long earliest, long latest) {
        this.earliest = earliest;
        this.latest = latest;
    }

    public boolean before(long timestamp) {
        return timestamp < earliest;
    }

    public boolean after(long timestamp)   {
        return timestamp > latest;
    }
}
```

As explained in AWS blog,[83] the error is calculated at each cluster node as ClockErrorBound. The real time value will always be within ClockErrorBound from the local clock time.

---

83. https://aws.amazon.com/blogs/mt/manage-amazon-ec2-instance-clock-accuracy-using-amazon-time-sync-service-and-amazon-cloudwatch-part-1

The error bounds are returned whenever date and time values are asked for.

```
public ClockBound now() {
    return now;
}
```

There are two properties guaranteed by the Clock-Bound API:

▪ Clock bounds should overlap across cluster nodes.

▪ For two time values t1 and t2, if t1 is less than t2, then clock_bound(t1).earliest is less than clock_bound(t2).latest across all cluster nodes.

Imagine we have three cluster nodes: Green, Blue, and Amber. Each node might have a different error bound. Let's say the error on Green is 1, on Blue, 2, and on Amber, 3. Figure 24.8 shows the clock bounds across the cluster nodes at time = 4.

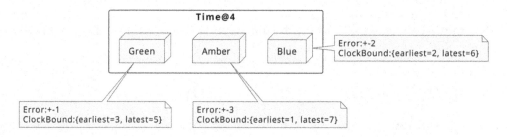

Figure 24.8 *Clock bounds across cluster nodes*

In this scenario, two rules need to be followed to implement the commit-wait.

▪ For any write operation, the clock bound's latest value should be picked as the timestamp. This will ensure that it is always higher than any timestamp assigned to previous write operations (considering the second rule below).

▪ Before storing the value, the system must wait until the write timestamp is less than the clock bound's earliest value.

This is because the earliest value is guaranteed to be lower than clock bounds' latest values across all cluster nodes. This write operation will be accessible to anyone reading with the clock-bound's latest value in the future. Also, this value is guaranteed to be ordered before any other write operation that may happen in the future.

class KVStore...

```
public void put(String key, String value) {
    ClockBound now = boundedClock.now();
```

```
        long writeTimestamp = now.latest;
        addPending(writeTimestamp);
        waitUntilTimeInPast(writeTimestamp);
        kv.put(new VersionedKey(key, writeTimestamp), value);
        removePending(writeTimestamp);
    }

    private void waitUntilTimeInPast(long writeTimestamp) {
        ClockBound now = boundedClock.now();
        while(now.earliest < writeTimestamp) {
            Uninterruptibles
                    .sleepUninterruptibly(now.earliest - writeTimestamp,
                        TimeUnit.MILLISECONDS);
            now = boundedClock.now();
        }
    }

    private void removePending(long writeTimestamp) {
        try {
            lock.lock();
            pendingWriteTimestamps.remove(writeTimestamp);

            //Signal to any waiting read requests.
            cond.signalAll();
        } finally {
            lock.unlock();
        }
    }

    private void addPending(long writeTimestamp) {
        try {
            lock.lock();
            pendingWriteTimestamps.add(writeTimestamp);
        } finally {
            lock.unlock();
        }
    }
```

To return to the Alice and Bob example above, when the new value for "title", "After Dawn", is written by Philip on server Green, the put operation on Green waits until the chosen write timestamp is below the earliest value of the clock bound. This guarantees that every other cluster node has a higher timestamp for the latest value of the clock bound. Figure 24.9 illustrates the following scenario. Green has an error bound of ± 1. So, with a put operation that starts at time 4 when it stores the value, Green will pick the latest value of the clock bound, which is 5. It then waits until the earliest value of the clock bound is above 5. Essentially, Green waits for the uncertainty interval before actually storing the value in the key-value store.

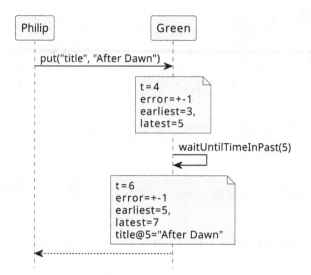

Figure 24.9 *Writes wait to cover the uncertainty interval.*

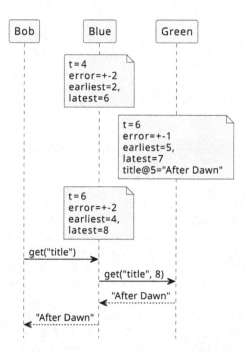

Figure 24.10 *Bob reads the new value following the uncertainty interval.*

When the value is made available in the key-value store, the clock bound's latest value is guaranteed to be higher than 5 on each and every cluster node. This means that Bob's request handled by Blue (Figure 24.10), as well as Alice's request handled by Amber (Figure 24.11), are guaranteed to get the latest value of the "title".

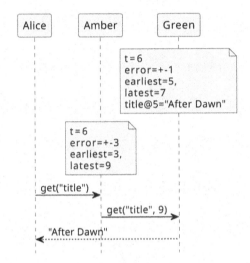

Figure 24.11   *Alice reads the new value following the uncertainty interval.*

We achieve the same outcome if Green has larger error bounds (Figure 24.12). A larger error bound results in a longer waiting period. Let's consider an error bound of ± 3. For a write occurring at time 4 on server Green, the clock bound values are (1, 7). The write timestamp is chosen as 7, and the write operation waits until the earliest clock bound value on Green exceeds 7. Neither Amber nor Blue can access the value before this point. Now, let's say Alice's read request is handled by Amber, which has an error bound of ± 2. Alice receives the latest value only when Amber can use a read timestamp of 7. At this juncture, every other cluster node is guaranteed to receive it at their respective server's clock bound's latest time value.

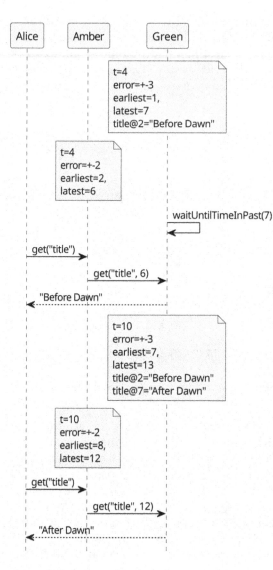

Figure 24.12   *Larger error bound causes longer wait.*

Read-Wait

When reading the value, the client will always pick the maximum value from the clock bound on its cluster node.

The cluster node that is receiving the request needs to make sure that once a response is returned at a specific request timestamp, there are no values written at that timestamp or a lower timestamp.

If the timestamp in the request is higher than the timestamp at the server, the cluster node will wait until the clock catches up before returning the response.

It will then check if there are any pending write requests at a lower timestamp which are not yet stored. If there are, then the read requests will pause until the requests are complete.

The server will then read the values at the request timestamp and return the value. This ensures that once a response is returned at a particular timestamp, no values will ever be written at a lower timestamp.

class KVStore...

```
final Lock lock = new ReentrantLock();
Queue<Long> pendingWriteTimestamps = new ArrayDeque<>();
final Condition cond  = lock.newCondition();

public Optional<String> read(long readTimestamp) {
    waitUntilTimeInPast(readTimestamp);
    waitForPendingWrites(readTimestamp);
    Optional<VersionedKey> max = kv.keySet().stream().max(Comparator.naturalOrder());
    if(max.isPresent()) {
        return Optional.of(kv.get(max.get()));
    }
    return Optional.empty();
}

private void waitForPendingWrites(long readTimestamp) {
    try {
        lock.lock();
        while (pendingWriteTimestamps
                .stream()
                .anyMatch(ts -> ts <= readTimestamp)) {

            cond.awaitUninterruptibly();
        }
    } finally {
        lock.unlock();
    }
}
```

As a final example shown in Figure 24.13, if Alice's read request at time 4 is handled by server Amber with an error bound interval of 3, it picks the latest time as 7 to read the "title". Meanwhile, Philip's write request is handled by Green with an error bound interval of 1, which picks 5 as the timestamp to store the value. Alice's read request waits until the earliest time at Green is past 7 and the pending write request is complete. It then returns the latest value with a timestamp below 7.

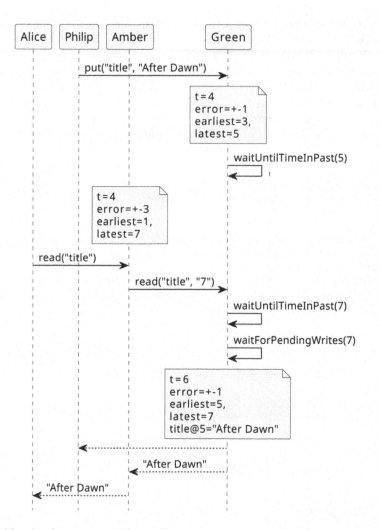

Figure 24.13   *Read requests wait for pending writes.*

Examples

- Google's TrueTime API provides a clock bound. Google Spanner uses it to implement commit-wait.

- AWS Time Sync Service ensures minimal clock drifts. It is possible to use the Clock Bound library[84] to implement waits to order the events across the cluster.

- CockroachDB implements read restart. It also has an experimental option to use commit-wait based on the configured maximum clock drift value.

- YugabyteDB implements read restart based on the configured maximum clock drift value.

---

84. https://github.com/aws/clock-bound

Part V

Patterns of Cluster Management

In a distributed system with multiple servers, it is essential to have a mechanism for managing server membership, detecting failures, and making decisions regarding data distribution. Moreover, this metadata must be stored in a fault-tolerant manner and accessible to clients.

In the following chapters, we will explore patterns that address these challenges, providing effective solutions for managing server clusters and ensuring reliable access to metadata.

Chapter 25

Consistent Core

*Maintain a smaller cluster providing stronger consistency to allow
the large data cluster to coordinate server activities without
implementing quorum-based algorithms.*

Problem

When a cluster needs to handle a lot of data, it uses more and more servers. For a cluster of servers, there are some common requirements, such as selecting a server to be the master for a particular task, managing group membership information, mapping data partitions to servers, and so on. This functionality requires a strong consistency guarantee of linearizability. The implementation also needs to be fault-tolerant. A common approach is to use a fault-tolerant consensus algorithm based on *Majority Quorum*. However, in quorum-based systems, throughput degrades with the size of the cluster.

Solution

Implement a smaller cluster of three to five nodes which provides linearizability guarantee as well as fault tolerance. A separate data cluster can use the small consistent cluster to manage metadata and for taking cluster-wide decisions with primitives like *Lease* (Figure 25.1). This way, the data cluster can grow to a large number of servers but still be able to do certain actions that need strong consistency guarantees using the smaller metadata cluster.

Providing linearizability along with fault tolerance needs consensus algorithms like Raft [Ongaro2014], Zab [Reed2008], or *Paxos* to be implemented.

While a consensus algorithm is an essential requirement to implement a consistent core, there are various aspects of client interaction—such as how a client finds the leader or how duplicate requests are handled—which are important

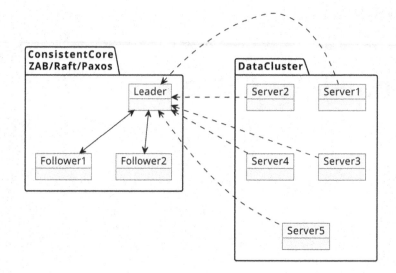

Figure 25.1 *Consistent core*

implementation decisions. There are also important considerations regarding safety and liveness. Paxos defines only the consensus algorithm, but these other implementation aspects are not well documented in the Paxos literature. Raft very clearly documents various implementation aspects, includes a reference implementation,[85] and is the most widely used algorithm today.

Since the entire cluster depends on the consistent core, it is critical to be aware of the details of the consensus algorithm used. Consensus implementations can run into liveness issues in some tricky network partition situations. For example, a Raft cluster can be disrupted by a partitioned server that can continuously trigger leader election unless special care is taken.

A typical interface of consistent core looks like this:

```
public interface ConsistentCore {
    CompletableFuture put(String key, String value);

    List<String> get(String keyPrefix);

    CompletableFuture registerLease(String name, long ttl);

    void refreshLease(String name);

    void watch(String name, Consumer<WatchEvent> watchCallback);
}
```

85. https://github.com/logcabin/logcabin

At a minimum, consistent core provides a simple key-value storage mechanism. It is used to store metadata.

Metadata Storage

The storage is implemented using consensus algorithms such as Raft. It is an implementation of *Replicated Log* where replication is handled by *Leader and Followers* and *High-Water Mark* is used to track successful replication using *Majority Quorum*.

Supporting Hierarchical Storage

Consistent core is generally used to store data for things like group membership or task distribution across servers. A common usage pattern is to scope the type of metadata with a prefix. For example, for group membership, the keys will look like /servers/1, servers/2, and so on. For tasks assigned to servers, the keys can be /tasks/task1, /tasks/task2. This data is generally read using all the keys with a specific prefix. For example, to get information about all the servers in the cluster, all the keys with the prefix /servers are read.

Here's an example usage.

Each server registers itself with the consistent core by creating its own key with the prefix /servers.

```
client1.setValue("/servers/1", "{address:192.168.199.10, port:8000}");

client2.setValue("/servers/2", "{address:192.168.199.11, port:8000}");

client3.setValue("/servers/3", "{address:192.168.199.12, port:8000}");
```

Clients can then get to know about all the servers in the cluster by reading keys with the prefix /servers:

```
assertEquals(client1.getValue("/servers"),
        Arrays.asList("{address:192.168.199.12, port:8000}",
                "{address:192.168.199.11, port:8000}",
                "{address:192.168.199.10, port:8000}"));
```

Because of this hierarchical nature of data storage, Apache ZooKeeper and Chubby [Burrows2006] provide a filesystem-like interface with the concept of parent and child nodes. Users can create directories and files, or nodes, inside the directories. etcd3 has a flat key space with the ability to get a range of keys.

Handling Client Interactions

One of the key features of consistent core is how a client interacts with the core. The following aspects are critical for clients to work with the consistent core.

Finding the Leader

Serializability and Linearizability

When read requests are handled by follower servers, it is possible that clients can get stale data, as the latest commits from the leader have not yet reached the followers. The order in which the updates are received by the client is still maintained but the updates might not be the most recent. This is the serializability guarantee as opposed to linearizability. Linearizability guarantees that every client gets the most recent updates. Clients can work with the serializability guarantee when they just need to read metadata and can tolerate stale metadata for a while. For operations like *Lease*, linearizability is strictly needed.

If the leader is partitioned from the rest of the cluster, clients can get stale values from the leader. Raft describes a mechanism to provide linearizable reads (see, for example, the etcd implementation of readIndex). YugabyteDB uses a technique called leader lease to achieve the same guarantee as described in the section "Bypassing the Log for Read Requests" of the *Replicated Log* pattern.

A similar situation can happen when followers are partitioned. A follower that's partitioned might not return the latest values to the client. To make sure the followers are not partitioned and are up-to-date with the leader, they need to query the leader and wait till they receive the latest updates before responding to the client. See the proposed Kafka design [Chen2020] as an example.

It's important that all the operations are executed on the leader, so a client library needs to find the leader server first. There are two approaches to do this.

- The follower servers in the consistent core know about the current leader, so if a client connects to a follower, the latter can return the address of the leader. The client can then directly connect to the leader identified in the response. It should be noted that the servers might be in the middle of a leader election when the client tries to connect. In that case, servers cannot return the leader address and the client needs to wait and try another server.

- Servers can implement a forwarding mechanism and forward all the client requests to the leader. This allows clients to connect to any server. Again, if servers are in the middle of a leader election, clients will need to retry until the leader election is successful and a legitimate leader is established.

  Products like ZooKeeper and etcd implement this approach because they allow some read-only requests to be handled by the follower servers. This avoids a bottleneck on the leader when a large number of clients are read-only. This also reduces complexity in the clients as they don't need to choose to connect to either leader or follower based on the type of the request.

A simple mechanism to find the leader is to try to connect to each server and send a request. The server responds with a redirect response if it's not the leader.

```
private void establishConnectionToLeader(List<InetAddressAndPort> servers) {
    for (var server : servers) {
        try {
            var socketChannel = new SingleSocketChannel(server,
                    10);
            logger.info("Trying to connect to " + server);
            var response = sendConnectRequest(socketChannel);
            if (isRedirectResponse(response)) {
                var redirectResponse =
                        deserialize(response.getMessageBody(),
                                RedirectToLeaderResponse.class);

                redirectToLeader(redirectResponse);
                break;
            } else if (isLookingForLeader(response)) {
                logger.info("Server is looking for leader. Trying next server");
                continue;
            } else { //we know the leader
                logger.info("Found leader. Establishing a new connection.");
                newPipelinedConnection(server);
                break;
            }
        } catch (IOException e) {
            logger.info("Unable to connect to " + server);
            //try next server
        }
    }
}

private boolean isLookingForLeader(RequestOrResponse requestOrResponse) {
    return requestOrResponse.getRequestId() == RequestId.LookingForLeader;
}

private void redirectToLeader(RedirectToLeaderResponse redirectResponse) {

    newPipelinedConnection(redirectResponse.leaderAddress);

    logger.info("Connected to the new leader "
            + redirectResponse.leaderServerId
            + " " + redirectResponse.leaderAddress
            + ". Checking connection");
}
```

Just establishing TCP connection is not enough—we need to know if the server can handle our requests. So clients send a special connection request for the server to acknowledge if it can serve requests or else redirect to the leader server.

```
private RequestOrResponse
        sendConnectRequest(SingleSocketChannel socketChannel)
            throws IOException {

    try {
        var request =
                new RequestOrResponse(new ConnectRequest(),
                nextRequestNumber.getAndIncrement());

        return socketChannel
                .blockingSend(request);

    } catch (IOException e) {
        resetConnectionToLeader();
        throw e;
    }
}
```

If an existing leader fails, the same technique is used to identify the newly elected leader from the cluster.

Once connected, the client maintains a *Single-Socket Channel* to the leader server.

Handling Duplicate Requests

In cases of failure, clients may try to connect to the new leader, resending the requests. But if those requests were already handled by the failed leader prior to failure, that might result in duplicates. Therefore, it's important to have a mechanism on the servers to ignore duplicate requests. The *Idempotent Receiver* pattern is used to implement duplicate detection.

Coordinating tasks across a set of servers can be done by using *Lease*. The same can be used to implement group membership and a failure detection mechanism.

State Watch is used to get notifications of changes to the metadata or time-bound leases.

Examples

- Google is known to use the Chubby lock service for coordination and metadata management.

- Apache Kafka uses Apache ZooKeeper to manage metadata and take decisions, such as a leader election for cluster master. The proposed architecture change [McCabe2020] in Kafka will replace ZooKeeper with its own Raft-based controller cluster.

- Apache BookKeeper uses ZooKeeper to manage cluster metadata.

- Kubernetes uses etcd for coordination, managing cluster metadata, and group membership information.

- All the big data storage and processing systems like HDFS,[86] Apache Spark,[87] Apache Flink[88] use Apache ZooKeeper for high availability and cluster coordination.

---

86. https://hadoop.apache.org
87. https://spark.apache.org
88. https://flink.apache.org

Chapter 26

Lease

Use time-bound leases for cluster nodes to coordinate their activities.

Problem

Cluster nodes need exclusive access to certain resources. But nodes can crash, be temporarily disconnected, or experience a process pause. Under these error scenarios, they should not keep the access to a resource indefinitely.

Solution

A cluster node can ask for a lease for a limited period of time, after which it expires. The node can renew the lease before it expires if it wants to extend the access. Implement the lease mechanism with *Consistent Core* to provide fault tolerance and consistency. Have a time-to-live value associated with the lease. Cluster nodes can create keys in a Consistent Core with a lease attached to it.

The leases are replicated with the *Leader and Followers* to provide fault tolerance. It's the responsibility of the node that owns the lease to periodically refresh it. *HeartBeat* is used by clients to refresh the time-to-live value in the Consistent Core. The leases are created on all the nodes in the Consistent Core, but only the leader tracks the lease timeouts. The timeouts are not tracked on the followers in the Consistent Core. This is because we need the leader to decide when leases expire, using its own monotonic clock, and then let the followers know. This makes sure that, like any other decision in the Consistent Core, nodes reach consensus about lease expiration.[89]

Wall Clocks Are Not Monotonic

Computers have two different mechanisms to represent time. The wall clock time, which represents the time of the day, is measured by a clock machinery generally built with a crystal oscillator. The known problem with oscillators is that they can drift away from the actual time of the day. To fix this, computers typically have a service like NTP set up, which checks the time of the day with time sources over the Internet and fixes the local time. Because of this, two consecutive readings of the wall clock time on a given server can have time going backwards. This makes the wall clock time unsuitable for measuring the time elapsed between some events. Computers have a different mechanism, called monotonic clock, which indicates elapsed time. The values of a monotonic clock are not affected by services like NTP. Two consecutive calls of a monotonic clock are guaranteed to get the elapsed time, so monotonic clocks are always used for measuring timeout values. This works well on a single server. But monotonic clocks on two different servers cannot be compared. All programming languages have an API to read both the wall clock and the monotonic clock—for example, in Java, System.currentMillis gives wall clock time and System.nanoTime gives monotonic clock time.

When a node from a Consistent Core becomes a leader, it starts tracking leases using its monotonic clock.

```
class ReplicatedKVStore...

  public void onBecomingLeader() {
      leaseTracker = new LeaderLeaseTracker(this, new SystemClock(), log);
      leaseTracker.start();
  }
```

Leader starts a scheduled task to periodically check for lease expiration.

```
class LeaderLeaseTracker...

  private ScheduledThreadPoolExecutor executor = new ScheduledThreadPoolExecutor(1);
  private ScheduledFuture<?> scheduledTask;
```

---

89. LogCabin, the reference implementation of Raft [Ongaro2015], has an interesting concept of cluster time, which is a logical clock maintained for the whole Raft cluster. With all the nodes in the cluster agreeing on the time, they can independently remove expired sessions. However, it requires heartbeat entries from leader to followers to be replicated and committed like any other log entries.

```
@Override
public void start() {
    scheduledTask = executor.scheduleWithFixedDelay(this::checkAndExpireLeases,
            leaseCheckingInterval,
            leaseCheckingInterval,
            TimeUnit.MILLISECONDS);
}

@Override
public void checkAndExpireLeases() {
    remove(expiredLeases());
}

private void remove(Stream<String> expiredLeases) {
    expiredLeases.forEach((leaseId) -> {
        //remove it from this server so that it doesnt cause trigger again.
        expireLease(leaseId);
        //submit a request so that followers know about expired leases
        submitExpireLeaseRequest(leaseId);
    });
}

private Stream<String> expiredLeases() {
    long now = System.nanoTime();
    Map<String, Lease> leases = kvStore.getLeases();
    return  leases.keySet().stream().filter(leaseId -> {
        Lease lease = leases.get(leaseId);
        return lease.getExpiresAt() < now;
    });
}
```

Followers start a no-op lease tracker.

class ReplicatedKVStore...

```
public void onCandidateOrFollower() {
    if (leaseTracker != null) {
        leaseTracker.stop();
    }
    leaseTracker = new FollowerLeaseTracker(this, leases);
}
```

The lease is represented simply:

```
public class Lease implements Logging {
    String name;
    long ttl;
    //Time at which this lease expires
    long expiresAt;

    //The keys from kv store attached with this lease
    List<String> attachedKeys = new ArrayList<>();
```

```
    public Lease(String name, long ttl, long now) {
        this.name = name;
        this.ttl = ttl;
        this.expiresAt = now + ttl;
    }

    public String getName() {
        return name;
    }

    public long getTtl() {
        return ttl;
    }

    public long getExpiresAt() {
        return expiresAt;
    }

    public void refresh(long now) {
        expiresAt = now + ttl;
    }

    public void attachKey(String key) {
        attachedKeys.add(key);
    }

    public List<String> getAttachedKeys() {
        return attachedKeys;
    }
}
```

When a node wants to create a lease, it connects with the leader of the Consistent Core and sends a request to create a lease. The register-lease request is replicated and handled similar to other requests in Consistent Core. The request is complete only when the *High-Water Mark* reaches the log index of the request entry in the replicated log.

class ReplicatedKVStore...

```
    private ConcurrentHashMap<String, Lease> leases = new ConcurrentHashMap<>();

    @Override
    public CompletableFuture<Response> registerLease(String name, long ttl) {
        if (leaseExists(name)) {
            return CompletableFuture
                    .completedFuture(
                            Response.error(RequestId.RegisterLeaseResponse,
                                DUPLICATE_LEASE_ERROR,
                                "Lease with name " + name + " already exists"));
        }
        return log.propose(new RegisterLeaseCommand(name, ttl));
    }
```

```
private boolean leaseExists(String name) {
    return leases.containsKey(name);
}
```

An important thing to note is where to validate for duplicate lease registration. Checking it before proposing the request is not enough, as there can be multiple in-flight requests. So the server also checks for duplicates when the lease is registered after successful replication (Figure 26.1).

class LeaderLeaseTracker...

```
private Map<String, Lease> leases;
@Override
public void addLease(String name, long ttl) throws DuplicateLeaseException {
    if (leases.get(name) != null) {
        throw new DuplicateLeaseException(name);
    }
    Lease lease = new Lease(name, ttl, clock.nanoTime());
    leases.put(name, lease);
}
```

Like any heartbeat mechanism, there is an assumption here that the server's monotonic clock is not faster than the client's monotonic clock. To take care of any possible rate difference, clients need to be conservative and send multiple heartbeats to the server within the timeout interval.

For example, ZooKeeper has a default session timeout of 10 seconds and uses 1/3 of the session timeout to send heartbeats. Apache Kafka, in its new architecture,[90] uses 18 seconds as lease expiration time, and heartbeat is sent every 3 seconds.

The node responsible for the lease connects to the leader and refreshes the lease before it expires. As discussed in HeartBeat, it needs to consider the network round trip time to decide on the time-to-live value and send refresh requests before the lease expires. The node can send refresh requests multiple times within the time-to-live interval to ensure that lease is refreshed in case of any issues. But the node also needs to make sure that not too many refresh requests are sent. It's reasonable to send a request after about half of the lease time is elapsed. This results in up to two refresh requests within the lease time. The client node tracks the time with its own monotonic clock.

---

90. https://cwiki.apache.org/confluence/display/KAFKA/KIP-631%3A+The+Quorum-based+Kafka+Controller
    #KIP631:TheQuorumbasedKafkaController-Configurations

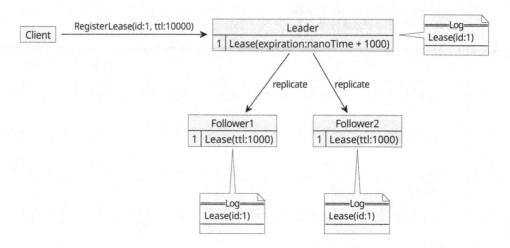

Figure 26.1 *Registering lease*

```
class LeaderLeaseTracker...

  @Override
  public void refreshLease(String name) {
      Lease lease = leases.get(name);
      lease.refresh(clock.nanoTime());
  }
```

Refresh requests are sent only to the leader of the Consistent Core, because only the leader is responsible for deciding when the lease expires (Figure 26.2).

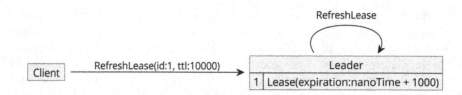

Figure 26.2 *Refreshing lease*

When the lease expires, it is removed from the leader, as Figure 26.3 demonstrates. It's also critical for this information to be committed to the Consistent Core. So the leader sends a request to expire the lease, which is handled like other requests in Consistent Core. Once the High-Water Mark reaches the proposed expire lease request, it's removed from all the followers.

```
class LeaderLeaseTracker...

    public void expireLease(String name) {
        getLogger().info("Expiring lease " + name);
        Lease removedLease = leases.remove(name);
        removeAttachedKeys(removedLease);
    }

    @Override
    public Lease getLeaseDetails(String name) {
        return leases.get(name);
    }
```

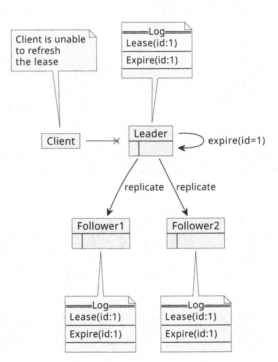

Figure 26.3 *Expiring lease*

Attaching the Lease to Keys in the Key-Value Storage

Apache ZooKeeper has a concept of sessions and ephemeral nodes. Its sessions are implemented with a mechanism similar to this pattern. Ephemeral nodes are attached to the session. Once the session expires, all the ephemeral nodes are removed from the storage.

A cluster needs to know if one of its nodes fails. It can do that by having the node take a lease from the *Consistent Core* and then attaching it to a self-identifying key stored within the Consistent Core. If the cluster node is running, it should renew the lease at regular intervals. Should the lease expire, the associated keys are removed. When the key is removed, an event indicating the node failure is sent to the interested cluster node, as discussed in the *State Watch* pattern.

A cluster node using Consistent Core creates a lease by making a network call:

```
consistentCoreClient.registerLease("server1Lease",
        Duration.ofSeconds(5));
```

It can then attach this lease to the self-identifying key it stores in the Consistent Core.

```
consistentCoreClient.setValue("/servers/1",
        "{address:192.168.199.10, port:8000}",
        "server1Lease");
```

When the Consistent Core receives the message to save the key in its key-value store, it also attaches the key to the specified lease.

```
class ReplicatedKVStore...

  private ConcurrentHashMap<String, Lease> leases = new ConcurrentHashMap<>();

class ReplicatedKVStore...

  private Response applySetValueCommand(Long walEntryId,
                                        SetValueCommand setValueCommand) {

      if (setValueCommand.hasLease()) {
          var lease = leases.get(setValueCommand.getAttachedLease());

          if (lease == null) {
              //The lease to attach is not available with the Consistent Core
              return Response.error(RequestId.SetValueResponse,
                  Errors.NO_LEASE_ERROR,
                  "No lease exists with name "
                          + setValueCommand.getAttachedLease(), 0);
          }

          lease.attachKey(setValueCommand.getKey());

      }
      kv.put(setValueCommand.getKey(),
              new StoredValue(setValueCommand.getValue(), walEntryId));
```

Once the lease expires, the Consistent Core also removes the attached keys from its key-value store.

```
class LeaderLeaseTracker...

  public void expireLease(String name) {
      getLogger().info("Expiring lease " + name);
      Lease removedLease = leases.remove(name);
      removeAttachedKeys(removedLease);
  }

  @Override
  public Lease getLeaseDetails(String name) {
      return leases.get(name);
  }

private void removeAttachedKeys(Lease removedLease) {
    if (removedLease == null) {
        return;
    }
    List<String> attachedKeys = removedLease.getAttachedKeys();
    for (String attachedKey : attachedKeys) {
        kvStore.remove(attachedKey);
    }
}
}
```

Handling Leader Failure

When the existing leader fails, a new leader for *Consistent Core* is elected. Once elected, the new leader starts tracking the leases.

The new leader refreshes all the leases it knows about (Figure 26.4). Note that the leases which were about to expire on the old leader get extended by the time-to-live value. This is not a problem, as it gives each client a chance to reconnect with the new leader and continue the lease (Figure 26.5).

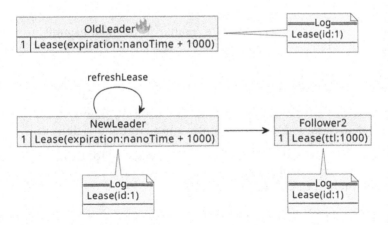

Figure 26.4 *New leader refreshes lease.*

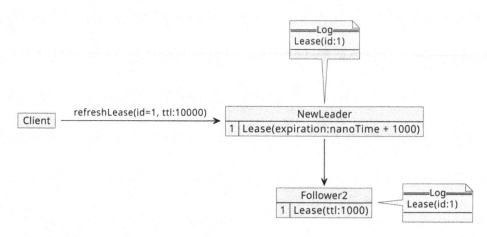

Figure 26.5 *Client connects to new leader.*

```
private void refreshLeases() {
    long now = clock.nanoTime();
    this.kvStore.getLeases().values().forEach(l -> {
        l.refresh(now);
    });
}
```

Examples

- Google's Chubby service implements the time-bound lease mechanism in a similar way.

- Apache ZooKeeper sessions are managed with mechanisms similar to replicated leases.

- Kafka uses time-bound leases to manage group membership and failure detection of Kafka brokers.

- etcd provides a time-bound lease facility used by clients to coordinate their activities as well as for group membership and failure detection.

- The DHCP protocol allows connecting devices to lease an IP address. The failover protocol[91] with multiple DHCP servers works similar to the implementation described here.

---

91. https://tools.ietf.org/html/draft-ietf-dhc-failover-12

Chapter 27

State Watch

Notify clients when specific values change on the server.

Problem

Clients are interested in changes to the specific values on the server. It's difficult for clients to structure their logic if they need to poll the server continuously to look for changes. If clients open too many connections to the server for watching changes, it can overwhelm the server.

Solution

Allow clients to register their interest with the server for specific state changes. The server notifies the interested clients when state changes happen. The client maintains a *Single-Socket Channel* with the server. The server sends state change notifications on this channel. Clients might be interested in multiple values, but maintaining a connection per watch can overwhelm the server. So clients can use a *Request Pipeline*.

With a simple key-value store example used in *Consistent Core*, a client can be interested when a value changes for a particular key or a key is removed. There are two parts to the implementation: the client-side implementation and the server-side implementation.

Client-Side Implementation

The client accepts the key and the function to be invoked when it gets watch events from the server. The client stores the function object for later invocation. It then sends the request to register the watch to the server.

```java
ConcurrentHashMap<String, Consumer<WatchEvent>> watches
        = new ConcurrentHashMap<>();

public void watch(String key, Consumer<WatchEvent> consumer) {
    watches.put(key, consumer);
    sendWatchRequest(key);
}

private void sendWatchRequest(String key) {
    requestSendingQueue.submit(new RequestOrResponse(new WatchRequest(key),
            correlationId.getAndIncrement()));
}
```

When a watch event is received on the connection, a corresponding consumer is invoked:

```java
this.pipelinedConnection
        = new PipelinedConnection(address, requestTimeoutMs, (r) -> {

    logger.info("Received response on the pipelined connection "
            + r.getRequestId());

    if (r.getRequestId() == RequestId.WatchEvent) {

        var watchEvent = deserialize(r.getMessageBody(),
                WatchEvent.class);

        var watchEventConsumer = getConsumer(watchEvent.getKey());

        watchEventConsumer.accept(watchEvent);
        //capture last watched index, in case of connection failure.
        lastWatchedEventIndex = watchEvent.getIndex();
    }
    completeRequestFutures(r);
});
```

Server-Side Implementation

When the server receives a watch registration request, it keeps the mapping of the pipelined connection on which the request is received and the keys.

```java
private Map<String, ClientConnection> watches = new HashMap<>();
private Map<ClientConnection, List<String>> connection2WatchKeys
                                = new HashMap<>();
```

```java
public void watch(String key, ClientConnection clientConnection) {
    logger.info("Setting watch for " + key);
    addWatch(key, clientConnection);
}

private synchronized void addWatch(String key,
                                   ClientConnection clientConnection) {

    mapWatchKey2Connection(key, clientConnection);
    watches.put(key, clientConnection);
}

private void mapWatchKey2Connection(String key,
                                    ClientConnection clientConnection) {

    List<String> keys = connection2WatchKeys.get(clientConnection);
    if (keys == null) {
        keys = new ArrayList<>();
        connection2WatchKeys.put(clientConnection, keys);
    }
    keys.add(key);
}
```

The ClientConnection wraps the socket connection to the client. It has the following structure. This structure remains the same for both blocking-IO-based servers and nonblocking-IO-based servers.

```java
public interface ClientConnection {
    void write(RequestOrResponse response);
    void close();
}
```

There can be multiple watches registered on a single connection. So it is important to store the mapping of connections to the lists of watch keys. When the client connection is closed, you need to remove all the associated watches:

```java
public void close(ClientConnection connection) {
    removeWatches(connection);
}

private synchronized void removeWatches(ClientConnection clientConnection) {
    var watchedKeys = connection2WatchKeys.remove(clientConnection);
    if (watchedKeys == null) {
        return;
    }
    for (String key : watchedKeys) {
        watches.remove(key);
    }
}
```

Using Reactive Streams

The example here shows writing the events directly to the pipelined connection. It is useful to have some type of backpressure at the application level. When too many events are generated, it's important to control the rate at which they can be sent. Keeping producers and consumers of the events in sync is an important consideration. An issue in etcd[92] is an example of how these considerations matter in production.

Reactive Streams[93] API makes it easier to write code with backpressure as a first-class concept. Protocols like RSocket[94] provide a structured way to implement this.

When specific events, such as setting a value for a key, happen on the server, the server notifies all the registered clients by constructing a relevant WatchEvent:

```
private synchronized void notifyWatchers(SetValueCommand setValueCommand,
                                         Long entryId) {

    logger.info("Looking for watches for " + setValueCommand.getKey());
    if (!hasWatchesFor(setValueCommand.getKey())) {
        return;
    }
    String watchedKey = setValueCommand.getKey();
    WatchEvent watchEvent = new WatchEvent(watchedKey,
                            setValueCommand.getValue(),
                            EventType.KEY_ADDED, entryId);
    notify(watchEvent, watchedKey);
}

private void notify(WatchEvent watchEvent, String watchedKey) {
    List<ClientConnection> watches = getAllWatchersFor(watchedKey);
    for (ClientConnection pipelinedClientConnection : watches) {
        try {
            getLogger().info("Notifying watcher of event "
                    + watchEvent +
                    " from "
                    + log.getServerId());
            pipelinedClientConnection.write(new RequestOrResponse(watchEvent));
        } catch (NetworkException e) {
            //remove watch if network connection fails.
            removeWatches(pipelinedClientConnection);
        }
    }
}
```

---

92. https://github.com/etcd-io/etcd/issues/11906
93. https://www.reactive-streams.org
94. https://rsocket.io

It is critical that the state related to watches can be accessed concurrently from the client request handling code and from the client connection handling code to close the connection. Therefore, all the methods accessing watch state need to be protected by locks.

Watches on Hierarchical Storage

Consistent Core mostly supports hierarchical storage. The watches can be set on a parent node, or prefix, of a key. Any change to the child node triggers the watches set on the parent node. For each event, the consistent core walks up the path to check if there are watches set up on ancestor nodes and send events to all those watches.

```
List<ClientConnection> getAllWatchersFor(String key) {
    List<ClientConnection> affectedWatches = new ArrayList<>();
    String[] paths = key.split("/");
    String currentPath = paths[0];
    addWatch(currentPath, affectedWatches);
    for (int i = 1; i < paths.length; i++) {
        currentPath = currentPath + "/" + paths[i];
        addWatch(currentPath, affectedWatches);
    }
    return affectedWatches;
}

private void addWatch(String currentPath,
                      List<ClientConnection> affectedWatches) {

    ClientConnection clientConnection = watches.get(currentPath);
    if (clientConnection != null) {
        affectedWatches.add(clientConnection);
    }
}
```

This allows a watch to be set up on a key prefix, such as "servers". Any key created with this prefix—"servers/1", "servers/2"—will trigger this watch.

Since the mapping of the function to be invoked is stored with the key prefix, it's important to walk the hierarchy to find the function to be invoked for the received event on the client side as well. An alternative can be to send the path for which the event was triggered along with the event, so that the client knows which watch caused the event to be sent.

Handling Connection Failures

The connection between client and server can fail at any time. For some use cases, this is problematic as the client might miss certain events when it's disconnected. For example, a cluster controller might be interested in knowing if some nodes have failed, which is indicated by events for removal of some keys. The client needs to tell the server about the last event it received. The client sends the last received event number when it resets the watch again. The server is expected to send all the events it has recorded from that event number onward.

In a *Consistent Core* client, it can be done when the client reestablishes the connection to the leader.

> **Pull-Based Design in Kafka**
>
> In a typical design for watches, the server pushes watch events to clients. Apache Kafka follows end-to-end pull-based design. In its new architecture [McCabe2020], the Kafka brokers are going to periodically pull metadata log from a Controller Quorum [McCabe2021], which itself is an example of Consistent Core. The offset-based pull mechanism allows a client, like any other Kafka consumer, to read events from the last known offset, avoiding loss of events.

```
private void connectToLeader(List<InetAddressAndPort> servers) {
    while (isDisconnected()) {
        logger.info("Trying to connect to next server");
        waitForPossibleLeaderElection();
        establishConnectionToLeader(servers);
    }
    setWatchesOnNewLeader();
}

private void setWatchesOnNewLeader() {
    for (String watchKey : watches.keySet()) {
        sendWatchResetRequest(watchKey);
    }
}

private void sendWatchResetRequest(String key) {
    var watchRequest =
            new RequestOrResponse(new SetWatchRequest(key,
                                                lastWatchedEventIndex),
            correlationId.getAndIncrement());

    pipelinedConnection.send(watchRequest);
}
```

The server numbers every event that occurs. For example, if the server is the Consistent Core, it stores all the state changes in a strict order and every change is numbered with the log index, as discussed in *Write-Ahead Log*. It is then possible for clients to ask for events starting from the specific index.

Deriving Events from the Key-Value Store

Events can be generated by looking at the current state of the key-value store, if it also numbers every change that happens and stores that number with each value.

When a client reestablishes connection to the server, it can set the watches again, also sending the last seen change number. The server can then compare it with the one stored with the value—if it's more than what client sent, it can resend the events to the client.

Deriving events from the key-value store can be a bit awkward as events need to be guessed. It might miss some events. For instance, if a key is created and then deleted while the client was disconnected, the create event will be missed.

```
private synchronized void eventsFromStoreState(String key, long stateChangesSince) {

    List<StoredValue> values = getValuesForKeyPrefix(key);
    for (StoredValue value : values) {
        if (values == null) {
            //the key was probably deleted send deleted event
            notify(new WatchEvent(key, EventType.KEY_DELETED), key);
        } else if (value.index > stateChangesSince) {
            //the key/value was created/updated after
            // the last event client knows about
            notify(new WatchEvent(key, value.getValue(),
                    EventType.KEY_ADDED, value.getIndex()), key);
        }
    }
}
```

Apache ZooKeeper uses this approach. The watches in ZooKeeper are also one-time triggers by default. Once the event is triggered, clients need to set the watch again if they want to receive further events. Some events can be missed before the watch is set again, so clients need to ensure they read the latest state so that they don't miss any updates.

Storing Event History

It's easier to keep a history of past events and reply to clients from the event history. The problem with this approach is that the event history needs to be limited, say to 1,000 events. If the client is disconnected for a longer duration, it might miss on events which are beyond the 1,000 events window.

Here's a simple implementation using Google Guava's EvictingQueue:

```
public class EventHistory implements Logging {
    Queue<WatchEvent> events = EvictingQueue.create(1000);
    public void addEvent(WatchEvent e) {
        getLogger().info("Adding " + e);
        events.add(e);
    }
```

```
public List<WatchEvent> getEvents(String key, Long stateChangesSince) {
    return this.events.stream()
            .filter(e -> e.getIndex() > stateChangesSince
                    && e.getKey().equals(key))
            .collect(Collectors.toList());
    }
}
```

When the client reestablishes the connection and resets watches, the events can be sent from history.

```
private void sendEventsFromHistory(String key, long stateChangesSince) {
    var events = eventHistory.getEvents(key, stateChangesSince);
    for (WatchEvent event : events) {
        notify(event, event.getKey());
    }
}
```

Using Multiversion Storage

To keep track of all the changes, it is possible to use multiversion storage. It keeps track of all the versions for every key and can easily get all the changes from the version asked for.

etcd from version 3 onward uses this approach.

Examples

- Apache ZooKeeper has the ability to set up watches on nodes. This is used by products like Apache Kafka for group membership and failure detection of cluster members.

- etcd has a watch implementation that is heavily used by Kubernetes for its resource watch implementation.[95]

---

95. https://kubernetes.io/docs/reference/using-api/api-concepts

Chapter 28

Gossip Dissemination

Use a random selection of nodes to pass on information to ensure it reaches all the nodes in the cluster without flooding the network.

Problem

In a cluster of nodes, each node needs to pass metadata it has to all the other nodes in the cluster, without depending on a shared storage. In a large cluster, if all servers communicate with all the other servers, a lot of network bandwidth can be consumed. Information should reach all the nodes even when some network links are experiencing issues.

Solution

Cluster nodes use gossip-like communication to propagate state updates. Each node selects a random node to pass the information it has. This is done at a regular interval, say every 1 second. Each time, a random node is selected to pass on the information.

Epidemics, Rumors, and Computer Communication

There are mathematical properties of epidemics which describe why they spread so fast. The mathematical branch of epidemiology studies how epidemics or rumors spread in a society. Gossip Dissemination is based on the mathematical models from epidemiology. The key feature of epidemics or rumors is that they spread very fast even if each person comes into contact with only a few individuals at random. An entire population can become infected with very few interactions per individual. More specifically, if n is the total number of people in a population, it takes interactions proportional to $\log(n)$ per individual, which is a very small number.

This property of epidemic spread is very useful to spread information across a set of processes. Even if a given process communicates with only a few processes at random, in a few communication rounds, all the nodes in the cluster will have the same information. HashiCorp has a very nice convergence simulator[96] to demonstrate how quickly the information spreads to the entire cluster, even with some network loss and node failures.

In large clusters, the following things need to be considered:

■ Put a fixed limit on the number of messages generated per server.

■ The messages should not consume a lot of network bandwidth. There should be an upper bound of, say, a few hundred kilobytes so you can be sure the applications' data transfer is not impacted by too many messages across the cluster.

■ Metadata propagation should tolerate network failures and a few server failures. It should reach all the cluster nodes even if some network links are down or a few servers have failed.

As discussed in the sidebar, gossip-style communication fulfills all these requirements.

Each cluster node stores the metadata as a list of key-value pairs associated with each node in the cluster:

```
class Gossip...

  Map<NodeId, NodeState> clusterMetadata = new HashMap<>();

class NodeState...

  Map<String, VersionedValue> values = new HashMap<>();
```

---

96. https://www.serf.io/docs/internals/simulator.html

At startup, each cluster node adds the metadata about itself that needs to be propagated to other nodes. Examples of metadata are the IP address and port the node listens on, the partitions it's responsible for, and so on. The Gossip instance needs to know about at least one other node to start the gossip communication. A well-known cluster node, which is used to initialize the Gossip instance, is called a seed node or an introducer. It's not a special node; any node can serve as one, as long as its address is configured on every node.

class Gossip...

```
public Gossip(InetAddressAndPort listenAddress,
              List<InetAddressAndPort> seedNodes,
              String nodeId) throws IOException {
    this.listenAddress = listenAddress;
    //filter this node itself in case its part of the seed nodes
    this.seedNodes = removeSelfAddress(seedNodes);
    this.nodeId = new NodeId(nodeId);
    addLocalState(GossipKeys.ADDRESS, listenAddress.toString());

    this.socketServer
            = new NIOSocketListener(newGossipRequestConsumer(),
                                    listenAddress);
}

private void addLocalState(String key, String value) {
    NodeState nodeState = clusterMetadata.get(listenAddress);
    if (nodeState == null) {
        nodeState = new NodeState();
        clusterMetadata.put(nodeId, nodeState);
    }
    nodeState.add(key, new VersionedValue(value, incremenetVersion()));
}
```

Each cluster node schedules a job to transmit the metadata it has to other nodes at regular intervals.

class Gossip...

```
private ScheduledThreadPoolExecutor gossipExecutor
        = new ScheduledThreadPoolExecutor(1);
private long gossipIntervalMs = 1000;
private ScheduledFuture<?> taskFuture;
public void start() {
    socketServer.start();
    taskFuture = gossipExecutor.scheduleAtFixedRate((()-> doGossip(),
                gossipIntervalMs,
                gossipIntervalMs,
                TimeUnit.MILLISECONDS);
}
```

When the scheduled task is invoked, it picks a small set of random nodes from the list of servers from the metadata map. A small constant number, called gossip fanout, determines how many nodes to pick as gossip targets. If nothing is known yet, it picks a random seed node and sends the metadata map it has to that node.

class Gossip...

```java
public void doGossip() {
    List<InetAddressAndPort> knownClusterNodes = liveNodes();
    if (knownClusterNodes.isEmpty()) {
        sendGossip(seedNodes, gossipFanout);
    } else {
        sendGossip(knownClusterNodes, gossipFanout);
    }
}

private List<InetAddressAndPort> liveNodes() {
    var nodes
            = clusterMetadata.values()
            .stream()
            .map(n ->
                    InetAddressAndPort
                            .parse(n.get(GossipKeys.ADDRESS).getValue()))
            .collect(Collectors.toSet());

    return removeSelfAddress(nodes);
}
```

Using UDP or TCP

Gossip communication assumes unreliable networks, so it can use UDP as a transport mechanism. But cluster nodes generally need some guarantee of quick convergence of state and therefore use TCP-based transport to exchange the gossip state. This is particularly useful when the nodes are spread across regions and communicate over a WAN.

```java
private void sendGossip(List<InetAddressAndPort> knownClusterNodes,
                       int gossipFanout) {

    if (knownClusterNodes.isEmpty()) {
        return;
    }

    for (int i = 0; i < gossipFanout; i++) {
        InetAddressAndPort nodeAddress = pickRandomNode(knownClusterNodes);
        sendGossipTo(nodeAddress);
    }
}
```

```
private void sendGossipTo(InetAddressAndPort nodeAddress) {
    try {
        getLogger().info("Sending gossip state to " + nodeAddress);
        var socketClient = new SocketClient(nodeAddress);
        var gossipStateMessage
                = new GossipStateMessage(this.nodeId, this.clusterMetadata);
        var request
                = createGossipStateRequest(gossipStateMessage);
        var response = socketClient.blockingSend(request);
        var responseState = deserialize(response);
        merge(responseState.getNodeStates());

    } catch (IOException e) {
        getLogger().error("IO error while sending gossip state to "
                + nodeAddress, e);
    }
}

private RequestOrResponse
        createGossipStateRequest(GossipStateMessage gossipStateMessage) {

    return new RequestOrResponse(gossipStateMessage, correlationId++);
}
```

The cluster node receiving the gossip message inspects the metadata it has and finds three things:

- The values which are in the incoming message but are not available in this node's state map

- The values which it has but the incoming gossip message does not have

- The higher version values that the node has for the values present in the incoming message

It then adds the missing values to its own state map. Whatever values were missing from the incoming message are returned as a response.

The cluster node sending the gossip message adds the values it gets from the gossip response to its own state.

class Gossip...

```
private void handleGossipRequest(Message<RequestOrResponse> request,
                                 ClientConnection clientConnection) {

    var gossipStateMessage = deserialize(request.getRequest());
    var gossipedState = gossipStateMessage.getNodeStates();
    getLogger().info("Merging state from " + clientConnection);
    merge(gossipedState);

    var diff = delta(this.clusterMetadata, gossipedState);
    var diffResponse = new GossipStateMessage(this.nodeId, diff);
```

```
            getLogger().info("Sending diff response " + diff);

        clientConnection
                .write(new RequestOrResponse(diffResponse,
                        request.getRequest().getCorrelationId())));
    }

public Map<NodeId, NodeState> delta(Map<NodeId, NodeState> fromMap,
                                    Map<NodeId, NodeState> toMap) {
    var delta = new HashMap<NodeId, NodeState>();
    for (NodeId key : fromMap.keySet()) {
        if (!toMap.containsKey(key)) {
            delta.put(key, fromMap.get(key));
            continue;
        }
        var fromStates = fromMap.get(key);
        var toStates = toMap.get(key);
        var diffStates = fromStates.diff(toStates);
        if (!diffStates.isEmpty()) {
            delta.put(key, diffStates);
        }
    }
    return delta;
}

public void merge(Map<NodeId, NodeState> otherState) {
    var diff = delta(otherState, this.clusterMetadata);
    for (var diffKey : diff.keySet()) {
        if(!this.clusterMetadata.containsKey(diffKey)) {
            this.clusterMetadata.put(diffKey, diff.get(diffKey));
        } else {
            NodeState stateMap = this.clusterMetadata.get(diffKey);
            stateMap.putAll(diff.get(diffKey));
        }
    }
}
```

This process happens every one second at each cluster node, each time selecting a different node to exchange the state.

Avoiding Unnecessary State Exchange

The above code example shows that the complete state of the node is sent in the gossip message. This is fine for a newly joined node, but once the state is up to date, it's unnecessary to send the complete state. The cluster node just needs to send the state changes since the last gossip. For this, each node maintains a version number which is incremented every time a new metadata entry is added locally.

```
class Gossip...

    private int gossipStateVersion = 1;

    private int incremenetVersion() {
        return gossipStateVersion++;
    }
```

Each value in the cluster metadata is maintained with a version number. This is an example of the *Versioned Value* pattern.

```
class VersionedValue...

    long version;
    String value;

    public VersionedValue(String value, long version) {
        this.version = version;
        this.value = value;
    }

    public long getVersion() {
        return version;
    }

    public String getValue() {
        return value;
    }
```

Each gossip cycle can then exchange states from a specific version.

```
class Gossip...

    private void sendKnownVersions(InetAddressAndPort gossipTo)
            throws IOException {
        var maxKnownNodeVersions = getMaxKnownNodeVersions();
        var knownVersionRequest =
                new RequestOrResponse(
                        new GossipStateVersions(maxKnownNodeVersions));

        var socketClient = new SocketClient(gossipTo);
        socketClient.blockingSend(knownVersionRequest);
    }

    private Map<NodeId, Long> getMaxKnownNodeVersions() {
        return clusterMetadata.entrySet()
                .stream()
                .collect(Collectors.toMap(e -> e.getKey(),
                        e -> e.getValue().maxVersion()));
    }
```

```
class NodeState...

    public long maxVersion() {
        return values.values()
                .stream()
                .map(v -> v.getVersion())
                .max(Comparator.naturalOrder())
                .orElse(Long.valueOf(0));
    }
```

The receiving node can then send the values only if the versions are greater than the ones in the request.

```
class Gossip...

    Map<NodeId, NodeState> getMissingAndNodeStatesHigherThan(Map<NodeId,
            Long> nodeMaxVersions) {

        var delta = new HashMap<NodeId, NodeState>();
        delta.putAll(higherVersionedNodeStates(nodeMaxVersions));
        delta.putAll(missingNodeStates(nodeMaxVersions));
        return delta;
    }

    private Map<NodeId, NodeState>
                    missingNodeStates(Map<NodeId, Long> nodeMaxVersions) {

        var delta = new HashMap<NodeId, NodeState>();
        List<NodeId> missingKeys = clusterMetadata
                .keySet()
                .stream()
                .filter(key -> !nodeMaxVersions.containsKey(key))
                .collect(Collectors.toList());

        for (NodeId missingKey : missingKeys) {
            delta.put(missingKey, clusterMetadata.get(missingKey));
        }
        return delta;
    }

    private Map<NodeId, NodeState>
                higherVersionedNodeStates(Map<NodeId, Long> nodeMaxVersions) {

        var delta = new HashMap<NodeId, NodeState>();
        var keySet = nodeMaxVersions.keySet();

        for (NodeId node : keySet) {
            var maxVersion = nodeMaxVersions.get(node);
            var nodeState = clusterMetadata.get(node);
            if (nodeState == null) {
                continue;
            }
```

```
                var deltaState = nodeState.statesGreaterThan(maxVersion);
                if (!deltaState.isEmpty()) {
                    delta.put(node, deltaState);
                }
            }
        }
        return delta;
    }
```

The gossip implementation in Apache Cassandra optimizes state exchange with a three-way handshake, where the node receiving the gossip message also sends the versions it needs from the sender, along with the metadata it returns. The sender can then immediately respond with the requested metadata. This avoids an extra message that otherwise would have been required.

The gossip protocol used in CockroachDB maintains state for each connected node. For each connection, it maintains the last version sent to that node and the version received from that node. This allows it to send "state since the last sent version" and ask for "state from the last received version."

Some other efficient alternatives can be used as well—for example, sending a hash of the entire map and doing nothing if the hash is the same.

Criteria for Node Selection to Gossip

Cluster nodes randomly select the node to send the gossip message to. An example implementation in Java can use java.util.Random:

class Gossip...

```
    private Random random = new Random();
    private InetAddressAndPort
                pickRandomNode(List<InetAddressAndPort> knownClusterNodes) {

        var randomNodeIndex = random.nextInt(knownClusterNodes.size());
        var gossipTo = knownClusterNodes.get(randomNodeIndex);
        return gossipTo;
    }
```

There can be other considerations, such as choosing the node that is least contacted with. For example, the gossip protocol in CockroachDB selects nodes this way.[97]

There are network-topology-aware [Gupta2006] ways of gossip target selection as well.

Any of these can be implemented modularly inside the pickRandomNode() method.

---

97. https://github.com/cockroachdb/cockroach/blob/master/docs/design.md

Group Membership and Failure Detection

Eventual Consistency

Information exchange with gossip protocols is eventually consistent by nature. Even if the gossip state converges very fast, there will be some delay before a new node is recognized by the entire cluster or a node failure is detected. Implementations using gossip protocol for information exchange need to tolerate eventual consistency.

For operations that require strong consistency, *Consistent Core* needs to be used.

It's a common practice to use both in the same cluster. For example, HashiCorp Consul uses gossip protocol for group membership and failure detection but also uses a Raft-based Consistent Core to store a strongly consistent service catalog.

Maintaining the list of available nodes in the cluster is one of the most common usage of gossip protocols. There are two approaches in use.

- SWIM [Das2002] uses a separate probing component which continuously probes different nodes in the cluster to detect if they are available. If it detects that the node is alive or dead, that result is propagated to the entire cluster with gossip communication. The prober randomly selects a node to send the gossip message. If the receiving node detects that this is new information, it immediately sends the message to a randomly selected node. This way, the failure of a node or a newly joined node in the cluster is quickly known to the entire cluster.

- The cluster node can periodically update its own state to reflect its heartbeat. This state is then propagated to the entire cluster through the gossip messages exchanged. Each cluster node can then check if it has received any update for a particular cluster node in a fixed amount of time or else mark that node as down. In this case, each cluster node independently determines if a node is up or down.

Handling Node Restarts

Versioned values do not work well if the node crashes or restarts, as all the in-memory state is lost. More importantly, the node can have different values for the same key. For example, a cluster node can start with a different IP address and port, or can start with a different configuration. *Generation Clock* can be used to mark generation with every value, so that when the metadata state is sent to a random cluster node, the receiving node can detect changes not just by the version number but also with the generation.

Note that this mechanism is not necessary for the core gossip protocol to work. But it's implemented in practice to make sure that the state changes are tracked correctly.

Examples

- Apache Cassandra uses gossip protocol for the group membership and failure detection of cluster nodes. Metadata for each cluster node, such as the tokens assigned to each cluster node, is also transmitted using gossip protocol.

- HashiCorp Consul uses SWIM gossip protocol for group membership and failure detection of consul agents.

- CockroachDB uses gossip protocol to propagate node metadata.

- Blockchain implementations such as Hyperledger Fabric[98] use gossip protocol for group membership and sending ledger metadata.

---

98. https://hyperledger-fabric.readthedocs.io/en/release-2.2/gossip.html

Chapter 29

Emergent Leader

*Order cluster nodes based on their age within the cluster to allow
nodes to select a leader without running an explicit election.*

Problem

Peer-to-peer systems treat each cluster node as equal: there is no leader. This
means there is no explicit leader election process as happens in the *Leader and
Followers* pattern. Sometimes the cluster also doesn't want to depend on a separate
Consistent Core to improve availability. However, there still needs to be one cluster
node acting as cluster coordinator for tasks such as assigning data partitions to
other cluster nodes and tracking when new cluster nodes join or fail and taking
corrective actions.

Solution

One of the common techniques used in peer-to-peer systems is to order cluster
nodes according to their age in the cluster. The oldest member of the cluster
plays the role of the coordinator. The coordinator is responsible for deciding on
membership changes and making cluster-wide decisions, such as ensuring the
distribution of *Fixed Partitions* across cluster nodes.

To form the cluster, one of the cluster nodes acts as a seed node or an introducer node. All the cluster nodes join the cluster by contacting the seed node.

> Various discovery mechanisms can be provided to find the node to join the cluster. For example, JGroups provides different discovery protocols.[99] Akka provides several discovery mechanisms[100] as well.

Every cluster node is configured with the seed node address. When a cluster node is started, it tries to contact the seed node to join the cluster.

```
class ClusterNode...

  MembershipService membershipService;
  public void start(Config config) {
      this.membershipService =  new MembershipService(config.getListenAddress());
      membershipService.join(config.getSeedAddress());
  }
```

The seed node could be any of the cluster nodes. It's configured with its own address as the seed node address and is the first node that is started. It immediately begins accepting requests. The age of the seed node is 1.

```
class MembershipService...

  Membership membership;
  public void join(InetAddressAndPort seedAddress) {
      var maxJoinAttempts = 5;

      for(int i = 0; i < maxJoinAttempts; i++){
          try {
              joinAttempt(seedAddress);
              return;
          } catch (Exception e) {
              logger.info("Join attempt "
                      + i + "from "
                      + selfAddress + " to "
                      + seedAddress + " failed. Retrying");
          }
      }
      throw new JoinFailedException("Unable to join the cluster after "
          + maxJoinAttempts + " attempts");
  }

  private void joinAttempt(InetAddressAndPort seedAddress)
          throws ExecutionException, TimeoutException {

      if (selfAddress.equals(seedAddress)) {
          int membershipVersion = 1;
          int age = 1;
```

99. https://docs.jboss.org/jbossas/docs/Clustering_Guide/beta422/html/jbosscache-jgroups-discovery.html
100. https://doc.akka.io/docs/akka-management/current/discovery/index.html

```
                updateMembership(new Membership(membershipVersion,
                        Arrays.asList(new Member(selfAddress,
                                age,
                                MemberStatus.JOINED)))));
                start();
                return;
        }
        long id = this.messageId++;
        var future = new CompletableFuture<JoinResponse>();
        var message = new JoinRequest(id, selfAddress);
        pendingRequests.put(id, future);
        network.send(seedAddress, message);

        var joinResponse = Uninterruptibles.getUninterruptibly(future, 5,
                TimeUnit.SECONDS);
        updateMembership(joinResponse.getMembership());
        start();
}

private void start() {
    heartBeatScheduler.start();
    failureDetector.start();
    startSplitBrainChecker();
    logger.info(selfAddress + " joined the cluster. Membership="
            + membership);
}

private void updateMembership(Membership membership) {
    this.membership = membership;
}
```

There can be more than one seed node, but any seed nodes start accepting requests only after they themselves join the cluster. Also, the cluster will remain functional if the seed node is down, but no new nodes will be able to join.

Non-seed nodes then send the join request to the seed node. The seed node handles the join request by creating a new member record and assigning its age. It updates its own membership list and sends messages to all the existing members with the new membership list. It then waits to make sure that the response is returned from every node, but will eventually return the join response even if the response is delayed.

```
class MembershipService...

public void handleJoinRequest(JoinRequest joinRequest) {
    handlePossibleRejoin(joinRequest);
    handleNewJoin(joinRequest);
}

private void handleNewJoin(JoinRequest joinRequest) {
    List<Member> existingMembers = membership.getLiveMembers();
```

```
        updateMembership(membership.addNewMember(joinRequest.from));

        var resultsCollector = broadcastMembershipUpdate(existingMembers);
        var joinResponse = new JoinResponse(joinRequest.messageId, selfAddress,
                membership);
        resultsCollector.whenComplete((response, exception) -> {
            logger.info("Sending join response from "
                    + selfAddress
                    + " to "
                    + joinRequest.from);

            network.send(joinRequest.from, joinResponse);
        });
    }
```

class Membership...

```
    public Membership addNewMember(InetAddressAndPort address) {
        var newMembership = new ArrayList<>(liveMembers);
        int age = yongestMemberAge() + 1;
        newMembership.add(new Member(address, age, MemberStatus.JOINED));
        return new Membership(version + 1, newMembership, failedMembers);
    }

    private int yongestMemberAge() {
        return liveMembers.stream().map(m -> m.age).max(Integer::compare)
                .orElse(0);
    }
```

If a node that's already part of the cluster is trying to rejoin after a crash, the failure detector state related to that member is cleared.

class MembershipService...

```
    private void handlePossibleRejoin(JoinRequest joinRequest) {
        if (membership.isFailed(joinRequest.from)) {
            //member rejoining
            logger.info(joinRequest.from
                    + " rejoining the cluster. Removing it from failed list");
            membership.removeFromFailedList(joinRequest.from);
        }
    }
```

That node is then added as a new member. Each member needs to be identified uniquely. It can be assigned a unique identifier at startup. This is a point of reference that makes it possible to detect that it is an existing cluster node that is rejoining.

The membership class maintains the list of live members as well as failed members. The members are moved from the live to failed list if they stop sending *HeartBeat,* as described in the "Failure Detection" section.

```
class Membership...

    List<Member> liveMembers = new ArrayList<>();
    List<Member> failedMembers = new ArrayList<>();

    public boolean isFailed(InetAddressAndPort address) {
        return failedMembers.stream().anyMatch(m -> m.address.equals(address));
    }
```

Sending Membership Updates to All the Existing Members

Membership updates are sent to all the other nodes concurrently. The coordinator also needs to track whether all the members successfully received the updates.

A common technique is to send a one-way request to all nodes and expect an acknowledgment message. Cluster nodes send acknowledgment messages to the coordinator to confirm receipt of the membership update. A ResultCollector object can track receipt of all the messages asynchronously: It is notified every time an acknowledgment is received for a membership update. It completes its future once the expected acknowledgment messages are received.

```
class MembershipService...

    private ResultsCollector
                broadcastMembershipUpdate(List<Member> existingMembers) {

        var resultsCollector = sendMembershipUpdateTo(existingMembers);
        resultsCollector.orTimeout(2, TimeUnit.SECONDS);
        return resultsCollector;
    }

    Map<Long, CompletableFuture> pendingRequests = new HashMap();
    private ResultsCollector
                sendMembershipUpdateTo(List<Member> existingMembers) {

        var otherMembers = otherMembers(existingMembers);
        var collector = new ResultsCollector(otherMembers.size());
        if (otherMembers.size() == 0) {
            collector.complete();
            return collector;
        }

        for (Member m : otherMembers) {
            var id = this.messageId++;
            var future = new CompletableFuture<Message>();
            future.whenComplete((result, exception) -> {
                if (exception == null){
                    collector.ackReceived();
                }
            });
            pendingRequests.put(id, future);
```

```
            network.send(m.address,
                    new UpdateMembershipRequest(id, selfAddress, membership));
        }
        return collector;
    }

class MembershipService...

  private void handleResponse(Message message) {
      completePendingRequests(message);
  }

  private void completePendingRequests(Message message) {
      var requestFuture = pendingRequests.get(message.messageId);
      if (requestFuture != null) {
          requestFuture.complete(message);
      }
  }

class ResultsCollector...

  class ResultsCollector {
      int totalAcks;
      int receivedAcks;
      CompletableFuture future = new CompletableFuture();

      public ResultsCollector(int totalAcks) {
          this.totalAcks = totalAcks;
      }

      public void ackReceived() {
          receivedAcks++;
          if (receivedAcks == totalAcks) {
              future.complete(true);
          }
      }

      public void orTimeout(int time, TimeUnit unit) {
          future.orTimeout(time, unit);
      }

      public void
          whenComplete(BiConsumer<? super Object, ? super Throwable> func) {

          future.whenComplete(func);
      }

      public void complete() {
          future.complete("true");
      }
  }
```

To see how ResultCollector works, consider a cluster with the nodes Athens, Byzantium, and Cyrene. Athens is acting as a coordinator. When a new node, Delphi, sends a join request to Athens, Athens updates the membership and sends the updateMembership request to Byzantium and Cyrene. It also creates a ResultCollector object to track acknowledgments. It records each acknowledgment received with ResultCollector. When it receives acknowledgments from both Byzantium and Cyrene, it responds to Delphi (Figure 29.1).

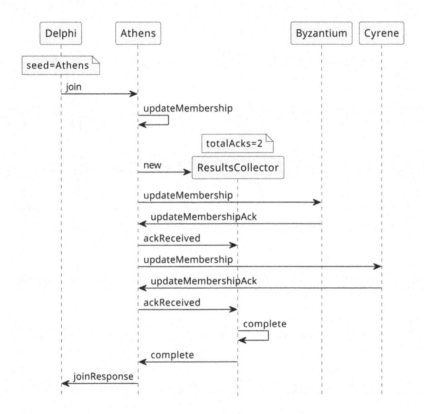

Figure 29.1 *Node join completes after membership is updated on all the nodes.*

Frameworks such as Akka use *Gossip Dissemination* and gossip convergence[101] to track whether updates have reached all cluster nodes.

---

101. https://doc.akka.io/docs/akka/current/typed/cluster-concepts.html#gossip-convergence

An Example Scenario

Consider another three nodes. Again, we'll call them Athens, Byzantium, and Cyrene. Athens acts as a seed node; the other two nodes are configured with Athens' address.

When Athens starts, it detects that it is itself the seed node. It immediately initializes the membership list and starts accepting requests (Figure 29.2).

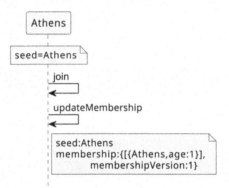

Figure 29.2 *Seed node starts*

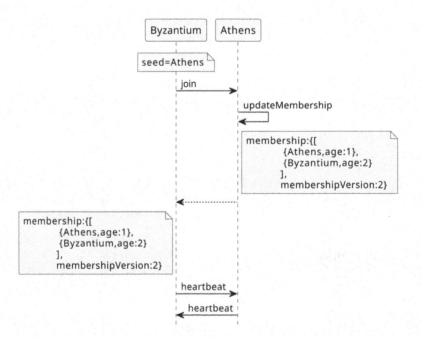

Figure 29.3 *Node joins the cluster by contacting the seed node.*

When Byzantium starts, it sends a join request to Athens. Even if Byzantium starts before Athens, it will keep trying to send join requests until it can connect to Athens. Athens finally adds Byzantium to the membership list and sends the updated membership list to Byzantium. Once Byzantium receives the response from Athens, it can start accepting requests (Figure 29.3).

With all-to-all heartbeating, Byzantium starts sending heartbeats to Athens, and Athens sends heartbeats to Byzantium.

Cyrene starts next. It sends join requests to Athens. Athens updates the membership list and sends the updated membership list to Byzantium. It then sends the join response with the membership list to Cyrene (Figure 29.4).

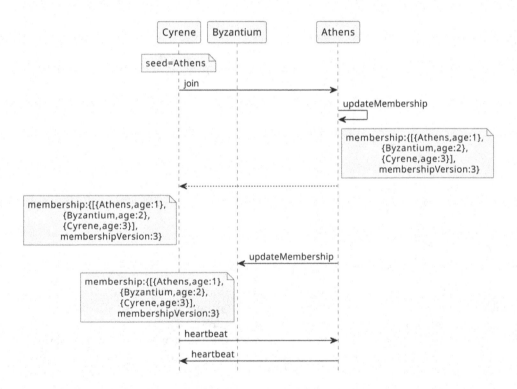

Figure 29.4 *Existing members get membership updates.*

With all to all heartbeating, Cyrene, Athens, and Byzantium all send heartbeats to each other.

Handling Missing Membership Updates

It's possible that some cluster nodes miss membership updates. There are two ways to handle this problem.

If all members are sending heartbeats to all other members, the membership version number can be sent as part of the heartbeat. The cluster node that handles the heartbeat can then ask for the latest membership.

```
class MembershipService...

    private void handleHeartbeatMessage(HeartbeatMessage message) {
        failureDetector.heartBeatReceived(message.from);
        if (isCoordinator()
                && (message.getMembershipVersion()
                    < this.membership.getVersion())) {

            membership.getMember(message.from)
                    .ifPresent(member -> {

                logger.info("Membership version in "
                        + selfAddress + "="
                        + this.membership.version
                        + " and in " + message.from
                        + "=" + message.getMembershipVersion());

                logger.info("Sending membership update from "
                        + selfAddress + " to " + message.from);

                sendMembershipUpdateTo(Arrays.asList(member));
            });
        }
    }
```

In the above example, if Byzantium misses a membership update from Athens, it will be detected when Byzantium sends a heartbeat to Athens. Athens can then send the latest membership to Byzantium (Figure 29.5).

Alternatively, each cluster node can check the latest membership list periodically—say, every one second—with other cluster nodes. If any of the nodes figures out that its member list is outdated, it can then ask for the latest membership list so it can update it. To be able to compare membership lists, a version number is maintained and incremented every time there is a change.

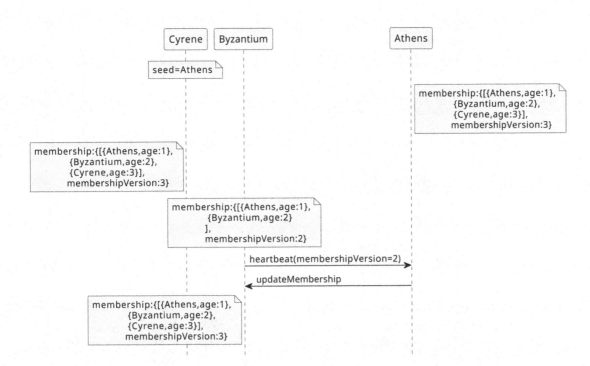

Figure 29.5 *Nodes detect missing membership using a version number.*

Failure Detection

In a simple case, all cluster nodes send heartbeats to all the other nodes. Each cluster node also runs a failure detector to check if heartbeats are missing from any of the cluster nodes. But only the coordinator marks the nodes as failed and communicates the updated membership list to all the other nodes. This makes sure that nodes don't unilaterally decide if some other node has failed. Hazelcast is an example of this implementation.

```
class MembershipService...

    private boolean isCoordinator() {
        Member coordinator = membership.getCoordinator();
        return coordinator.address.equals(selfAddress);
    }

    TimeoutBasedFailureDetector<InetAddressAndPort> failureDetector
            = new TimeoutBasedFailureDetector<InetAddressAndPort>(Duration.ofSeconds(2));
```

```
private void checkFailedMembers(List<Member> members) {
    if (isCoordinator()) {
        removeFailedMembers();
    } else {
        //if failed member consists of coordinator,
        // then check if this node is the next coordinator.
        claimLeadershipIfNeeded(members);
    }
}

void removeFailedMembers() {
    var failedMembers =
        checkAndGetFailedMembers(membership.getLiveMembers());
    if (failedMembers.isEmpty()) {
        return;
    }
    updateMembership(membership.failed(failedMembers));
    sendMembershipUpdateTo(membership.getLiveMembers());
}
```

Avoiding All-to-All Heartbeating

All-to-all heartbeating is not feasible in large clusters. Typically, each node will receive heartbeats from only a few other nodes. If a failure is detected, it's broadcasted to all the other nodes including the coordinator.

For example, in Akka, a node ring is formed by sorting network addresses so that each cluster node only sends heartbeats to a few cluster nodes. Apache Ignite arranges all the nodes in the cluster in a ring so that each node only sends heartbeat to the node next to it. Hazelcast[102] uses all-to-all heartbeat.

Any membership changes, because of nodes being added or node failures, need to be broadcast to all the other cluster nodes. A node can connect to every other node to send the required information. *Gossip Dissemination* can be used to broadcast this information.

Split Brain

Even though a single coordinator node decides when to mark another node as down, there's no explicit leader election to select which node acts as a coordinator. Every cluster node expects a heartbeat from the existing coordinator node; if it doesn't get a heartbeat in time, it can then claim to be the coordinator and remove the existing coordinator from the memberlist.

```
class MembershipService...

private void claimLeadershipIfNeeded(List<Member> members) {
    var failedMembers = checkAndGetFailedMembers(members);
```

---

102. https://hazelcast.com/

```
        if (!failedMembers.isEmpty() && isOlderThanAll(failedMembers)) {
            var newMembership = membership.failed(failedMembers);
            updateMembership(newMembership);
            sendMembershipUpdateTo(newMembership.getLiveMembers());
        }
    }

    private boolean isOlderThanAll(List<Member> failedMembers) {
        return failedMembers.stream().allMatch(m -> m.age < thisMember().age);
    }

    private List<Member> checkAndGetFailedMembers(List<Member> members) {
        List<Member> failedMembers = members
                .stream()
                .filter(this::isFailed)
                .map(member ->
                        new Member(member.address,
                                member.age,
                                member.status))
                .collect(Collectors.toList());

        failedMembers.forEach(member -> {
            failureDetector.remove(member.address);
            logger.info(selfAddress + " marking " + member.address + " as DOWN");
        });
        return failedMembers;
    }

    private boolean isFailed(Member member) {
        return !member.address.equals(selfAddress)
                && failureDetector.isMonitoring(member.address)
                && !failureDetector.isAlive(member.address);
    }
```

This can create a situation where two or more subgroups form in an existing cluster, each subgroup considering the others to have failed. This is called a *split brain problem*.

Consider a five-node cluster: Athens, Byzantium, Cyrene, Delphi, and Ephesus. If Athens receives heartbeats from Delphi and Ephesus, but stops getting heartbeats from Byzantium and Cyrene, it marks both Byzantium and Cyrene as failed.

Byzantium and Cyrene could send heartbeats to each other but stop receiving heartbeats from Cyrene, Delphi, and Ephesus. Byzantium, being the second oldest member of the cluster, then becomes the coordinator. So two separate clusters are formed, one with Athens as the coordinator and the other with Byzantium as the coordinator (Figure 29.6).

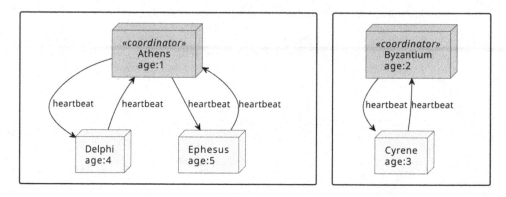

Figure 29.6 *Partial connectivity leads to a split brain.*

Handling Split Brain

One common way to handle the split brain issue is to check whether there are enough members to handle any client request, and reject the request if there are not enough live members. For example, Hazelcast allows you to configure the minimum cluster size to execute any client request.

```
public void handleClientRequest(Request request) {
    if (!hasMinimumRequiredSize()) {
        throw new NotEnoughMembersException("Requires minimum 3 members " +
                "to serve the request");
    }
}

private boolean hasMinimumRequiredSize() {
    return membership.getLiveMembers().size() > 3;
}
```

The part which has the majority of the nodes continues to operate. The nodes in the minority stop serving client requests. As explained in the Hazelcast documentation, there will always be a time window[103] before this mechanism comes into effect.

The problem can be avoided if cluster nodes are not marked as down unless it's guaranteed that this won't cause a split brain. For example, Akka recommends that you don't have nodes marked as down[104] through the failure detector; instead, you can use its split brain resolver[105] component.

103. https://docs.hazelcast.com/imdg/4.2/network-partitioning/split-brain-protection#time-window-for-split-brain-protection

104. https://doc.akka.io/docs/akka/2.5/cluster-usage.html#auto-downing-do-not-use-

105. https://doc.akka.io/docs/akka-enhancements/current/split-brain-resolver.html

Recovering from Split Brain

The coordinator runs a periodic job to check if it can connect to the failed nodes. If a connection can be established, it sends a special message indicating that it wants to trigger a split brain merge.

If the receiving node is the coordinator of a subcluster, it will check to see if the cluster that is initiating the request is part of a minority group. If it is, it will send a merge request. The coordinator of the minority group, upon receiving the merge request, will execute the merge request on all the nodes in the minority subgroup.

class MembershipService...

```
splitbrainCheckTask = taskScheduler.scheduleWithFixedDelay(() -> {
            searchOtherClusterGroups();
        },
        1, 1, TimeUnit.SECONDS);
```

class MembershipService...

```
private void searchOtherClusterGroups() {
    if (membership.getFailedMembers().isEmpty()) {
        return;
    }
    var allMembers = new ArrayList<Member>();
    allMembers.addAll(membership.getLiveMembers());
    allMembers.addAll(membership.getFailedMembers());
        if (isCoordinator()) {
        for (Member member : membership.getFailedMembers()) {
            logger.info("Sending SplitBrainJoinRequest to "
                    + member.address);

            network.send(member.address,
                    new SplitBrainJoinRequest(messageId++,
                            this.selfAddress,
                            membership.version,
                            membership.getLiveMembers().size())));
        }
    }
}
```

If the receiving node is the coordinator of the majority subgroup, it asks the sending coordinator node to merge with itself.

class MembershipService...

```
private void handleSplitBrainJoinMessage(
        SplitBrainJoinRequest splitBrainJoinRequest) {

    logger.info(selfAddress + " Handling SplitBrainJoinRequest from "
            + splitBrainJoinRequest.from);
```

```
        if (!membership.isFailed(splitBrainJoinRequest.from)) {
            return;
        }

        if (!isCoordinator()) {
            return;
        }

        if(splitBrainJoinRequest.getMemberCount()
                < membership.getLiveMembers().size()) {
            //requesting node should join this cluster.
            logger.info(selfAddress
                    + " Requesting "
                    + splitBrainJoinRequest.from
                    + " to rejoin the cluster");
            network.send(splitBrainJoinRequest.from,
                    new SplitBrainMergeMessage(splitBrainJoinRequest.messageId,
                            selfAddress));
        } else {
            //we need to join the other cluster
            mergeWithOtherCluster(splitBrainJoinRequest.from);
        }
    }

    private void mergeWithOtherCluster(
            InetAddressAndPort otherClusterCoordinator) {

        askAllLiveMembersToMergeWith(otherClusterCoordinator);
        //initiate merge on this node.
        handleMerge(new MergeMessage(messageId++,
                selfAddress, otherClusterCoordinator));
    }

    private void askAllLiveMembersToMergeWith(
            InetAddressAndPort mergeToAddress) {

        List<Member> liveMembers = membership.getLiveMembers();
        for (Member m : liveMembers) {
            network.send(m.address,
                    new MergeMessage(messageId++, selfAddress, mergeToAddress));
        }
    }
}
```

In our last example shown in Figure 29.7, when Athens can communicate with Byzantium, it will ask Byzantium to merge with itself.

The coordinator of the smaller subgroup then asks all the cluster nodes inside its group to trigger a merge. The merge operation shuts down the cluster nodes and rejoins them to the coordinator of the larger group.

In this example, Byzantium and Cyrene shut down and rejoin Athens to form a full cluster again (Figure 29.8).

```
class MembershipService...

  private void handleMerge(MergeMessage mergeMessage) {
      logger.info(selfAddress + " Merging with " + mergeMessage.getMergeToAddress());
      shutdown();
      //join the cluster again through the other cluster's coordinator
      taskScheduler.execute(() -> {
          join(mergeMessage.getMergeToAddress());
      });
  }
```

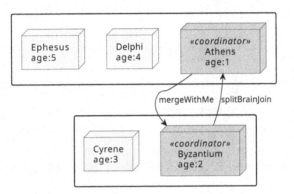

Figure 29.7 *Triggering split brain merge*

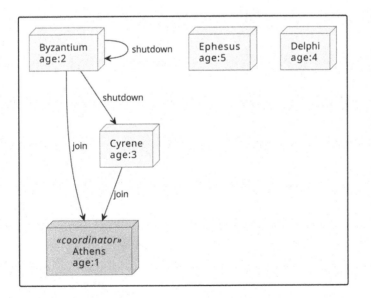

Figure 29.8 *Nodes rejoin after split brain merge.*

Comparison with Leader and Followers

Let's compare this pattern with *Leader and Followers*. The leader-follower setup, as used by patterns like *Consistent Core*, does not function unless the leader is chosen by running an election. This guarantees that the *Majority Quorum* of cluster nodes have an agreement about who the leader is. In the worst case, if an agreement isn't reached, the system will be unavailable to process any requests. In other words, it prefers consistency over availability.

The emergent leader, on the other hand, will always have some cluster node acting as a leader for processing client requests. In this case, availability is preferred over consistency.

Examples

- In JGroups, the oldest member is the coordinator that decides on membership changes.

- In Akka, the oldest member of the cluster runs actor singletons, such as the shard coordinator which decides on the placement of *Fixed Partitions* across cluster nodes.

- In-memory data grids, such as Hazelcast and Apache Ignite, have the oldest member act as the cluster coordinator.

Part VI

Patterns of Communication between Nodes

When nodes in a cluster communicate with each other, efficient utilization of the network becomes crucial. It is important to manage connections effectively, avoiding the creation of unnecessary connections between nodes. Additionally, optimizing network bandwidth usage can reduce latency and improve overall throughput.

In this part, we will explore commonly used patterns that focus on maximizing network utilization while facilitating communication among cluster nodes.

Chapter 30

Single-Socket Channel

Maintain the order of the requests sent to a server by using a single
TCP connection.

Problem

When using *Leader and Followers*, we need to ensure that messages between the leader and each follower are kept in order, with a retry mechanism for any lost messages. We need to do this while keeping the cost of new connections low, so that opening connections doesn't increase the system's latency.

Solution

Fortunately, the long-used and widely available TCP protocol provides all these necessary characteristics. We can get what we need by ensuring all communication between a follower and its leader goes through a single-socket channel (Figure 30.1). The follower then serializes the updates from the leader using a *Singular Update Queue*.

Once a connection to a node is open, the node never closes it and continuously reads it for new requests. Nodes use a dedicated thread per connection to read and write requests. A thread per connection isn't needed if nonblocking-IO is used.

Here's a simple thread-based implementation:

```
class SocketHandlerThread...

  @Override
  public void run() {
      isRunning = true;
      try {
          //Continues to read/write to the socket connection till it is closed.
```

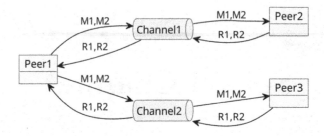

Figure 30.1 *Single-socket channel*

```
        while (isRunning) {
            handleRequest();
        }
    } catch (Exception e) {
        getLogger().debug(e);
        closeClient(this);
    }
}

private void handleRequest() {
    RequestOrResponse request = clientConnection.readRequest();
    server.accept(new Message<>(request,
                               request.getRequestId()
    ), clientConnection);
}

public void closeConnection() {
    clientConnection.close();
}
```

The node reads requests and submits them to a Singular Update Queue for processing. Once the node has processed the request, it writes the response back to the socket.

Whenever a node establishes a communication, it opens a single-socket connection that's used for all requests with the other party.

class SingleSocketChannel...

```
public class SingleSocketChannel implements Closeable {
    final InetAddressAndPort address;
    final int heartbeatIntervalMs;
    private Socket clientSocket;
    private final OutputStream socketOutputStream;
    private final InputStream inputStream;

    public SingleSocketChannel(InetAddressAndPort address,
                               int heartbeatIntervalMs) throws IOException {
        this.address = address;
```

```
                this.heartbeatIntervalMs = heartbeatIntervalMs;
                clientSocket = new Socket();
                clientSocket
                        .connect(new InetSocketAddress(address.getAddress(),
                                address.getPort()), heartbeatIntervalMs);
                //set socket read timeout to be more than heartbeat.
                clientSocket.setSoTimeout(heartbeatIntervalMs * 10);
                socketOutputStream = clientSocket.getOutputStream();
                inputStream = clientSocket.getInputStream();
            }

        public RequestOrResponse blockingSend(RequestOrResponse request)
                throws IOException {

            writeRequest(request);
            var responseBytes = readResponse();
            return deserialize(responseBytes);
        }

        private void writeRequest(RequestOrResponse request) throws IOException {
            var dataStream = new DataOutputStream(socketOutputStream);
            var messageBytes = serialize(request);
            dataStream.writeInt(messageBytes.length);
            dataStream.write(messageBytes);
        }
```

It's important to keep a timeout on the connection so it doesn't block indefinitely in case of errors. We use *HeartBeat* to periodically send requests over the socket channel to keep it alive. This timeout is generally kept as a multiple of the heartbeat interval to allow for network round trip time and some possible network delays. It's reasonable to set the connection timeout at, say, 10 times the heartbeat interval.

class SocketListener...

```
    private void setReadTimeout(Socket clientSocket) throws SocketException {
        clientSocket.setSoTimeout(config.getHeartBeatIntervalMs() * 10);
    }
```

Sending requests over a single channel can create problems with *head-of-line blocking*. To avoid this, we can use a *Request Pipeline*.

Examples

- ZooKeeper uses a single-socket channel[106] and a thread per follower to do all the communication.

---

106. https://zookeeper.apache.org/doc/r3.4.13/zookeeperInternals.html

- Kafka uses a single-socket channel between follower and leader partitions to replicate messages.

- The reference implementation of the Raft consensus algorithm, LogCabin, uses single-socket channel to communicate between the leader and the followers.

Chapter 31

Request Batch

Combine multiple requests to optimally utilize the network.

Problem

If a lot of requests are sent to cluster nodes with a small amount of data, network latency and the request processing time (including serialization and deserialization of the request on the server side) can add significant overhead.

For example, in a network with 1Gbps capacity, if the latency and request processing time is 100 microseconds and the client is sending hundreds of requests at the same time, it will significantly limit the overall throughput even though each request is just a few bytes.

Solution

Combine multiple requests together into a single request batch. The batch of the request will be sent to the cluster node for processing, with each request processed in exactly the same manner as an individual request. The node will then respond with a batch of responses.

As an example, consider a distributed key-value store where a client sends requests to store multiple key-value records on the server. When the client receives a call to send the request, it does not immediately send it over the network—instead, it keeps a queue of requests to be sent.

```
class Client...

    LinkedBlockingQueue<RequestEntry> requests = new LinkedBlockingQueue<>();

    public CompletableFuture send(SetValueRequest setValueRequest) {
        var requestId = enqueueRequest(setValueRequest);
        var responseFuture = trackPendingRequest(requestId);
        return responseFuture;
    }

    private int enqueueRequest(SetValueRequest setValueRequest) {
        var requestId = nextRequestId();
        var requestBytes = serialize(setValueRequest, requestId);
        requests.add(new RequestEntry(requestBytes, clock.nanoTime()));
        return requestId;
    }

    private int nextRequestId() {
        return requestNumber++;
    }
```

The time at which the request is enqueued is tracked and is later used to decide if the request can be sent as part of the batch.

```
class RequestEntry...

    class RequestEntry {
        byte[] serializedRequest;
        long createdTime;

        public RequestEntry(byte[] serializedRequest, long createdTime) {
            this.serializedRequest = serializedRequest;
            this.createdTime = createdTime;
        }
    }
```

The node then tracks the pending requests to be completed when a response is received. Each request will be assigned a unique request number used to map the response and complete the request.

```
class Client...

    Map<Integer, CompletableFuture> pendingRequests = new ConcurrentHashMap<>();

    private CompletableFuture trackPendingRequest(Integer correlationId) {
        var responseFuture = new CompletableFuture();
        pendingRequests.put(correlationId, responseFuture);
        return responseFuture;
    }
```

The client starts a separate task which continuously tracks the queued requests.

class Client...

```
  public Client(Config config,
                InetAddressAndPort serverAddress,
                SystemClock clock) {

      this.clock = clock;
      this.sender = new Sender(config, serverAddress, clock);
      this.sender.start();
  }
```

class Sender...

```
  @Override
  public void run() {
      while (isRunning) {
          var maxWaitTimeElapsed =
                  requestsWaitedFor(config.getMaxBatchWaitTime());
          var maxBatchSizeReached = maxBatchSizeReached(requests);

          if (maxWaitTimeElapsed || maxBatchSizeReached) {
              RequestBatch batch = createBatch(requests);
              try {
                  var batchResponse = sendBatchRequest(batch, address);
                  handleResponse(batchResponse);

              } catch (IOException e) {
                  batch
                          .getPackedRequests()
                          .stream()
                          .forEach(r -> {
                      pendingRequests
                              .get(r.getCorrelationId())
                              .completeExceptionally(e);
                  });
              }
          }
      }
  }

  private RequestBatch createBatch(LinkedBlockingQueue<RequestEntry> requests) {
      var batch = new RequestBatch(MAX_BATCH_SIZE_BYTES);
      var entry = requests.peek();
      while (entry != null && batch.hasSpaceFor(entry.getRequest())) {
          batch.add(entry.getRequest());
          requests.remove(entry);
          entry = requests.peek();
      }
      return batch;
  }
```

```
class RequestBatch...

  public boolean hasSpaceFor(byte[] requestBytes) {
      return batchSize() + requestBytes.length <= maxSize;
  }

  private int batchSize() {
      return requests.stream().map(r->r.length).reduce(0, Integer::sum);
  }
```

There are two checks to be done by the sender task:

■ Check if enough requests have accumulated to fill the batch to the maximum configured size.

```
class Sender...

    private boolean maxBatchSizeReached(Queue<RequestEntry> requests) {
        return accumulatedRequestSize(requests) > MAX_BATCH_SIZE_BYTES;
    }

    private int accumulatedRequestSize(Queue<RequestEntry> requests) {
        return requests
                .stream()
                .map(re -> re.size())
                .reduce((r1, r2) -> r1 + r2)
                .orElse(0);
    }
```

■ We cannot wait forever for the batch to be filled in, so we configure a small amount of wait time and check if the request has been added more than the wait time ago.

```
class Sender...

    private boolean requestsWaitedFor(long batchingWindowInMs) {
        var oldestPendingRequest = requests.peek();
        if (oldestPendingRequest == null) {
            return false;
        }
        var oldestEntryWaitTime =
                clock.nanoTime() - oldestPendingRequest.createdTime;
        return oldestEntryWaitTime > batchingWindowInMs;
    }
```

Once any of these conditions has been fulfilled, the batch request is sent to the server. The server unpacks the batch request and processes each of the individual requests.

```
class Server...

  private void handleBatchRequest(RequestOrResponse batchRequest,
                                  ClientConnection clientConnection) {
```

```
        var batch = deserialize(batchRequest.getMessageBody(),
                RequestBatch.class);
        var requests = batch.getPackedRequests();
        var responses = new ArrayList<RequestOrResponse>();
        for (RequestOrResponse request : requests) {
            var response = handleSetValueRequest(request);
            responses.add(response);
        }

        sendResponse(batchRequest,
                clientConnection,
                new BatchResponse(responses));
    }

    private RequestOrResponse handleSetValueRequest(RequestOrResponse request) {
        var setValueRequest =
                deserialize(request.getMessageBody(),
                        SetValueRequest.class);

        kv.put(setValueRequest.getKey(), setValueRequest.getValue());

        var response
                = new RequestOrResponse(new StringResponse(RequestId.SetValueResponse,
                                    "Success".getBytes()), request.getCorrelationId());

        return response;
    }
```

The client receives the batch response and completes all the pending requests.

class Sender...

```
    private void handleResponse(BatchResponse batchResponse) {
        var responseList = batchResponse.getResponseList();
        logger.debug("Completing requests from "
                + responseList.get(0).getCorrelationId()
                + " to "
                + responseList.get(responseList.size() - 1)
                .getCorrelationId());

        responseList
                .stream()
                .forEach(r -> {
            var completableFuture =
                    pendingRequests.remove(r.getCorrelationId());
            if (completableFuture != null) {
                completableFuture.complete(r);
            } else {
                logger.error("no pending request for " + r.getCorrelationId());
            }
        });
    }
```

Technical Considerations

The batch size should be chosen based on the size of individual messages and available network bandwidth, as well as the observed latency and throughput improvements under real-life load. Sensible defaults are set assuming smaller message sizes and the optimal batch size for server-side processing. For example, Apache Kafka has a default batch size of 16Kb. It also has a configuration parameter called linger.ms with the default value of 0. However, if the messages are bigger, a higher batch size might work better.

Having a too large batch size will likely only offer diminishing returns. For example, a batch size in megabytes can add further overhead in terms of processing. This is why the batch size parameter is typically tuned based on observations made during performance testing.

Request batching is generally used along with *Request Pipeline* to improve the overall throughput and latency.

When the retry-backoff policy is used to send requests to cluster nodes, the entire batch request will be retried. However, the cluster node might have processed part of the batch already. To ensure the retry works, you should implement *Idempotent Receiver*.

Examples

- Apache Kafka supports batching of the producer requests.

- Batching is also used when saving data to disk. For example, Apache BookKeeper implements batching in a similar way to flush the log to the disk.

- Nagel's algorithm is used in TCP to batch multiple smaller packets together to improve the overall network throughput.

Chapter 32

Request Pipeline

Improve latency by sending multiple requests on the connection without
waiting for the response of the previous requests.

Problem

Communicating between servers within a cluster using *Single-Socket Channel* can
cause performance issues if requests need to wait for responses to previous requests. To achieve better throughput and latency, the request queue on the
server should be filled enough to make sure the server capacity is fully utilized.
For example, when *Singular Update Queue* is used within a server, it can always
accept more requests, until the queue fills up, while it's processing a request. If
only one request is sent at a time, most of the server capacity is unnecessarily
wasted.

Solution

Nodes send requests to other nodes without waiting for responses from previous
requests. This is achieved by creating two separate threads, one for sending requests over a network channel and the other for receiving responses from the
network channel (Figure 32.1).

The sender node sends the requests over the socket channel, without waiting
for response:

```
class SingleSocketChannel...

  public void sendOneWay(RequestOrResponse request) throws IOException {
      var dataStream = new DataOutputStream(socketOutputStream);
      byte[] messageBytes = serialize(request);
      dataStream.writeInt(messageBytes.length);
```

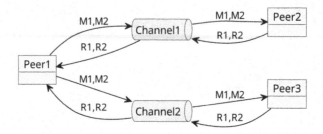

Figure 32.1 *Request pipeline*

```
    dataStream.write(messageBytes);
}
```

A separate thread is started to read responses:

class ResponseThread...

```
class ResponseThread extends Thread implements Logging {
    private volatile boolean isRunning = false;
    private SingleSocketChannel socketChannel;

    public ResponseThread(SingleSocketChannel socketChannel) {
        this.socketChannel = socketChannel;
    }

    @Override
    public void run() {
        try {
            isRunning = true;
            logger.info("Starting responder thread = " + isRunning);
            while (isRunning) {
                doWork();
            }

        } catch (IOException e) {
            getLogger().error(e); //thread exits if stopped or there is IO error
        }
    }

    public void doWork() throws IOException {
        RequestOrResponse response = socketChannel.read();
        logger.info("Read Response = " + response.getRequestId());
        processResponse(response);
    }
}
```

The response handler can immediately process the response or submit it to a Singular Update Queue.

There are two issues with the request pipeline.

If requests are continuously sent without waiting for the response, the node accepting the request can be overwhelmed. For this reason, there is an upper limit on how many requests can be kept in-flight at a time. Any node can send up to the maximum number of requests to other nodes. Once the maximum in-flight requests are sent without receiving a response, no more requests are accepted and the sender is blocked. A very simple strategy to limit maximum in-flight requests is to use a blocking queue to keep track of requests. The queue is initialized with the number of requests which can be in-flight. Once the response is received for a request, it's removed from the queue to create room for more requests. Here, the maximum of five in-flight requests are accepted per socket connection:

```
class RequestLimitingPipelinedConnection...

  private Map<InetAddressAndPort, ArrayBlockingQueue<RequestOrResponse>>
        inflightRequests = new ConcurrentHashMap<>();

  private int maxInflightRequests = 5;

  public void send(InetAddressAndPort to,
                   RequestOrResponse request) throws InterruptedException {

    var requestsForAddress = inflightRequests.get(to);

    if (requestsForAddress == null) {
        requestsForAddress = new ArrayBlockingQueue<>(maxInflightRequests);
        inflightRequests.put(to, requestsForAddress);
    }
    requestsForAddress.put(request);
```

The request is removed from the in-flight request queue once the response is received.

```
class RequestLimitingPipelinedConnection...

  private void consume(SocketRequestOrResponse response) {
      var correlationId = response.getRequest().getCorrelationId();
      var requestsForAddress = inflightRequests.get(response.getAddress());
      var first = requestsForAddress.peek();
      if (correlationId != first.getCorrelationId()) {
          throw new RuntimeException(
                  "First response should be for the first request");
      }
      requestsForAddress.remove(first);
      responseConsumer.accept(response.getRequest());
  }
```

Handling failures while maintaining ordering guarantees becomes tricky to implement. Let's say there are two in-flight requests. The first request failed and retried. The server might have processed the second request before the retried first request reaches the server.

Servers need some mechanism to make sure out-of-order requests are rejected. Otherwise, there's always a risk of messages getting reordered in case of failures and retries. For example, Raft always sends the previous log index that is expected with every log entry. If the previous log index does not match, the server rejects the request. Kafka can allow `max.in.flight.requests.per.connection` to be more than one, with its idempotent producer implementation assigning a unique identifier to each message batch that is sent to the broker. The broker can then check the sequence number of the incoming request and reject it if the requests are out of order.

Examples

- All consensus algorithms, such as Zab [Reed2008] and Raft [Ongaro2014], support request pipelines.

- Apache Kafka encourages clients to use request pipelining to improve throughput.

References

[Alexander1977] Alexander, Christopher, Max Jacobson, with Sara Ishikawa, Murray Silverstein, Ingrid Fiksdahl-King, and Shlomo Angel. *A Pattern Language*. Oxford University Press, New York, 1977. ISBN 978-0195019193.

[Arulraj2016] Arulraj, Joy, Matthew Perron, and Andrew Pavlo. "Write-Behind Logging." In: *Proc. VLDB Endow.*, 10, 4, November 2016, pp. 337–348. https://doi.org/10.14778/3025111.3025116, accessed on August 21, 2023.

[Berenson1995] Berenson, Hal, Phil Bernstein, Jim Gray, Jim Melton, Elizabeth O'Neil, and Patrick O'Neil. "A Critique of ANSI SQL Isolation Levels." In: *SIGMOD Rec.*, Volume 24, Number 2, May 1995, pp. 1–10, DOI: 10.1145/568271.223785. https://doi.org/10.1145/568271.223785, accessed on August 27, 2023.

[Birman2012] Birman, Kenneth P. *Guide to Reliable Distributed Systems*. Springer, 2012. ISBN 978-1-4471-2415-3.

[Brewer1999] Fox, A. and E. A. Brewer. "Harvest, Yield and Scalable Tolerant Systems." In: *Proc. of the Seventh Workshop Hot Topics in Operating Systems (HotOS '99)*, IEEE CS, 1999, pp. 174–178. https://dl.acm.org/doi/10.5555/822076.822436, accessed on August 21, 2023.

[Burrows2006] Burrows, Mike. "The Chubby Lock Service for Loosely-Coupled Distributed Systems." In: *Proceedings of the 7th Symposium on Operating Systems Design and Implementation (OSDI '06)*, Seattle, 2006, pp. 335–350.

[Cahill2009] Cahill, Michael J., Uwe Röhm, and Alan D. Fekete. "Serializable Isolation for Snapshot Databases." In: *ACM Trans. Database Syst.*, Volume 34, Number 4, 2009, pp. 20:1–20:42, DOI: 10.1145/1620585.1620587. https://doi.org/10.1145/1620585.1620587, accessed on August 27, 2023.

[Castro1999] Castro, Miguel and Barbara Liskov. "Practical Byzantine Fault Tolerance." In: *Proceedings of the Third Symposium on Operating Systems Design and Implementation (OSDI '99)*, New Orleans, 1999, pp. 173–186. https://dl.acm.org/doi/10.5555/296806.296824, accessed on August 21, 2023.

[Chen2020] Chen, Boyang. *KIP-650: Enhance Kafkaesque Raft Semantics*. https://cwiki.apache.org/confluence/display/KAFKA/KIP-650%3A+Enhance+Kafkaesque+Raft+semantics#KIP650:Enhance KafkaesqueRaftsemantics-Non-leaderLinearizableRead, accessed on September 4, 2023.

[Das2002] Das, Abhinandan, Indranil Gupta, and Ashish Motivala. "SWIM: Scalable Weakly-Consistent Infection-Style Process Group Membership Protocol." In: *Proceedings International Conference on Dependable Systems and Networks*, Washington, 2002, pp. 303–312, DOI: 10.1109/DSN.2002.1028914. https://doi.org/10.1109/DSN.2002.1028914, accessed on August 21, 2023.

[Dean2009] Dean, Jeaf. *Keynote LADIS 2009 Conference.* https://www.cs.cornell.edu/projects/ladis2009/talks/dean-keynote-ladis2009.pdf, accessed on August 21, 2023.

[Demirbas2014] Demirbas, Murat, Marcelo Leone, Bharadwaj Avva, Deepak Madeppa, and Sandeep S. Kulkarni. *Logical Physical Clocks and Consistent Snapshots in Globally Distributed Databases.* 2014. https://api.semanticscholar.org/CorpusID:15965481, accessed on August 15, 2023.

[Fischer1985] Fischer, Michael J., Nancy A. Lynch, and Michael S. Paterson. "Impossibility of Distributed Consensus with One Faulty Process." In: *Journal of the ACM*, volume 32, number 2, April 1985, pp. 374–382, DOI: 10.1145/3149.214121. https://doi.org/10.1145/3149.214121, accessed on August 21, 2023.

[Fowler2005] Fowler, Martin. *Event Sourcing.* https://martinfowler.com/eaaDev/EventSourcing.html, accessed on August 15, 2023.

[Gamma1994] Gamma, Erich, Richard Helm, Ralph Johnson, and John Vlissides. *Design Patterns: Elements of Reusable Object-Oriented Software.* Addison-Wesley, 1995. ISBN 0201633612.

[Goetz2006] Goetz, Brian, Tim Peierls, Joshua Bloch, Joseph Bowbeer, David Holmes, and Doug Lea. *Java Concurrency in Practice.* Addison-Wesley Professional, 2006. ISBN 0321349601.

[Gupta2006] Gupta, Indranil, Anne-Marie Kermarrec, and Ayalvadi J. Ganesh. "Efficient and Adaptive Epidemic-Style Protocols for Reliable and Scalable Multicast." In: *IEEE Trans. Parallel Distrib. Syst.*, Volume 17, Number 7, pp. 593–605. DOI: 10.1109/TPDS.2006.85. https://doi.org/10.1109/TPDS.2006.85, accessed on August 21, 2023.

[Gustafson2018] Gustafson, Jason. *KIP-392: Allow Consumers to Fetch from Closest Replica.* https://cwiki.apache.org/confluence/display/KAFKA/KIP-392%3A+Allow+consumers+to+fetch+from+closest+replica, accessed on August 15, 2023.

[Gustafson2023] Gustafson, Jason. *KIP-595: A Raft Protocol for the Metadata Quorum.* https://cwiki.apache.org/confluence/display/KAFKA/KIP-595%3A+A+Raft+Protocol+for+the+Metadata+Quorum, accessed on August 21, 2023.

[Hayashibara2004] Hayashibara, Naohiro, Xavier Défago, Rami Yared, and Takuya Katayama. "The φ Accrual Failure Detector." In: *Proceedings of the 23rd IEEE International Symposium on Reliable Distributed Systems*, 2004, pp. 66–78. https://www.researchgate.net/publication/29682135_The_ph_accrual_failure_detector, accessed on August 21, 2023.

[Howard2016] Howard, Heidi, Dahlia Malkhi, and Alexander Spiegelman. "Flexible Paxos: Quorum Intersection Revisited." In: *arXiv preprint arXiv:1608.06696*, 2016. https://arxiv.org/abs/1608.06696, accessed on August 21, 2023.

[Hunt2010] Hunt, Patrick, Mahadev Konar, Flavio P. Junqueira, and Benjamin Reed. "ZooKeeper: Wait-Free Coordination for Internet-Scale Systems." In: *Proceedings of the 2010 USENIX Annual Technical Conference (ATC '10)*, USENIX Association, Berkeley, 2010, pp. 11–11. https://www.usenix.org/legacy/event/atc10/tech/full_papers/Hunt.pdf, accessed on August 21, 2023.

[Lamport1978] Lamport, Leslie. "Time, Clocks, and the Ordering of Events in a Distributed System." In: *Communications of the ACM*, Volume 21, Number 7, July 1978, pp. 558–565. DOI: 10.1145/359545.359563.

[Lamport1998] Lamport, Laslie. "The Part-Time Parliament." In: *ACM Transactions on Computer Systems (TOCS)*, 16(2), pp. 133–169, May 1998. http://lamport.azurewebsites.net/pubs/lamport-paxos.pdf, accessed on August 21, 2023.

[Lamport2001] Lamport, Laslie. "Paxos Made Simple." In: *ACM SIGACT News (Distributed Computing Column)*, November 2001. https://lamport.azurewebsites.net/pubs/paxos-simple.pdf, accessed on August 21, 2023.

[Liskov2012] Liskov, Barbara and James Cowling. "Viewstamped Replication Revisited." In: *MIT Technical Report MIT-CSAIL-TR-2012-021*, July 2012. http://pmg.csail.mit.edu/papers/vr-revisited.pdf, accessed on August 21, 2023.

[Malkhi2013] Malkhi, Dahlia and Jean-Philippe Martin. "Spanner's Concurrency Control." In: *Proceedings of the Twenty-Fourth ACM Symposium on Operating Systems Principles (SOSP '13)*, Farmington, ACM, September 2013, pp. 358–372, DOI: 10.1145/2517349.2517350. https://www.microsoft.com/en-us/research/publication/spanners-concurrency-control, accessed on August 27, 2023.

[McCabe2020] McCabe, Colin. *KIP-500: Replace ZooKeeper with a Self-Managed Metadata Quorum.* https://cwiki.apache.org/confluence/display/KAFKA/KIP-500%3A+Replace+ZooKeeper+with+a+Self-Managed+Metadata+Quorum, accessed on August 21, 2023.

[McCabe2021] McCabe, Colin. *KIP-631: The Quorum-Based Kafka Controller.* https://cwiki.apache.org/confluence/display/KAFKA/KIP-631%3A+The+Quorum-based+Kafka+Controller, accessed on August 21, 2023.

[Moraru2013] Moraru, Iulian, David G. Andersen, and Michael Kaminsky. "There Is More Consensus in Egalitarian Parliaments." In: *Proceedings of the Twenty-Fourth ACM Symposium on Operating Systems Principles (SOSP '13)*, Farmington, 2013, pp. 358–372, DOI: 10.1145/2517349.2517350. https://doi.org/10.1145/2517349.2517350, accessed on August 21, 2023.

[Ongaro2014] Ongaro, Diego. *Consensus: Bridging Theory and Practice.* Ph.D. thesis, Stanford University, August 2014. https://web.stanford.edu/~ouster/cgi-bin/papers/OngaroPhD.pdf, accessed on August 21, 2023.

[Ongaro2015] Ongaro, Diego. *LogCabin.appendEntry(5, "Cluster Clock, etc").* https://ongardie.net/blog/logcabin-2015-02-27, accessed on August 21, 2023.

[Peng2010] Peng, Daniel and Frank Dabek. "Large-Scale Incremental Processing Using Distributed Transactions and Notifications." In: *Proceedings of the 9th USENIX Symposium on Operating Systems Design and Implementation*, 2010.

[Qin2015] Qin, Jiangjie. *Kafka Controller Redesign*. https://cwiki.apache.org/confluence/display/ KAFKA/Kafka+Controller+Redesign, accessed on August 15, 2023.

[Rao2014] Rao, Jun. *Kafka Controller Internals*. https://cwiki.apache.org/confluence/display/ KAFKA/Kafka+Controller+Internals, accessed on August 21, 2023.

[Reed2008] Reed, Benjamin and Flavio P. Junqueira. "A Simple Totally Ordered Broadcast Protocol." In: *Proceedings of the 2nd Workshop on Large-Scale Distributed Systems and Middleware (LADIS '08)*, ACM, New York, 2008, pp. 1–6. https://dl.acm.org/doi/abs/10.1145/ 1529974.1529978, accessed on August 21, 2023.

[Rystsov2018] Rystsov, Denis. "CASPaxos: Replicated State Machines without logs." In: *arXiv preprint arXiv:1802.07000*, 2018. https://arxiv.org/abs/1802.07000, accessed on August 21, 2023.

[Schneider1990] Schneider, Fred B. "Implementing Fault-Tolerant Services Using the State Machine Approach: A Tutorial." In: *ACM Comput. Surv.*, 22, 4, December 1990, pp. 299–319. https://doi.org/10.1145/98163.98167, accessed on August 21, 2023.

[Stopford2021] Stopford, Ben. *KIP-101—Alter Replication Protocol to Use Leader Epoch Rather Than High Watermark for Truncation*. https://cwiki.apache.org/confluence/display/KAFKA/KIP-101+ -+Alter+Replication+Protocol+to+use+Leader+Epoch+rather+than+High+Watermark+for+Truncation, accessed on August 21, 2023.

[Thomson2011a] Thompson, Martin. *Single Writer Principle*. 22 September 2011. https://mechanical-sympathy.blogspot.com/2011/09/single-writer-principle.html, accessed on August 21, 2023.

[Thomson2011b] Thompson, Martin, Dave Farley, Michael Barker, Patricia Gee, and Andrew Stewart. *Disruptor: High Performance Alternative to Bounded Queues for Exchanging Data between Concurrent Threads*. May 2011. https://lmax-exchange.github.io/disruptor/files/ Disruptor-1.0.pdf, accessed on August 21, 2023.

[Tunnicliffe2023] Tunnicliffe, Sam. *CEP-21: Transactional Cluster Metadata*. https://cwiki.apache. org/confluence/display/CASSANDRA/CEP-21%3A+Transactional+Cluster+Metadata, accessed on August 15, 2023.

[Welsh2001] Welsh, Matt, David Culler, and Eric Brewer. "SEDA: An Architecture for Well-Conditioned, Scalable Internet Services." In: *Proceedings of the Eighteenth ACM Symposium on Operating Systems Principles (SOSP '01)*, October 2001, pp. 230–243. https://dl.acm.org/doi/10.1145/502034.502057, accessed on August 21, 2023.

[XA1991] The Open Group. "Distributed Transaction Processing: The XA Specification." In: *X/Open CAE Specification*, December 1991. https://pubs.opengroup.org/onlinepubs/ 009680699/toc.pdf, accessed on September 2, 2023.

Index

Register Your Product at informit.com/register

Access additional benefits and save up to 65%* on your next purchase

- Automatically receive a coupon for 35% off books, eBooks, and web editions and 65% off video courses, valid for 30 days. Look for your code in your InformIT cart or the Manage Codes section of your account page.

- Download available product updates.

- Access bonus material if available.**

- Check the box to hear from us and receive exclusive offers on new editions and related products.

InformIT—The Trusted Technology Learning Source

InformIT is the online home of information technology brands at Pearson, the world's leading learning company. At informit.com, you can

- Shop our books, eBooks, and video training. Most eBooks are DRM-Free and include PDF and EPUB files.

- Take advantage of our special offers and promotions (informit.com/promotions).

- Sign up for special offers and content newsletter (informit.com/newsletters).

- Access thousands of free chapters and video lessons.

- Enjoy free ground shipping on U.S. orders.*

Offers subject to change.

*** Registration benefits vary by product. Benefits will be listed on your account page under Registered Products.*

Connect with InformIT—Visit informit.com/community

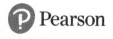 Pearson

Addison-Wesley • Adobe Press • Cisco Press • Microsoft Press • Oracle Press • Peachpit Press • Pearson IT Certification • Que